高中英文句型總整理

序

　　我很慶幸李端老師能夠為莘莘學子寫了這本《高中英文句型總整理》參考書。

　　李端老師是我認識的英文老師中最有學養的一位。他治學嚴謹，對英語及英國文學的造詣極深，所以常春藤出版的諸多叢書多經由他及本人的審校才能付梓。一年前當他表示要撰寫本書時，我就欣然同意，深信這一定是一本好書，也樂見其成。果不其然，這本書推出後，立即造成學校及讀者搶購。因為它內容精確，解說簡明。

　　李端老師以優異成績畢業於台大外文研究所，專研修辭及英國文學。教書空閒時間，只喜歡看書，繼續充實自己的知識，在現今日趨浮燥虛華的社會，這種『書痴型』的學者已難得一見了，而常春藤就喜歡與這樣的人為伍，因為我們都是一群熱愛英文的工作者。有李老師相伴，編輯室的所有同仁每天的生活既充實又愉快。他的認真態度也成了所有同仁的楷模，並直接提升了同仁的英文功力。

　　在本書第五次付印的前夕，我特別寫了這些話語，一則感謝李老師寫了這本好書，二則也期望所有的讀者都能靠閱讀本書而在英文應試的能力上獲得大幅提升，考上理想的大學，終而像我們一樣，成為熱愛英文的狂熱份子。

於台北常春藤書廊

前言

　　古今中外任何一種語言皆有其「文法」。「文法」其實就是吾人造句、寫作的基本原則。我們自己的國語文如此，英文自然也不例外。因此，要學好英文的人，必定要有扎實的文法基礎。比方來說，文法是英文的「根本」或「骨幹」，而單字、片語不過是其「枝葉」或「皮毛」而已。換言之，如果沒有文法概念，單字、片語背了再多也沒有用。所謂「皮之不存，毛將焉附」就是這個道理。在國內有很多孩子從幼稚園就學英文，可是為什麼大多數的學生唸到高中、大學，甚至研究所還無法「突破瓶頸」呢？問題就出在他們沒有把文法基礎打好。

　　有鑑於此，本人特別編寫了這本《高中英文句型總整理》，其特色如下：

1. 共 20 個單元，從句子，子句到介系詞的介紹，面面俱到。

2. 句型條舉分明，詳加比較並附解說。

3. 例句簡單實用，易記好背。

4. 契合考試趨勢，融入歷屆試題。

5. 提昇閱讀寫作能力，畢其功於一役。

目錄

五大句型

要點 1

完全不及物動詞的句型：

1. S + Vi

   Tastes differ.

   （人各有所好。）

2. S + Vi + adv

   My parents live nearby.

   （我的父母住在附近。）

   He will resign from the Cabinet.

   （他將自內閣辭職。）

說明：

主詞 (S) 和動詞 (V) 是組成英文句子的兩大要素。動詞一般可按是否需接『受詞』而有及物 (vt.) 和不及物 (vi.) 之分。不及物動詞又可分為『完全』和『不完全』兩種。當主詞+完全不及物動詞時，句意即完整（全）。唯此類動詞亦可視情況需要在其後加上副詞、副詞片語／子句等。值得注意的是，多數動詞兼有及物和不及物的用法。

聯考題型

1. "Money _____," as the saying goes.
   (A) speaks   (B) talks   (C) says   (D) tells

2. Our chemistry teacher was on a one-month sick leave, so the principal had to find a teacher to _____ for her. (94 指考)
   (A) recover   (B) navigate   (C) rehearse   (D) substitute

3. It's not easy to quit smoking. As you know, old habits _____ hard.
   (A) work   (B) think   (C) die   (D) look

4. The ground is slippery. Hold onto the rope and don't let _____. (93 學測)
   (A) go   (B) down   (C) up   (D) slip

5. A: "Which do you like better, coffee or tea?"
   B: "Either will _____."
   (A) do   (B) make   (C) take   (D) work

6. Hundreds of people _____ in the desert storm and many more were left homeless. (91 指考)
   (A) perished   (B) inspired   (C) mistreated   (D) dismissed

7. Mary is nearly fifty, but she could _____ as 35 or so.
   (A) look upon   (B) pass   (C) refer to   (D) regard

8. Helen _____ with anger when she saw her boyfriend kissing an attractive girl. (92 學測)
   (A) collided   (B) exploded   (C) relaxed   (D) defeated

9. Old soldiers never die; they _____ away.
   (A) walk   (B) look   (C) give   (D) fade

10. Jenny _____ when she was praised by her teacher for writing an excellent English composition. (90 聯招)
    (A) blushed   (B) bloomed   (C) blamed   (D) blessed

11. J.K. Rowling's *Harry Potter* series _____ like hot cakes.
    (A) sells   (B) works   (C) looks   (D) tastes

12. During the process of evolution, man has shown remarkable ability to _____. (88 推甄)
    (A) adorn   (B) adopt   (C) adore   (D) adapt

13. It _____ that I was out for lunch when Tom came to my office.
    (A) happened   (B) occurred   (C) found   (D) pretended

14. If I can help you with the project, don't _____ to call me. (87 推甄)
    (A) concern   (B) hesitate   (C) notify   (D) submit

15. To be honest with you, what _____ is nothing but a faint memory of him.
    (A) remains   (B) reminds   (C) leaves   (D) stays

1. 常言道：『會叫的狗不咬人。』

   試譯：＿＿＿＿＿＿＿＿＿＿＿＿＿＿＿＿＿＿＿＿＿＿＿＿＿

2. 如果你堅持下去就會成功。

   試譯：＿＿＿＿＿＿＿＿＿＿＿＿＿＿＿＿＿＿＿＿＿＿＿＿＿

3. 你相信他的構想真的可行嗎？

   試譯：＿＿＿＿＿＿＿＿＿＿＿＿＿＿＿＿＿＿＿＿＿＿＿＿＿

4. 那名交通警察恰好是我的表哥。

   試譯：＿＿＿＿＿＿＿＿＿＿＿＿＿＿＿＿＿＿＿＿＿＿＿＿＿

5. 人瑞就是活到一百或更多歲數的人。

   試譯：A centenarian is one who ＿＿＿＿＿＿＿＿＿＿＿＿＿

要點 2

不完全不及物動詞的句型：須接主詞補語

> S + Vi + SC（主詞補語）
>
> Nick is a good-for-nothing.（名詞作補語）
>
> （尼克一無是處。）
>
> The soup tastes funny.（形容詞作補語）
>
> （這道湯的味道怪怪的。）
>
> I feel cheated.（過去分詞作補語）
>
> （我有受騙的感覺。）
>
> The Lakers' performance was disappointing.（現在分詞作補語）
>
> （湖人隊的表現真令人失望。）

We remain <u>in the dark</u>.（介詞片語作補語）

（我們仍然毫無所悉。）

說明：

不完全不及物動詞（亦稱連綴動詞）須接主詞補語句意才能完整。此類動詞有：

1. be
2. seem, appear
3. become, come, go, get, grow, turn, fall, drop
4. feel, look, sound, smell, taste
5. remain, stay, keep
6. prove

聯考題型

1. It's not my fault. You are _____.
   (A) blaming   (B) blamed   (C) to blame   (D) to be blamed

2. Thousands of people flooded into the city to join the demonstration; as a result, the city's transportation system was almost _____. (94指考)
   (A) testified   (B) paralyzed   (C) stabilized   (D) dissatisfied

3. You'd better carry an umbrella with you. It looks _____ outside.
   (A) raining   (B) rained   (C) like rain   (D) as rain

4. If you want to borrow magazines, tapes, or CDs, you can visit the library. They are all _____ there. (94學測)
   (A) sufficient   (B) marvelous   (C) impressive   (D) available

5. My grandfather often _____ asleep when watching TV.
   (A) falls   (B) goes   (C) drops   (D) gets

6. As the tallest building in the world, Taipei 101 has become a new _____ of Taipei City. (93學測)
   (A) incident   (B) geography   (C) skylight   (D) landmark

7. It sounds _____ a good idea.
   (A) like   (B) as   (C) being   (D) to be

8. Victor's classmates are very _____ of him because he has just received a new cell phone for his birthday. (92指考)
   (A) arrogant　　　(B) envious　　　(C) beloved　　　(D) logical

9. Uncle George _____ dead of a heart attack at the age of 41.
   (A) grew　　　(B) turned　　　(C) fell　　　(D) dropped

10. All the flights to and from Kaohsiung were _____ because of the heavy thunderstorm. (92學測)
    (A) advised　　　(B) disclosed　　　(C) cancelled　　　(D) benefited

11. One of the gangsters turned _____ and gave the police the details of their robbery.
    (A) informant　　　(B) an informant　　　(C) the informant　　　(D) informed

12. Jack doesn't look _____, but he is, in fact, excellent at sports, especially baseball. (91指考)
    (A) athletic　　　(B) graceful　　　(C) enthusiastic　　　(D) conscientious

13. The boat turned _____ when it made an abrupt turn.
    (A) upside　　　(B) turtle　　　(C) inside　　　(D) tortoise

14. Our team will certainly win this baseball game because all the players are highly _____. (91學測)
    (A) illustrated　　　(B) estimated　　　(C) motivated　　　(D) dominated

15. Peter must be a heavy smoker because his breath smells strongly _____ tobacco.
    (A) of　　　(B) like　　　(C) with　　　(D) about

翻譯造句

1. 這個古董證實為一件膺品。 (prove)

   試譯：＿＿＿＿＿＿＿＿＿＿＿＿＿＿＿＿＿＿＿＿＿＿＿＿

2. 我希望你的夢想可以成真。 (come)

   試譯：＿＿＿＿＿＿＿＿＿＿＿＿＿＿＿＿＿＿＿＿＿＿＿＿

3. 務必保持聯絡。 (keep)

   試譯：＿＿＿＿＿＿＿＿＿＿＿＿＿＿＿＿＿＿＿＿＿＿＿＿

4. 很多青少年成為毒品的受害者。 (fall)

　　試譯：＿＿＿＿＿＿＿＿＿＿＿＿＿＿＿＿＿＿＿＿

5. 為了保持苗條，她一天只吃一餐。 (stay)

　　試譯：＿＿＿＿＿＿＿＿＿＿＿＿＿＿＿＿＿＿＿＿

要點 3

完全及物動詞的句型：

　　S + Vt + O

　　I hate <u>the smell</u> of cigarettes.（名詞作受詞）

（我討厭聞到菸味。）

　　We all respect <u>him</u>.（代名詞作受詞）

（我們都尊敬他。）

　　History repeats <u>itself</u>.（反身代名詞作受詞）

（歷史會重演的。）

　　Many people enioy <u>going</u> on vacation.（動名詞作受詞）

（許多人喜歡去度假。）

　　They decided <u>to wait and see</u>.（不定詞作受詞）

（他們決定等候看看再說。）

　　You know <u>what to do</u>, don't you?（名詞片語作受詞）

（你知道該做什麼，是嗎？）

　　I don't see <u>how this new model is any better than the old one</u>.（名詞子
句作受詞）

（我看不出這新機種比舊的好在哪裡。）

說明：

受詞的形式有：

1. 名詞

2. 代名詞（含 oneself/itself）

3. 動名詞

4. 不定詞

5. 名詞片語（疑問字 + 不定詞）

6. 名詞子句（that/where等 + S + V ...）

聯考題型

1. I'm not joking at all. I really mean _____.
   (A) business   (B) nothing   (C) itself   (D) everything

2. Irene does not throw away used envelopes. She _____ them by using them for taking telephone messages.
   (A) designs   (B) recycles   (C) disguises   (D) manufactures

3. Mr. Kim is speaking now. You can have your _____ later.
   (A) saying   (B) say   (C) said   (D) to say

4. Though Dr. Wang has been away from his hometown for over ten years, he can still _____ his old house clearly. (94指考)
   (A) nominate   (B) visualize   (C) prolong   (D) sprinkle

5. Let's _____ a coin to decide who goes first.
   (A) dump   (B) cast   (C) toss   (D) flap

6. Jordan's performance _____ his teammates and they finally beat their opponents to win the championship. (92指考)
   (A) signaled   (B) promoted   (C) opposed   (D) inspired

7. This stuff is more durable and bears _____.
   (A) wash   (B) washing   (C) washer   (D) to wash

8. The young couple decided to _____ their wedding until all the details were well taken care of. (92學測)
   (A) announce   (B) maintain   (C) postpone   (D) simplify

9. Mr. Evans is a very influential person in the government. Whatever he says _____ weight.
   (A) gains (B) loses (C) carries (D) brings

10. Now that my computer is connected to the Internet, I can browse e-papers, send and receive e-mail, and _____ software. (91指考)
    (A) upset (B) overcharge (C) undertake (D) download

11. When I entered the classroom, Miss Wang was calling the _____.
    (A) role (B) roll (C) names (D) heads

12. At the closing ceremony of the Olympic Games, all the athletes _____ good-bye to the audience. (90學測)
    (A) charmed (B) waved (C) dared (D) gazed

13. She devotes _____ full-time to the fashion business.
    (A) it (B) itself (C) her (D) herself

14. Faced with a problem, you have to _____ it first, and then try to find a solution. (90聯招)
    (A) resemble (B) analyze (C) concentrate (D) substitute

15. _____ Billy will show up only God knows.
    (A) If (B) Whether (C) As (D) So

翻譯造句

1. 我還很餓，可否再來一客？ (helping/serving)

   試譯：＿＿＿＿＿＿＿＿＿＿＿＿＿＿＿＿＿＿＿＿＿＿＿＿＿＿＿

2. 彼德不但親自下廚而且也洗衣服。 (cooking; laundry)

   試譯：＿＿＿＿＿＿＿＿＿＿＿＿＿＿＿＿＿＿＿＿＿＿＿＿＿＿＿

3. 如果你不是指她，那你究竟是指誰？ (mean)

   試譯：＿＿＿＿＿＿＿＿＿＿＿＿＿＿＿＿＿＿＿＿＿＿＿＿＿＿＿

4. 從今以後我不會再冒任何風險了。 (chance)

   試譯：＿＿＿＿＿＿＿＿＿＿＿＿＿＿＿＿＿＿＿＿＿＿＿＿＿＿＿

5. 瑪麗有好幾通電話要打。 (make)

試譯：＿＿＿＿＿＿＿＿＿＿＿＿＿＿＿＿＿＿＿＿＿＿

要點 4

授與動詞的句型：

S + Vt + IO + DO
= S + Vt + DO + 介詞 + IO

I will buy you a digital camera.
= I will buy a digital camera <u>for</u> you.
（我會買一台數位相機給你。）
The sun gives us light and heat.
= The sun gives light and heat <u>to</u> us.
（太陽給我們光與熱。）

說明：

1. 凡及物動詞需接兩個受詞（一為間接受詞，一為直接受詞）者，稱為『授與動詞』。
2. 間接受詞 (IO) 指人；直接受詞 (DO) 指物。
3. 直接受詞在前，間接受詞在後時，其間應置適當的介系詞。
4. 搭配介詞 to 的動詞有：bring, give, grant, deliver, deny, do, lend, offer, owe, pay, sell, send, show, teach, tell 等。
5. 搭配介詞 for 的動詞有：buy, choose, get, leave, make, order, save 等。
6. 有些片語屬固定用法，如 do me a favor 不能說成 do a favor to me。

1. She said she would sue the doctor because he had _____ treatment to her.
   (A) denied (B) offered (C) paid (D) sent

2. On receiving my letter of complaint, the hotel manager sent me a written _____. (92指考)
   (A) consent (B) scandal (C) lecture (D) apology

3. I think I'll ask Henry for help. He _____ me a favor.
   (A) does (B) pays (C) owes (D) gives

4. A litte garlic will _____ some flavor to the sauce.
   (A) send (B) lend (C) put (D) show

5. The U.S. embassy urged the government to _____ an amnesty to all political prisoners.
   (A) grant (B) pay (C) send (D) forgive

6. _____ a piece of cake for me. I'll eat it when I'm back.
   (A) Give (B) Have (C) Save (D) Pass

7. You can rest assured that we will _____ your order to your door.
   (A) delay (B) deliver (C) deny (D) delete

8. _____ your pass to the guard at the entrance.
   (A) Expose (B) Enter (C) Show (D) Shake

9. The naughty boy needs _____ a lesson.
   (A) teach (B) teaching (C) to teach (D) taught

10. As a matter of fact, I _____ him no grudge.
    (A) treat (B) owe (C) leave (D)bear

11. Amy is _____ a reward to anyone who can help find her lost dog.
    (A) offering (B) offending (C) pretending (D) predicting

12. His uncle managed to _____ him a full-time job at a local factory.
    (A) get (B) receive (C) supply (D) seek

13. If I am out, please leave a message _____ my assistant.
    (A) to (B) for (C) with (D) by

14. That old man leaves everything _____ his only son in his will.
    (A) to (B) for (C) with (D) by

15. Leave some whiskey _____ me. Don't drink it all.
    (A) to   (B) for   (C) with   (D) by

翻譯造句

1. 老媽已為我們烤好一個大蛋糕。 (bake)

   試譯：_____

2. 一罐可樂不會對你的健康造成傷害。 (do)

   試譯：_____

3. 把胡椒粉遞給我，好嗎？ (pass)

   試譯：_____

4. 這家百貨公司正為迎接新年提供特別的折扣。 (offer)

   試譯：_____

5. 一名警察向她指示前往機場的路線。 (show)

   試譯：_____

不完全及物動詞的句型：須接受詞補語

S + Vt + O + <u>OC</u>（受詞補語）

This movie has made him <u>a megastar</u>. (名詞作補語)

（這部電影已經使他成為一位超級巨星。）

She managed to keep herself <u>busy</u>. (形容詞作補語)

（她設法使自己忙碌些。）

Don't keep me <u>waiting</u>. (現在分詞作補語)

（不要讓我等候。）

George had his bike <u>stolen</u> yesterday. (過去分詞作補語)

（喬治的腳踏車昨天被偷了。）

I could not make them <u>believe</u> me. (原形動詞作補語)

（我無法使他們相信我說的話。）

He'd like me <u>to come</u> earlier. (不定詞作補語)

（他要我早點到。）

說明：

不完全及物動詞接了受詞後，仍需再接受詞補語方可使句意完整。如同主詞補語說明主詞，受詞補語則說明受詞。現在分詞作補語有『主動』之意；過去分詞則表『被動』之意。

聯考題型

1. Turn down the music ! It's driving me _____.
   (A) craze   (B) madness   (C) guts   (D) nuts

2. Without much contact with the outside world for many years, John found many technological inventions _____ to him. (94學測)
   (A) natural   (B) common   (C) foreign   (D) objective

3. Although I tried very hard to communicate with that foreigner, I still could not make myself _____ in English.
   (A) understand   (B) understood   (C) understanding   (D) to understand

4. Science makes _____ the use of new materials and new methods of producing objects. (92指考)
   (A) possible   (B) possibly   (C) possibility   (D) possibilities

5. I saw a dog bite a man, but have you ever seen a dog _____ by a man?
   (A) bite   (B) biting   (C) to bite   (D) bitten

6. These two photographs are too small. Let's have them _____. (84聯招)
   (A) increased   (B) formalized   (C) enlarged   (D) expanded

7. Why don't you get someone _____ your broken windows?
   (A) repair   (B) to repair   (C) repairing   (D) repaired

8. Jane and Sue are twins, but they seem to have nothing _____. (87推甄)
   (A) in common   (B) in comparison   (C) in contact   (D) in contrast

9. Don't set the dog _____. He might attack people.
   (A) lose   (B) loose   (C) lost   (D) losing

10. Do not leave the door open. Please keep it _____.
    (A) close   (B) closed   (C) closely   (D) closing

11. They did not say anything to help me out. They just left me there _____ for words.
    (A) fumble   (B) fumbled   (C) fumbling   (D) to fumble

12. I like my coffee _____. How about you?
    (A) nice and strong   (B) strong and nice   (C) nicely strong   (D) strongly nice

13. The President appointed him _____ of State.
    (A) Secretary   (B) a Secretary   (C) the Secretary   (D) his Secretary

14. The bully threatened to _____ the small boy black and blue.
    (A) beat   (B) hit   (C) strike   (D) lick

15. We found the old man _____ to himself again.
    (A) mutter   (B) muttering   (C) to mutter   (D) and mutter

1. 我不知不覺地就隨著音樂起舞。 (find)

   試譯：_____

2. 你應該去量一下體溫。 (have)

   試譯：_____

3. 多次的失敗造就了今天的我。 (make)

   試譯：_____

4. 讓我來幫你做家事吧。 (help)

   試譯：_____

5. 市長留下好幾個問題沒有回答。 (leave)

   試譯：_____

Unit 2　　　　　四種句子

要點 1

直述句的句型：

1. S + V + (O) ...

   He hailed a taxi to take him home.

   （他攔了一部計程車載他回家。）

2. There/Here + is/are + S（限名詞）.

   There is a cat lying on the floor.

   （有一隻貓躺在地板上。）

說明：

直述句是英文句子最常見的類型。除了用There/Here或否定副詞（片語）開頭的句子須倒裝之外（詳見 Unit 16），直述句一律按五大句型的結構呈現。值得注意的是『主詞』可用下列方式表達：

1. 名詞
2. 代名詞
3. 動名詞（片語）
4. 不定詞（片語）
5. the + 形容詞（指人時多為複數用法）
6. 名詞片語
7. 名詞子句

聯考題型

1. There will _____ no charge for our after-sale service.

   (A) be 　　　　(B) have 　　　　(C) take 　　　　(D) bring

2. Cheese, powdered milk, and yogurt are common _____. (94學測)

   (A) produces 　　(B) products 　　(C) productions 　　(D) productivities

3. Both her parents live in the States, but _____ remain in England.
   (A) he   (B) him   (C) his   (D) himself

4. _____ in love is always magical. It feels eternal as if love will last forever. (94學測)
   (A) Falling   (B) Feeling   (C) Sinking   (D) Signing

5. To err _____ human; to forgive, divine.
   (A) makes   (B) is   (C) has   (D) takes

6. The current tallest, at 101 floors, ____ the Taipei 101 in Taiwan. (94指考)
   (A) is   (B) are   (C) being   (D) to be

7. Whether _____ the job offer kept me wide awake all night.
   (A) accept   (B) to accept   (C) accepting   (D) accepted

8. _____ hummingbirds can travel far as well as fast is shown by their yearly migrations between the United States and Central and South America. (84聯招)
   (A) What   (B) That   (C) Which   (D) Where

9. The temple _____ performances of Taiwanese opera every year as an expression of gratitude to the Goddess of Mercy. (93指考)
   (A) stages   (B) stands   (C) spreads   (D) spends

10. It does not matter whether you are a Christian or Buddhist. _____ matters is your attitude toward life.
    (A) It   (B) That   (C) What   (D) Those

11. _____ with an intellectual like Mr. Williams broadens my horizons.
    (A) Chat   (B) Chatting   (C) Chatted   (D) Chatter

12. _____ for hidden meanings is to identify with the poet, to ask the poet's questions. (93指考)
    (A) To read   (B) Read   (C) Reader   (D) Being read

13. The rich _____ not always happy, but the poor _____ usually unhappy.
    (A)is ... is   (B) are ... are (C) has ... has (D) have ... have

14. A _____ failure temporarily darkened the whole city, and it was not until two hours later that electricity was restored. (91指考)
    (A) power   (B) powered   (C) powering   (D) powerful

15. What one is _____ more important than what one has.
    (A) is   (B) has   (C) seem   (D) far

1. 凡是說那句話的人就是騙子。(whoever)

   試譯：_____

2. 談戀愛是一回事，結婚是另一回事。(falling)

   試譯：_____

3. 對於這位末期病人而言，繼續活下去則受罪更多。(to go on)

   試譯：For the terminally ill patient, _____

4. 你的鼓勵對我意義重大。(mean)

   試譯：_____

5. 這棟房子沒人住，地板上四散著垃圾。(deserted; scattered)

   試譯：_____

要點 2

疑問句的句型：

1. 助動詞 / Be + S ... ?（直接問句）

   = S + V + (O) + whether/if + S + V ...（間接問句）

   Does she have a driver's license?

   （她持有駕照嗎？）

   = I'd like to know whether she has a driver's license.

2. 疑問字 + 助動詞 / be + S …?（直接問句）

   = S + V + (O) + 疑問字 + S + V …（間接問句）

   Where are you headed?

（你要前往哪裡？）

= Tell me where you are headed.

3. Do/Did + S + $\begin{vmatrix} \text{ask, hear, know} \\ \text{mention, say, tell} \end{vmatrix}$ + 疑問字 + S + V …？

   Do you know where he comes from?（回答Yes/No）

   （你知道他是哪裡人嗎？）

4. 疑問字 + do/did + S + $\begin{vmatrix} \text{believe, guess, imagine} \\ \text{suppose, think, say} \end{vmatrix}$ + (S) + V …？

   Where do you think he comes from?（回答地點）

   （你認為他是哪裡人？）

5. S + V + (O) ..., don't/isn't + S（代名詞）？（附加問句）

   Peter likes blondes, doesn't he?

   （彼德喜歡金髮女郎，是不是？）

聯考題型

1. _____ you didn't keep your promise?
   (A) Why　　　　(B) How　　　　(C) What for　　　(D) How come

2. But does our society encourage our children to break the rules? I'm afraid the answer is _____. (94學測)
   (A) no　　　　(B) not　　　　(C) none　　　　(D) nothing

3. A: What do you do?
   B: _____.
   (A) How do you do?　　　　　　(B) Nice to meet you.
   (C) I'm jogging now.　　　　　　(D) I'm a lawyer.

4. _____ I say "a lot of dime"? Oh, I'm really sorry. I meant to say "a lot of time." (94指考)
   (A) Did　　　　(B) Do　　　　(C) May　　　　(D) Shall

5. Mary: How often do you have your hair cut?

George: _____.

(A) Two weeks 　　　　　　(B) Two weeks ago

(C) Every two weeks 　　　(D) Until two weeks

6. _____ you someone who practically lives in front of the computer — a mouse potato? (91指考)

(A) Do 　　　(B) Have 　　　(C) Are 　　　(D) Will

7. (A) Who do you think you are? 　　(B) Who do you think are you?

(C) Do you think who you are? 　　(D) Do you think who are you?

8. That is why, every once in a while, _____ to escape into the world of fantasy. (91學測)

(A) we like 　　(B) do we like 　　(C) like us 　　(D) are we like

9. Jack seldom goes swimming in the morning, _____?

(A) does Jack 　(B) doesn't Jack 　(C) does he 　(D) doesn't he

10. Flight Attendant: Excuse me, would you like the chicken or the beef?

Passenger: _____ (88聯招)

(A) Yes, please. 　(B) No way. 　(C) Chicken soup. (D) Beef, please

11. Let's go grab a bite before the movie, _____?

(A) shall we 　(B) will you 　(C) may we 　(D) can you

12. Tom: Don't forget tomorrow night at my home.

Bill: No, I won't. Do you mind if I bring a friend?

Tom: _____.

Bill: See you then. (85聯招)

(A) Yes, it's a good idea. 　　(B) No, you'd better not.

(C) Certainly, I do. 　　　　(D) Not at all. You're all welcome.

13. A: Do you have the time?

B: _____.

(A) Yes, I'm free now. 　　(B) No, I must hurry.

(C) Sorry, I forgot. 　　　(D) It's three twenty.

14. Kevin: How do you find my sister?

Hart: _____.

(A) She's very intelligent. 　　(B) Not me. It's someone else.

(C) The police did. 　　　　(D) You must be kidding.

15. John has to apologize, _____ he?

(A) hasn't 　(B) must 　(C) does 　(D) doesn't

1. 你有沒有告訴過我她想要什麼？

   試譯：＿＿＿＿＿＿＿＿＿＿＿＿＿＿＿＿＿＿＿＿＿＿＿＿

2. 你曾經告訴過我她想要什麼啊？

   試譯：＿＿＿＿＿＿＿＿＿＿＿＿＿＿＿＿＿＿＿＿＿＿＿＿

3. 老闆多久會回來？

   試譯：＿＿＿＿＿＿＿＿＿＿＿＿＿＿＿＿＿＿＿＿＿＿＿＿

4. 你到底是指誰啊？

   試譯：＿＿＿＿＿＿＿＿＿＿＿＿＿＿＿＿＿＿＿＿＿＿＿＿

5. 他要在這裡待多久？

   試譯：＿＿＿＿＿＿＿＿＿＿＿＿＿＿＿＿＿＿＿＿＿＿＿＿

要點 3

感嘆句的句型：

1. How +
   ① adj. + (a + n.) + S + V !
   ② adv. + S + V !

   How beautiful (a girl) she is !
   （她是多麼美麗啊！）

   How beautifully she dances !
   （她舞跳得多美啊！）

2. What +
   ① a(n) + (adj.) + n. + S + V !
   ② (adj.) + 複數/不可數 n. + S + V !

What a handsome boy he is !

= How handsome a boy he is !

（他是多麼英俊蕭灑啊！）

What a fool he is !

= What a foolish man he is !

（他是多麼愚蠢啊！）

What nice people they are !

= How nice these people are !

（他們這些人真親切啊！）

What freedom they enjoy !

（他們享有何等自由啊！）

說明：

how 是副詞，直接修飾其後的形容/副詞。What 是形容詞，可直接引導名詞。

聯考題型

1. Wow ! Can you believe your eyes? _____ it is !
   (A) What a gorgeous view   (B) How a gorgeous view
   (C) What view gorgeous   (D) How view gorgeous

2. What a small computer ! Does it really _____? (86推甄)
   (A) bite   (B) type   (C) work   (D) use

3. _____ to shop on the Internet !
   (A) It is how easy   (B) How easy it is (C) It is what easy (D) What easy it is

4. Wife: Sweetheart. You'll never believe this. I just won the lottery !
   Husband: _____ I don't believe it. (86聯招)
   (A) Cheer up !   (B) Good work !   (C) That's awful !   (D)Good heavens !

5. (A) What sweet music it is !   (B) How sweet music it is !
   (C) What music it is sweet !   (D) How music it is sweet !

6. Paul: I've just passed my college entrance exam.

David: _____.

Paul: I feel so relieved now. (84聯招)

(A) Well done !　　(B) What a pity !　　(C) How awful !　　(D) Cheer up !

7. _____ strange neighbors you have !

(A) How　　　　　(B) What　　　　(C) Which　　　　(D) Whether

8. Alice: Guess what?

John: _____. (83聯招)

(A) What?

(B) Sure, what can I do for you?

(C) I'm glad you are having a good time.

(D) Really? What a pleasant surprise !

9. _____ awful weather we are having !

(A) What　　　　　(B) How　　　　(C) So　　　　(D) If

10. _____ fast rumors are spreading !

(A) What　　　　　(B) How　　　　(C) Too　　　　(D) Such

翻譯造句

1. 真是巧啊！我也正要去購物。

試譯：_____

2. 你看，她走路的姿勢多優雅啊！

試譯：_____

3. 你的老弟真是個天才唉！

試譯：_____

4. 你聽，雨下得多大啊！

試譯：_____

5. 在這裡遇到你真是令人驚喜啊！

試譯：_____

祈使/願句的句型：

1. 原形動詞 + (O)…　（肯定的命令/要求）

   Take out the trash !

   （把垃圾拿出去倒！）

   Be a good boy !

   （要當個好男孩！）

2. Don't / Never + 原形動詞 + (O)…　（否定的命令/要求）

   Don't rely on others for everything.

   （不要事事依賴別人。）

   Never say die.

   （不要氣餒。）

3. Let me / us / him + 原形動詞　（請求）

   Let me give you a word of advice.

   （讓我給你一句忠告好了。）

4. May + S + 原形動詞…　（祈願）

   May you live long and be happy !

   （祝你長命百歲，幸福美滿！）

說明：

原形動詞 + (O)…，and / or + S + V…表『做…然後 / 否則就…。』

1. _____ yourself a minimum of 30 minutes to do exercise every day.
   (A) Giving　　　(B) Give　　　(C) To give　　　(D) Given

2. "Look, mate ! Don't _____ do that again. You scared the living daylights out of me !" (94指考)
   (A) ever　　　(B) never　　　(C) yourself　　　(D) think

3. The Post Office? Oh, go straight and _____ left at the lights. You can't miss it.
   (A) turn　　　(B) turned　　　(C) turning　　　(D) to turn

4. _____ "geocaching," for example. Hikers looking for something a little different on their treks created a global hunting game. (93指考)
   (A) Make　　　(B) Take　　　(C) Look　　　(D) Cite

5. If you have a speech to make, _____ it short and sweet.
   (A) make　　　(B) take　　　(C) look　　　(D) cite

6. _____ the instructions closely, and you will find it easy to assemble the bicycle. (87推甄)
   (A) Read　　　(B) Keep　　　(C) Follow　　　(D) Offer

7. Don't _____ off more than you can chew.
   (A) pay　　　(B) get　　　(C) turn　　　(D) bite

8. Take heart and _____ your goal for as long as it takes. (87聯招)
   (A) hang on to　　(B) keep out of　　(C) go back on　　(D) get it straight

9. _____ sorry, or you'll be punished by your dad.
   (A) Say　　　(B) Admit　　　(C) Tell　　　(D) Claim

10. Tim: Someone left a schoolbag on the bus.
    Sam: _____ there is a name inside the bag. (86推甄)
    (A) Look whether　(B) See if　　　(C) Find out　　　(D) Take care

11. _____ sure to punch in when you get to work.
    (A) Be　　　(B) Make　　　(C) Feel　　　(D) For

12. "Let's go Dutch," John said to Paul after eating dinner at a restaurant. (86聯招)
    (A) find another restaurant　　　(B) share expenses
    (C) travel to Holland　　　(D) leave right away

13. One more mistake, _____ you are fired.
   (A) and (B) but (C) or (D) for

14. _____ God bless our country and people.
   (A) May (B) Might (C) Will (D) Would

15. Never _____ ashamed to admit that the fault is yours.
   (A) look (B) looking (C) be (D) being

翻譯造句

1. 要就接受，不要就算了。 (take)

   試譯： _____

2. 不要讓你自己成為一個傻瓜。 (make)

   試譯： _____

3. 再加把勁，那麼你就會成功。 (One...)

   試譯： _____

4. 請坐！ (Be...)

   試譯： _____

5. 願有情人終成眷屬。 (May...)

   試譯： _____

名詞子句

1. 帶 that 的名詞子句（接於 Vt 之後 that 可省略）

   We believe (that) John is innocent.

   （我們相信約翰是無辜的。）

2. 帶 whether/if 的名詞子句

   She asked whether/if I liked pizza.

   （她問我是否喜歡披薩。）

3. 帶 who/what/why/where/how 等『疑問字』的名詞子句

   Please tell me what happened.（what 為疑問代名詞）

   （請告訴我發生了什麼事。）

4. 帶 whoever/what/whatever 等『複合關代』的名詞子句

   He showed me what he had bought. (what = the thing which)

   （他亮出他買的東西給我看。）

說明：

英文有『句子』和『子句』之分。不論是直述句或祈使句，『句子』可以獨立使用。『子句』不能獨立使用，必須附屬於某一句子。打個比方，句子是『大人』，可以獨立。子句是還不能獨立的『小孩子』，必須有人來『帶』。因此，子句須有　that/whether/what 等來帶。子句的型式為 that/whether/what + S + V …（不倒裝）

1. I'm not sure _____ my girlfriend will come or not.
   (A) when　　　　(B) that　　　　　(C) whether　　　(D) of

2. These photos will show _____ smoking damages your health. (94學測)
   (A) when　　　　(B) how　　　　　(C) where　　　　(D) what

3. I'm sure _____ he will make it to the wedding.
   (A) when　　　　　(B) that　　　　　(C) whether　　　　　(D) if

4. The 7,000 pieces－full statues, heads and carved inscriptions－are breathtaking not only for their individual beauty but also for _____ they represent. (94指考)
   (A) what　　　　　(B) which　　　　　(C) that　　　　　(D) when

5. The prize will go to _____ sings best.
   (A) who　　　　　(B) whom　　　　　(C) whoever　　　　　(D) whomever

6. Another requirement was _____ he should have large ears, upward-slanting eyes and eyebrows. (93學測)
   (A) what　　　　　(B) whether　　　　　(C) why　　　　　(D) that

7. Who he is _____ no concern of mine.
   (A) is　　　　　(B) does　　　　　(C) makes　　　　　(D) takes

8. About 60 million years ago Gondwana broke up into _____ later became South America, Africa, Antarctica, India and Australia. (92學測)
   (A) which　　　　　(B) where　　　　　(C) what　　　　　(D) that

9. _____ the earth is round is known to everybody.
   (A) That　　　　　(B) How　　　　　(C) When　　　　　(D)What

10. I have no doubt _____ your older brother will stage a comeback in the next election.
   (A) that　　　　　(B) whether　　　　　(C) if　　　　　(D) about

1. 名詞子句作主詞（接單數動詞）

Whatever he says makes sense.

（他說的任何一句話都有道理。）

Whether my dad will agree is still unknown.

（我老爸是否會同意還不知道。）

2. 名詞子句作受詞

I know **who stole your bike**.（Vt 的受詞）

（我知道誰偷了你的腳踏車。）

We are concerned about **whether it will clear up this afternoon**.（介系詞的受詞）

（我們關心今天下午是否會放晴。）

說明：

表『是否…』的名詞子句置於句首作主詞時，限用 whether（if 不可）引導。另外，置於介系詞之後也限用 whether（if 不可）引導。

翻譯造句

1. 她會選擇哪一個無關緊要。 (matter)

   試譯：_____

2. 告訴我該輪到誰了。 (whose)

   試譯：_____

3. 他當時為何要辭職，我們一直不解。 (mystery)

   試譯：_____

4. 我不知道他們是否會結婚。 (wonder)

   試譯：＿＿＿＿＿＿＿＿＿＿＿＿＿＿＿＿＿＿＿＿

5. 你知道 David 如何謀生嗎？ (how)

   試譯：＿＿＿＿＿＿＿＿＿＿＿＿＿＿＿＿＿＿＿＿

要點 3

名詞子句作補語/同位語

1. S + be + 名詞子句（主詞補語）

   The fact is that he no longer works here.

   （事實是他已經不在這裡工作了。）

   This is what Mom told me.

   （這是老媽告訴我的。）

2. 名詞子句作受詞補語

   S + make + O + what (ever) + S + be.

   Hard work has made him what he is today.

   （努力使他有今天的成就。）

3. 名詞 + that + S + V …（同位語）

   The news that he died is confirmed.（主詞同位語）

   （他過世的消息已獲得證實。）

   比較：The news (that) he told me is true.（形容詞子句）

   （他告訴我的那則消息是真的。）

說明：

引導名詞子句的 that 是一個『連接詞』，本身不具任何意義。下列兩種情形的 that 不能省略：(1) 置於句首引導子句作主詞時；(2) 引導子句作名詞同位語時。

1. 問題之一是我沒有足夠的現金。

   試譯：_____

2. 他的意見是你應暫緩出國。

   試譯：_____

3. 她的父母造就了今日的她。

   試譯：_____

4. 男人比女人優越的想法是錯誤的。

   試譯：_____

5. 我有信心你會獲得那筆獎學金。

   試譯：_____

要點 4

that 引導的名詞子句接於若干特殊形容詞之後

$$S + be + \begin{vmatrix} \text{afraid, ashamed, aware,} \\ \text{confident, convinced,} \\ \text{delighted, determined} \\ \text{glad, sorry, sure, worried} \end{vmatrix} + \text{(that)} + S + V \cdots$$

I'm afraid that the typhoon will come.

（恐怕颱風會來。）

Jack is glad that you are his partner now.

（傑克很高興你已經是他的合夥人。）

She is worried that he may walk out on her.

（她擔心他或許會棄她而去。）

說明：

I'm afraid that …是 I'm afraid of the likelihood that … 之略。Jack is glad that …
為 Jack is glad of the fact that …之略。She is worried that …是 She is worried
about the possibility that …之略。因此這種 that 子句是名詞子句。

翻譯造句

1. 我對自己犯下這個錯誤引以為恥。 (ashamed)

   試譯：＿＿＿＿＿＿＿＿＿＿＿＿＿＿＿＿＿＿＿＿＿＿＿＿＿＿＿

2. 你知道你該對這件事情負責嗎？ (aware)

   試譯：＿＿＿＿＿＿＿＿＿＿＿＿＿＿＿＿＿＿＿＿＿＿＿＿＿＿＿

3. 我深信我們這次做對了。 (convinced)

   試譯：＿＿＿＿＿＿＿＿＿＿＿＿＿＿＿＿＿＿＿＿＿＿＿＿＿＿＿

4. 我們很高興期末考試總算結束了。 (delighted)

   試譯：＿＿＿＿＿＿＿＿＿＿＿＿＿＿＿＿＿＿＿＿＿＿＿＿＿＿＿

5. 你確定沒忘了什麼吧？ (sure)

   試譯：＿＿＿＿＿＿＿＿＿＿＿＿＿＿＿＿＿＿＿＿＿＿＿＿＿＿＿

要點 1

（簡單）關係代名詞引導的形容詞子句

先行詞　　　格	主格	受格	所有格
人	who	who(m)	① whose　② of whom
事物	which	which	① whose　② of which
人事物	that	that	

① 關係代名詞 = 連接詞 + 代名詞。

② 先行詞→關係代名詞所指的人或事物。

③ 關係代名詞所引導的子句是形容詞子句（因其修飾先行詞，即其前之名詞）。

④ 使用關係代名詞須先考慮其先行詞（人或事物），但該關代的格則由該形容詞子句的需要決定。

⑤ that 之前不可有介系詞或逗點。

⑥ 主格關代之後的動詞單複數應與先行詞一致。

⑦ 受格的關代 (whom, which, that) 一般可以省略，前有介系詞或逗點則否。

⑧ 主格關代一般不省略，若欲省略，須將其動詞約化為 v-ing 或 p.p.。

⑨ 關係詞與先行詞之間沒有逗點時為限定用法，有逗點為補述用法。

　　Tom is the man <u>who/that won the prize</u>.（主格）

（湯姆就是得獎的那個人。）

　　They are the foreigners <u>who(m)/that I mentioned</u>.（受格）

（他們就是我曾提及的老外。）

　　A child <u>whose parents are dead is called an orphan</u>.（所有格）

（父母雙亡的小孩就是孤兒。）

　　This is the dog <u>which/that bit me yesterday</u>.（主格）

（昨天咬我的就是這隻狗。）

　　The novel <u>which/that you lent me</u> is interesting.（受格）

（你借我的那本小說很有趣。）

We live in a house <u>whose roof may collapse at any time</u>.（所有格）

（我們住在一棟屋頂隨時可能塌下來的房子。）

聯考題型

1. For those people _____ work requires much sitting, brisk walking is strongly recommended.
   (A) who   (B) whom   (C) whose   (D) that

2. It consists of nearly one hundred islands, _____ many are famous for their pure white-sand beaches. (94指考)
   (A) which   (B) that   (C) of which   (D) of that

3. Good writing is an acquired skill _____ constant practice.
   (A) requiring   (B) which require   (C) required   (D) that requiring

4. Jet lag, _____ by traveling between time zones, is becoming a common problem for frequent travelers. (94學測)
   (A) is caused   (B) caused   (C) which caused   (D) causing

5. On the MRT I met a foreigner _____ I thought was your English teacher.
   (A) who   (B) whom   (C) whose   (D) which

6. All the students are required to attend the two-day orientation program so that they can have a complete understanding of the university _____ they are admitted to. (93指考)
   (A) when   (B) where   (C) which   (D) who

7. He fears nothing _____ knows nothing.
   (A) who   (B) which   (C) when   (D) if

8. A person _____ exercises regularly is more likely to look young. (92學測)
   (A) who   (B) do   (C) take   (D) when

9. This is the gentleman _____ I've been waiting.
   (A) who   (B) whom   (C) for who   (D) for whom

10. Less than 3 percent of the world's water is fresh, and most of _____ is trapped in polar ice or buried underground in springs too deep to reach. (91指考)
    (A) which   (B) it   (C) what   (D) them

11. This is the electronic toy _____ I paid 50 dollars.
    (A) which   (B) for which   (C) that   (D) for that

12. I spent three years in Paris, during _____ time I studied both French literature and philosophy.
    (A) that   (B) this   (C) which   (D) much

13. Look up in the dictionary the word _____ meaning you do not understand.
    (A) what   (B) which   (C) that   (D) whose

14. The motorcyclist _____ down by a van has been sent to a nearby hospital.
    (A) run   (B) running   (C) ran   (D) to run

15. Look at the blind man and the Seeing Eye dog _____ are crossing the street !
    (A) which   (B) who   (C) that   (D) they

翻譯造句

1. 窗子破掉那棟房子好像鬧鬼。 (haunted)

   試譯：_____

2. 鬍子長長的那個老人是我爺爺。

   試譯：_____

3. 她就是你曾經提到的女孩嗎？

   試譯：_____

4. 他就是警方正在尋找的那個人。

   試譯：_____

5. 當時乘客很少，都逃離開沒有受傷。（非限定用法）

   試譯：_____

複合關係代名詞 = 先行詞 + 關係代名詞（引導名詞子句）

1. whoever（主格）= anyone who
2. who(m)ever（受格）= anyone whom
3. whosever（所有格，已罕用）= anyone whose

凡⋯之人

　　We will invite <u>whoever is willing to come</u>.（主格）

（凡是願意來的人都在我們邀請之列。）

　　The boss can employ <u>who(m)ever he likes</u>.（受格）

（老闆想僱用誰就僱用誰。）

4. what = ① the thing(s) <u>which</u> →指事物（主/受格）
　　　　　 ② the person <u>that</u> →指身分/地位/人品（作補語）

　　She didn't want to give up <u>what seemed to be her last hope</u>.（主格）

（她不想放棄這個似乎是她最後希望的機會。）

　　<u>What he said</u> is true.（受格）

（他當時說的是千真萬確的。）

　　Have confidence, and you can become <u>what you want to be</u>.（補語）

（有信心，你就可以成為你想成為的那種人。）

5. Whatever = anything which → 指任何東西

　　Help yourself to <u>whatever you want to eat</u>.

（想吃任何東西的話，請自取。）

6. whichever = any one of those that → 其中的任一人/物

　　I have five daughters. You may marry <u>whichever you like</u>.

（我有五個女兒。你可以娶你喜歡的任何一個。）

1. Go and discuss the problem with _____ is in charge there.
   (A) who   (B) whom   (C) whoever   (D) whomever

2. To be active, you must dare to rebel, and courageously express your own outlook and take pride in _____ makes you unique. (94學測)
   (A) what   (B) that   (C) which   (D) where

3. _____ seems easy at first will often turn out to be difficult in the end.
   (A) What   (B) It   (C) Which   (D) That

4. Now, you are free to say _____ you want to say.
   (A) whoever   (B) however   (C) whatever   (D) whichever

5. Here we have a variety of ties. You may choose _____ goes with your suit.
   (A) what   (B) whatever   (C) which   (D) whichever

1. 現在的他已非昔日的他了。(what)

   試譯：_____

2. 你的任何東西就是我的。(whatever)

   試譯：_____

3. 把這本小冊子送給想要的任何人。(whoever)

   試譯：_____

4. 我們工作三班制。你可以挑選最適合你的其中之一班。(whichever)

   試譯：We work in three shifts. _____

5. 他們對我所建議的事項不感興趣。(what)

   試譯：_____

關係形容詞（= 連接詞 + 形容詞）的句型

1. <u>which</u> + n. + S + V … →而這個…

   The code was written in Hebrew, <u>which</u> language I don't understand.

   （這個密碼是用希伯來文寫的，而這種語文是我不懂的。）

2. <u>whichever</u> + n. + S + V … →（其中的）任一…

   You may take <u>whichever</u> seat you like.

   （你可以坐你喜歡的任何一個位子。）

3. <u>what</u> few/little + (n.) + S + V … →僅有的…

   I spent <u>what</u> little time I had with my family.

   （我將僅有的一點點時間拿來與家人共度。）

4. <u>whatever</u> + n. + S + V … →無論什麼的…

   You may write on <u>whatever</u> subject you choose.

   （你可以寫你所選的任何題目。）

聯考題型

1. I stayed in Rome for five years, during _____ time I devoted myself to art.
   (A) that   (B) this   (C) what   (D) which

2. My dad did not read many books. But _____ few books he ever read, he read very carefully.
   (A) which   (B) what   (C) whichever   (D) whatever

3. The soldier decided to go on fighting. He wouldn't give up _____ little hope he had.
   (A) which   (B) what   (C) how   (D) where

4. You may take _____ route you like to get there.
   (A) which   (B) what   (C) whichever   (D) whatever

5. I'm willing to pay _____ price you ask.
   (A) whichever   (B) whatever   (C) whoever   (D) however

翻譯造句

1. 我準備接受我能獲得的任何幫助。 (whatever)

   試譯：_____

2. 他說的不多，但句句充滿著智慧。 (what)

   試譯：_____

3. 他們要我戒菸，而這個勸告我並沒有接受。 (which)

   試譯：_____

4. 你可以選擇最適合你的任何一種方法。 (whichever)

   試譯：_____

5. 我把身上僅有的一點點錢都給了那名乞丐。 (what)

   試譯：_____

先行詞（時間/地點/原因） + 關係副詞（＝介系詞 + 關代）…

1. the time + <u>when</u> (= at/in/on/during which)

2. the place + <u>where</u> (= at/in/on which)

3. the reason + <u>why</u> (= for which)

4. the way (that/in which) = <u>how</u>

   Can you tell me the time <u>when</u> he will arrive? (= at which)

   （你能否告訴我他何時可抵達？）

   This is the place <u>where</u> we first met. (= in which)

   （這就是我們初次相遇的地方。）

   Give me the reason <u>why</u> you hate him. (= for which)

   （跟我說明你痛恨他的理由。）

   I love to watch <u>the way/how</u> she sings.

   （我很喜歡看她唱歌的樣子。）

說明：

作關係副詞時 how 沒有先行詞。作關係副詞的 when, where, why 可由 that 代替，在口語中還經常被省略，如：The reason(that) these chairs are so expensive is that they are made by hand.（這些椅子這麼貴是因為手工打造的。）關係副詞 when 和 where 有『限定用法』和『非限定用法』之分。另外，關係副詞兼有連接詞和副詞的功能，引導形容詞子句。

1. Please tell me the exact time _____ the plane will take off.
   (A) which   (B) when   (C) how   (D) where

2. Women, similarly, expect men to feel and behave _____ women do. (94學測)
   (A) when   (B) where   (C) why   (D) the way

3. The summer vacation is the only part of the year _____ I am free.
   (A) when   (B) which   (C) where   (D) how

4. But the collection is not in a museum, and it is not open to visitors. It is held in unknown, guarded warehouses _____ only a few people can see it. (94指考)
   (A) which   (B) where   (C) until   (D) unless

5. He stayed there till Saturday _____ he was bound for Tokyo.
   (A) when   (B) , when   (C) and when   (D) which

6. They went to Kaohsiung _____ they spent three days visiting friends and relatives.
   (A) where   (B) , where   (C) there   (D) here

7. Economic consequences are often most serious in developing countries _____ poultry raising is an important source of income. (93指考)
   (A) that   (B) until   (C) although   (D) where

8. Nick is very selfish. This is _____ I don't like about him.
   (A) where   (B) why   (C) because   (D) what

9. Once used, the bags are sealed and stored for the flight back to the earth, _____ they are disposed of. (92學測)
   (A) where   (B) what   (C) which   (D) whether

10. The clearest demonstration of how much people value freedom is _____ they vote with their feet when they have no other way to vote.
    (A) where   (B) why   (C) while   (D) the way

1. 他出生在他祖母去世的那一天。 (when)

   試譯：_____

2. 那是一個我從未去過的小島。 (where)

   試譯：_____

3. 告訴我你為何寧可獨居。 (why)

   試譯：_____

4. 這就是我瘦身的方式。 (how)

   試譯：_____

5. 我不喜歡他看著我的方式。 (the way)

   試譯：_____

要點 5

準關係代名詞 but, as, than 的句型

1. There is no + n + <u>but</u> + (S) + V …→沒有…不…(but = that...not)

   There is no one <u>but</u> admires your courage.（主格）

   = There is no one <u>that</u> does <u>not</u> admire your courage.

   （沒有人不欽佩你的勇氣。）

   There is nothing <u>but</u> I can do.（受格）

   = There is nothing <u>that</u> I cannot do.

   （沒有一件我不能做的事。）

   注意：主格的準關代所接的動詞單複數須與其先行詞一致。

2.

$\left.\begin{array}{l} \text{such (a)} \cdots \\ \text{the same} \\ \text{as ...} \end{array}\right\}$ + n. + as $\cdots \rightarrow$ 像$\cdots$的$\cdots$

Such of you <u>as</u> wish to leave may do so now.（主格）

（你們當中想走的人現在可以離開了。）

There is no such person <u>as</u> you mentioned.（受格）

（並沒有你提及的這個人。）

Animals feel the same pain <u>as</u> we do.（受格）

（動物疼痛的感覺和我們相同。）

3. 比較級 + (n.) + than $\cdots \rightarrow$ 比$\cdots$更$\cdots$的$\cdots$

There is more to this problem <u>than</u> meets the eye.（主格）

（這個問題可不是表面看來那麼簡單。）

We have more problems <u>than</u> we can imagine.（受格）

（我們的問題多到無法想像。）

| 聯考題型

1. *The Bible* says that money is the root of all evil; however, there is no one but _____ money.
   (A) love 　　(B) loves 　　(C) loving 　　(D) to love

2. There are few people but _____ going on vacation.
   (A) love 　　(B) loves 　　(C) loving 　　(D) to love

3. Mary wears the same watch _____ I do.
   (A) that 　　(B) when 　　(C) as 　　(D) but

4. He is as rich a man _____ ever lived.
   (A) that 　　(B) who 　　(C) as 　　(D) so

5. Farmers trap and kill such animals _____ are harmful to the crop.
   (A) that 　　(B) which 　　(C) who 　　(D) as

6. To err is human. Who is there _____ errs?
   (A) but   (B) that   (C) without   (D) never

7. I'll pay you back _____ much as I owe you.
   (A) so   (B) that   (C) this   (D)as

8. Don't give your children more money than _____.
   (A) they need it   (B) they are necessary
   (C) is needed   (D) are needed

9. This is the same bike _____ I lost yesterday. It's mine.
   (A) that   (B) as   (C) when   (D) but

10. Read only such books _____ are worth reading.
    (A) as   (B) that   (C) which   (D) those

翻譯造句

1. 我們當中沒有人不支持你的。 (but)

   試譯：_____

2. 很少人不喜歡被讚美的。 (but)

   試譯：_____

3. 要提防那些諂媚你的人。 (as)

   試譯：_____

4. 這個問題跟我們去年遇到的類似。 (as)

   試譯：_____

5. 她賺的錢比我多很多。 (more)

   試譯：_____

1. which 和 as 均可以以其前面的句子（子句）為先行詞，但用法略有異同。
   ① which 和 as 皆可作 be 動詞的主詞。
   ② which 和 as 皆可作及物 V. 之受詞。
   ③ which 可作一般 V 之主詞，as 不可（be 除外）。
   ④ as 引導的子句可提至句首，which不可。

2. 先行詞是人，但所指的非本人，乃是指其身分（地位）時，其關代不可用who(whom)，限用 which (或 that)，不過 that 之前不可有逗點。

聯考題型

1. He married the girl, _____ he had hoped for many years.
   (A) who   (B) whom   (C) as   (D) that

2. He married the girl, _____ he had scarcely known for two weeks.
   (A) that   (B) whom   (C) as   (D) which

3. She invited us to dinner, _____ was very kind of her.
   (A) who   (B) it   (C) as   (D) that

4. He is a southerner, _____ I know from his accent.
   (A) who   (B) whom   (C) as   (D) that

5. _____ is usual with her, Mary is late again.
   (A) As   (B) It   (C) What   (D) Which

6. She won a gold medal, _____ delighted her very much.
   (A) who   (B) that   (C) as   (D) which

7. George said nothing about the phone call, _____ made his wife very angry.
   (A) that   (B) which   (C) as   (D) it

8. If I were his wife, _____ I am not, I would get divorced.
   (A) who   (B) whom   (C) that   (D) which

9. He wanted to be a policeman, _____ he is now.
   (A) who   (B) whom   (C) that   (D) which

10. He wanted to be a policeman, _____ his father opposed.
    (A) who   (B) whom   (C) that   (D) which

副詞子句

引導時間副詞子句的 when, while, as 之用法

1. when + S + V …→當…之時（常表一點時間）

   When (you are) faced with danger, you should keep a cool head.
   （當你面臨危險時，應保持冷靜。）

2. while + S + V …→當…之時（常表一段時間）

   While (I was) taking a walk, I met a foreigner.
   （我在散步時遇到一名老外。）

3. as = ① when ② while

4. whenever + S + V …→每當…

   = every/each time + S + V …

   Whenever I hear that song, I think of you.
   （每當我聽到那首歌就想到你。）

說明：

while 亦有表『對比/照』的用法。這個 while 的意思相當於 whereas。while 另有表『雖然/儘管』的用法，這個 while 的意思相當於 although/though。

1. How could I convince him _____ he chose not to listen?
   (A) when　　　　(B) while　　　　(C) that　　　　(D) whether

2. _____ a small child, he would pick up a broom and pretend to be playing the guitar for the entertainment of family guests. (94學測)
   (A) Since　　　　(B) For　　　　(C) To　　　　(D) As

3. Mary sprained her ankle _____ playing tennis.
   (A) while   (B) whether   (C) where   (D) though

4. _____ all bird species are thought to be susceptible to infection, domestic poultry flocks are especially vulnerable to infections that can rapidly reach epidemic proportions. (93指考)
   (A) Not   (B) While   (C) Since   (D) Unless

5. _____ a man's heart stops beating, he dies.
   (A) When   (B) While   (C) Unless   (D) Until

6. _____ a Dalai Lama died, a search began for his reincarnation. (93學測)
   (A) However   (B) Forever   (C) Whenever   (D) Whoever

7. _____ people across the world criticized Jackson as an unfit father, child protection groups called on German police to take action against the pop legend. (92指考)
   (A) As   (B) Like   (C) What   (D) Such

8. _____ I agree with you, I do not think your way is the best.
   (A) As   (B) When   (C) While   (D) If

9. The north of the country continues to grow richer, _____ the south grows poorer.
   (A) when   (B) while   (C) even   (D) ever

10. We got to the check-in desk just _____ they were about to close.
    (A) as   (B) like   (C) for   (D) where

克漏字

Everything changes over time, and human languages are no exception.

Languages change as human beings __1__, but the changes are made over periods of centuries instead of years. __2__ made at special times, the changes are all but imperceptible to the speakers. __3__ you look in the mirror each morning, you are not aware of having changed from the day before. Yet the time will come __4__ you are no longer a child, but a man; no longer a young man, but a middle-aged, and then an elderly, man. Languages die, too, like individuals. They may fall into disuse. However,

___5___ they live, they change.

1. (A) are   (B) make   (C) do   (D) take

2. (A) Before   (B) After   (C) If   (D) Unless

3. (A) However   (B) Even   (C) Like   (D) As

4. (A) while   (B) when   (C) but   (D) until

5. (A) while   (B) however   (C) whereas   (D) whether

要點 2

搭配 since 的句型:

1. S + have/has + pp. + (ever) since +
   - ① S + 過去式 V.
   - ② 過去的時間
   - ③ ✕

   I have worked here <u>since</u> I moved to Taipei.（連接詞）
   （自從我搬到台北就一直在此地工作。）
   I have worked here <u>since</u> 2003.（介系詞）
   （自從2003年以來我一直在此地工作。）
   I have worked here <u>since</u>.（副詞）
   （自從那時以來我一直在此地工作。）

2. since + S + 一般 V …→因為/既然…

   Since you are living here, I'll often drop by to see you.
   （既然你目前住在這裡,我會常過來看你。）

   ※ since = now (that) = seeing (that) 表『因為/既然』。

1. It's been a long time since we first _____.
   (A) meet   (B) met   (C) meeting   (D) to meet

2. _____ then, the theory has been elaborated and even extended to explain the positive effect of birth order on intelligence. (94指考)
   (A) Since   (B) And   (C) Just   (D) Back

3. His wife left him five years ago, and he has never seen her _____.
   (A) before   (B) now   (C) soon   (D) since

4. Still others say that aliens were responsible for the growth of highly evolved civilizations which have _____ perished, including the Incan and Mayan civilizations and the legendary Atlantis. (93學測)
   (A) since   (B) ever   (C) even   (D) once

5. Do not blame yourself anymore. I've forgiven you _____.
   (A) long ago   (B) long since   (C) since long   (D) too long

6. Since the terrorist attack on America on September 11, hundreds of new security measures _____ put in place to make Americans safer, or at least feel safer. (92指考)
   (A) are   (B) were   (C) will be   (D) have been

7. I think I have to go on a diet again _____ I'm a little overweight.
   (A) until   (B) unless   (C) since   (D) otherwise

8. Since it was a holiday, I _____ in bed an extra hour. (92學測)
   (A) stay   (B) stayed   (C) have stayed   (D) had stayed

9. _____ my computer is connected to the Internet, I can browse e-papers, send and receive e-mail, and download software. (91指考)
   (A) Now what   (B) Now that   (C) See that   (D) Make sure

10. _____ have you ever been concerned about my feelings?
   (A) Since then   (B) Since when   (C) Since ever   (D) Since long

注意：

when 所引導的子句需視其在整個句中的功用來決定其為何種子句（where/why 引導的子句亦同）。

Do you know <u>when he'll come back</u>?（名詞子句作受詞）

（你知道他何時會回來嗎？）

Tell me the time <u>when he'll be back</u>.（形容詞子句修飾名詞 time）

（請告訴我他回來的時間。）

Give him the letter <u>when he's back</u>.（副詞子句修飾動詞 give）

（他回來時把這封信交給他。）

 要點 3

搭配 until/till 的句型

1. S + V … <u>until</u> + $\begin{cases} ① \text{ 時間} \\ ② \text{ S + V } … \end{cases}$ →直到…

I was employed by a manufacturing company <u>until</u> last month.（介系詞）

（我受僱於一家製造業公司一直到上個月。）

He stayed there <u>until</u> she came back.（連接詞）

（他待在哪裡直到她回來。）

2. S + be/助動詞 + <u>not</u> …<u>until</u> …→直到…才…

Dad did <u>not</u> go to bed <u>until</u> midnight.

（老爸直到午夜才就寢。）

Bob was <u>not</u> aware of the gravity of the situation <u>until</u> he found out the truth.

（直到發現真相後鮑伯才知道情況的嚴重性。）

說明：

1.not 可因句子變化需要代之以 none/nothing/never/hardly 等否定字。

2.Not until + (S + V) 置於句首時，其後的主要子句須倒裝。

聯考題型

1. But the first colony of the red fire ants was not found _____ 1942 by a 13-year-old boy in his backyard. (94學測)
   (A) since　　　(B) until　　　(C) when　　　(D) unless

2. Not until she was 35 _____.
   (A) she got married　　　(B) she was married
   (C) married she　　　　 (D) was she married

3. It was not until the 1970's _____ the modern American football game came into being.
   (A) that　　　(B) when　　　(C) before　　　(D) then

4. People _____ know the blessing of good health until they lose it.
   (A) usually　　(B) hardly　　(C) truly　　(D) justly

5. The supermarket is open _____ eleven p.m. on Fridays.
   (A) to　　　(B) till　　　(C) for　　　(D) through

克漏字

You do not possess anything unless you begin to use it. You buy a beefsteak and transfer it from the butcher's icebox to your __1__. But you do not __2__ the beefsteak in the most important sense __3__ you have got it into your bloodstream. __4__, books must be digested and __5__ in your mind to do you any good.

1. (A) taste　　　(B) own　　　(C) delight　　　(D) health

2. (A) own   (B) owe   (C) reserve   (D) deserve

3. (A) when   (B) after   (C) until   (D) if

4. (A) Otherwise   (B) Likewise   (C) Similar   (D) Contrary

5. (A) informed   (B) fetched   (C) drilled   (D)absorbed

翻譯造句

1. 星期天我通常睡到中午。 (till...)

   試譯：

2. 直到你離開家很久之後你才會想家。 (not... until...)

   試譯：

3. 直到隔天早上事情就發生了。 (nothing)

   試譯：

4. 直到失去自由時人們才知道自由之可貴。 (Not until...)

   試譯：

5. 直到 25 歲時他才獨立，不再依靠父母。 (It was...)

   試譯：

表『一…就…』的句型

1. As soon as + S + V …, S + V …

   As soon as she saw me, she walked away.

   （她一看到我就走開了。）

2. The moment/minute/instant + S + V …, S + V …

   The moment you come, we'll start.

   （你一來我們就開始。）

3. S + had + no sooner + pp. + than + S + 過去式 V …

   = S + had + | hardly | + pp. + | when | + S + 過去式 V …
            | scarcely | | before |

   I had no sooner made the phone call than I regretted it.

   （我一打完電話就後悔了。）

4. On/Upon + V-ing …, S + V …

   On alighting from the plane, we went straight to the hotel.

   （一下飛機我們就直奔飯店。）

5. At the + n + (of sth), S + V …

   At the sight of blood, she will faint.

   （一見到血她就會暈倒。）

6. Directly/Immediately + S + V …, S + V …（英式用法）

   I'll let you know immediately he shows up.

   （他一現身我馬上通知你。）

7. Once + S + V …, S + V …

Once you get to know everybody else, you'll love the place.

（你一旦認識了大家，你就會喜歡這個地方。）

聯考題型

1. Andy rushed out of his office _____ the fire alarm went off.
   (A) as much as   (B) as long as   (C) as soon as   (D) as far as

2. But jet lag becomes a problem _____ we have passed through three or four time zones. (94學測)
   (A) once   (B) like   (C) even   (D) though

3. They came to blows _____ they met each other.
   (A) the first   (B) the minute   (C) the second   (D) the way

4. On receiving my letter of complaint, the hotel manager sent me a written ____. (92指考)
   (A) consent   (B) scandal   (C) lecture   (D) apology

5. No sooner had I walked out of my office _____ I heard the telephone ringing.
   (A) than   (B) when   (C) before   (D) after

6. As soon as the couple realized that they didn't love each other anymore, they _____. (92學測)
   (A) fell off   (B) cut in   (C) broke up   (D) stood by

7. Hardly had he sat down _____ his cellphone rang.
   (A) and   (B) but   (C) that   (D) when

8. Zoe was rather healthy when she was found, and _____ under the care of the orphanage she was very happy. (90推甄)
   (A) once   (B) ever   (C) that   (D) justly

9. The _____ I saw him, I knew he was the man of my dreams.
   (A) way   (B) instant   (C) look   (D) beginning

10. I see you're busy right now, Sue. As soon as you _____, I'd like to talk to you for a few minutes. (89推甄)
    (A) finish   (B) finished   (C) are finishing   (D) will finish

Human beings are indeed social animals. __1__ we are born, our society begins to transform us from mere biological beings into social __2__. Every human being at every stage of history is born into a society and is molded by __3__ society from his or her earliest years. __4__ has been said, the individual would be both speechless and mindless if __5__ away from society.

1. (A) The moment   (B) The occasion   (C) The location   (D) The condition

2. (A) status   (B) elite   (C) customs   (D) ones

3. (A) that   (B) what   (C) which   (D) it's

4. (A) It   (B) As   (C) Like   (D) What

5. (A) taking   (B) to take   (C) taken   (D) took

要點 5

表『目的』和『結果』的句型

1. S + V … + │so that   │+ S +may/can + 原 V …(表目的)
             │in order that│

Peter studied hard so that he might win the scholarship.
（彼德努力用功，為了要得那筆獎學金。）

2. S + V … + │to   │+ 原 V …（表目的）
             │so as to │
             │in order to│

We eat to live, not live to eat.
（吾人為生而食，非為食而生。）

3. S + V … + | with a view to | + v-ing … （表目的）
              | with an eye to |

They had their house renovated with a view to selling it.
（為了求售他們將房子重新整修。）

4. S + V … + | so … | + that + S + V … （表結果）
              | such … |

She was so frightened that she could not say a word.
（她害怕到一句話也說不出來。）

注意：

so 接 adj 或 adv，但是 such 接 n 為主。

| 聯考題型

1. Regular checks are required _____ safety standards to be maintained.
   (A) in order to   (B) in order that   (C) in order for   (D) in order with

2. Nowadays people have to pass various tests for professional certificates _____ they can be qualified for a well-paying job. (94指考)
   (A) so that   (B) such that   (C) so as   (D) such as

3. They are _____ devoted fans of Beckham that they have collected a lot of pictures of him.
   (A) so   (B) such   (C) too   (D) very

4. Julie wants to buy a portable computer _____ she can carry it around when she travels. (93學測)
   (A) so that   (B) such that   (C) so as   (D) such as

5. I drove at a steady 50 mph _____ save fuel.
   (A) so as to   (B) such as to   (C) with a view to   (D) with an eye to

6. The clown has such a funny face _____ children enjoy watching.
   (A) which   (B) that   (C) as   (D) like

7. The clown has such a funny face _____ children enjoy watching it.
   (A) which   (B) that   (C) as   (D) like

8. The book is written in _____ English as you can understand.
   (A) as easy   (B) so easy   (C) such easy   (D) too easy

9. _____ was her carelessness that she lost both her passport and traveler's checks.
   (A) It   (B) So   (C) Such   (D) All

10. _____ careless was my mom that she forgot to turn off the gas stove.
   (A) Such   (B) So   (C) Too   (D) How

克漏字

Most people in the world have to work to live. The way people make a living is always __1__ on the principle of "give and take." That is, people must give something to society before (or after) they take anything from it. On the other hand, society needs contributions from all __2__ of life to be sound and solid. Each member of society, therefore, contributes in a different way. For instance, there is a __3__ difference between ordinary workers and artists. The former work to earn money __4__ they can enjoy those things in life which are not his work. The __5__, however, make money by their works of art in order that they may go on working.

1. (A) base   (B) based   (C) basing   (D) to base

2. (A) types   (B) sorts   (C) species   (D) walks

3. (A) steady   (B) sinister   (C) striking   (D) similar

4. (A) so that   (B) so much   (C) such that   (D) such much

5. (A) later   (B) latter   (C) last   (D) latest

1. 當時的演講很沉悶，所以我睡著了。 (such)

   試譯：＿＿＿＿＿＿＿＿＿＿＿＿＿＿＿＿＿＿＿＿＿＿＿＿＿

2. （我們）休息是為了走更遠的路。 (so that)

   試譯：＿＿＿＿＿＿＿＿＿＿＿＿＿＿＿＿＿＿＿＿＿＿＿＿＿

3. 她打開窗戶好讓一些新鮮的空氣進來。 (so as to)

   試譯：＿＿＿＿＿＿＿＿＿＿＿＿＿＿＿＿＿＿＿＿＿＿＿＿＿

4. 電視如此有影響力以致於它可以讓任何人一夕成名。 (so … that)

   試譯：＿＿＿＿＿＿＿＿＿＿＿＿＿＿＿＿＿＿＿＿＿＿＿＿＿

5. 我早起為的是要看日出。 (in order to)

   試譯：＿＿＿＿＿＿＿＿＿＿＿＿＿＿＿＿＿＿＿＿＿＿＿＿＿

要點 6

表『唯恐/以免…』的句型

    S + V … lest + S + (should) + 原 V …
  = S + V … in case (that) + S + V …
  = S + V … for fear (that) + S + V …
  = S + V … for fear of + V-ing …

Jack turned down the TV lest he should miss the telephone ringing.
（傑克把電視的聲音關小以免漏接電話。）

注意：

in case (that) S + V …表示『如果…』時，相當於 if + S + V …的用法。

1. I put on warm clothes _____ catching cold.
   (A) in spite of　　(B) for fear of　　(C) instead of　　(D) afraid of

2. She drove as fast as possible lest she _____ late.
   (A) would be　　(B) could be　　(C) was　　(D) be

3. The prince disguised himself as a beggar _____ he should be recognized.
   (A) so that　　(B) such that　　(C) lest　　(D) in fear

4. Take some more money with you _____ you need it.
   (A) in case　　(B) in order　　(C) in place　　(D) in fact

5. I refrained from drinking too much wine _____ that I should forget myself.
   (A) for fear　　(B) in fear　　(C) with fear　　(D) by fear

克漏字

Albert Einstein deserves our respect not only because he was a great scientist but also because he led a simple life. While he was undaunted by the __1__ of science, he believed in a life of simplicity. He led a very simple life lest he __2__ waste his time and energy. He went around __3__ old clothes and seldom wore a hat. He shaved with the same soap __4__ he used for his bath. It was simply because he felt using two different kinds of soap made life too complicated for his own __5__.

1. (A) necessity　　(B) complexity　　(C) density　　(D) levity

2. (A) should　　(B) would　　(C) could　　(D) might

3. (A) on　　(B) with　　(C) in　　(D) by

4. (A) which　　(B) that　　(C) when　　(D) but

5. (A) like　　(B) likeness　　(C) likelihood　　(D) liking

表『因為』的句型

1. <u>because</u> + S + V …

Because he is rich, he can afford such luxuries.

（因為他有錢，他買得起這些奢侈品。）

2. <u>for</u> + S + V …（置於主要子句之後）

He must be very rich, for he can afford such luxuries.

（他一定很有錢，因為他買得起那些奢侈品。）

3. <u>as</u> + S + V …

You should not stay up late, as you are in poor health.

（你不應該熬夜到很晚，因為你健康欠佳。）

4. <u>since</u> + S + V …

Since you are busy now, I'll come later.

（既然你現在正忙著，我晚一點再來。）

注意：

1. for 亦可接名詞或 v-ing 表原因。

2. since = now (that) = seeing as = seeing (that), 唯 now (that) 引導的子句限用現在式動詞。

3. $\left. \begin{array}{l} \text{because of = out of = on account of} \\ \text{= due to = owing to = thanks to} \end{array} \right\}$ + n.

1. _____ because Amy is young and pretty, it does not mean she can be a good secretary.
(A) Just   (B) Right   (C) Mere   (D) Partly

2. _____ computers are getting less expensive, they are widely used in schools and offices today. (94學測)
(A) Though   (B) For   (C) As   (D) If

3. My friend kept yawning _____ lack of sleep.
(A) because   (B) since   (C) as   (D) for

4. In Taiwan, using electronic devices is prohibited on domestic flights _____ it interferes with the communication between the pilots and the control tower. (93指考)
(A) because   (B) though   (C) even   (D) unless

5. You may turn to John for help _____ he was your boss.
(A) now that   (B) since   (C) due to   (D) only

6. _____ there are a number of species of firefly, the males of each kind flash their own particular signal. (93學測)
(A) As   (B) For   (C) If   (D) Ever since

7. I went to watch the ceremony _____ curiosity.
(A) out of   (B) away from   (C) up to   (D) in between

8. _____ many students were kept in the dark about the lecture, the attendance was much smaller than expected. (92指考)
(A) Now that   (B) For   (C) Because   (D) Owing to

9. Maybe we should throw a party, _____ that your birthday is next Friday.
(A) see   (B) seeing   (C) seen   (D) to see

10. Our team will certainly win the baseball game _____ all the players are highly motivated. (91學測)
(A) because   (B) unless   (C) until   (D) though

What is the essential difference between man and animals? Man differs from the lower animals in part ___1___ whatever one generation of man gains is passed on to the next, ___2___ that each generation of man starts with a little advantage over the ___3___ that went before it. Most species of animals, on the other hand, have little to offer to their ___4___. The knowledge and skills they can give their young are very ___5___.

1. (A) that　　　(B) because　　(C) since　　　(D) as

2. (A) so　　　　(B) all　　　　(C) such　　　(D) in

3. (A) time　　　(B) age　　　　(C) one　　　(D) other

4. (A) offspring　(B) future　　　(C) charge　　(D) company

5. (A) ample　　　(B) practical　　(C) abstract　(D) limited

要點 8

表『條件』的句型

1. If + S + V …, S + V …→如果…

   If we miss the last bus, we'll have to walk home.

   （如果我們錯過最後一班公車，我們將必須走路回家。）

2. Unless + S + V …, S + V …→除非…

   I can't help you unless you tell me what's wrong.

   （除非你告訴我哪裡出差錯，否則我無法幫你。）

3. As/So long as + S + V …, S + V …→只要…

   = On condition (that) + S + V …, S + V …

= Provided/Providing (that) + S + V…, S + V…

= Only if + S + V…, S + V…

My parents don't care what I work at as long as I am happy.

（只要我快樂我父母不在乎我做什麼工作。）

4. Given (that) + S + V…, S + V… →要是考慮到…

= Considering (that) + S + V…, S + V…

Given that he is so young, he has done a fairly good job.

（要是考慮到他還這麼年輕，他表現得相當好了。）

注意：

if 亦可代之以 assuming (that) 或 suppose/supposing (that)。

聯考題型

1. _____ that conflict is inevitable, we need to know how to manage it.
   (A) Give   (B) Giving   (C) Given   (D) To give

2. Beauty standards vary with culture. In Samoa a woman is not considered attractive _____ she weighs more than 200 pounds. (94學測)
   (A) however   (B) but   (C) even   (D) unless

3. Any book will do _____ it is interesting.
   (A) as soon as (B) as far as   (C) as much as   (D) as long as

4. If you exercise regularly, your blood _____ will be improved, and you will feel more energetic. (94指考)
   (A) fatigure   (B) tranquility   (C) fragrance   (D) circulation

5. _____ that your boss should find out, what should you do?
   (A) Suppose   (B) Supposed   (C) Surprise   (D) Surprised

6. If people keep polluting the rivers, no fish there will survive _____. (93學測)
   (A) at all cost (B) for a long while (C) in the long run (D) by no means

7. _____ you are divorced, what are you going to do then?
   (A) Assume   (B) Assuming   (C) Presume   (D) Presuming

8. _____ old newspapers are stacking up in your house, there are options other than tossing them out or selling them to a recycler. (93指考)
    (A) For   (B) Because   (C) If   (D) Until

9. Take a sweater with you _____ you catch a cold.
    (A) unless   (B) if   (C) in that   (D) in case

10. But _____ that Christmas is just a few weeks away, here is a gift idea. (90學測)
    (A) given   (B) give   (C) giving   (D) to give

克漏字

Some parents like to make a comparison between their children. They tend to do so especially when one of their children does not live up to their __1__. But all parents ought to remember that each child of theirs is an __2__. Besides, every child would like to be treated __3__. Therefore, __4__ children should hear their parents compare them, they would feel that they are being unfairly treated. Parents should realize this and accept each child for __5__ he or she is.

1. (A) expectations   (B) proposals   (C) explanations   (D) programs

2. (A) alien   (B) elite   (C) individual   (D) offender

3. (A) such as   (B) as such   (C) so as   (D) as so

4. (A) when   (B) while   (C) unless   (D) if

5. (A) what   (B) who   (C) how   (D) where

表『雖然／儘管…』的句型

1. <u>Though/Although</u> + S + V …, S + V …

Although he is known to only a few now, he has potential.

（雖然目前認識他的人不多，但是他有潛力。）

2. $\left.\begin{array}{l}\text{（零冠詞）N} \\ \text{Adj} \\ \text{Adv} \\ \text{V}\end{array}\right\}$ + <u>as/though</u> + S + （助動詞）+ (V) …, S + V …

<u>Scholar</u> as he is, he is lacking in common sense.（零冠詞）

（他雖為學者，可是缺乏常識。）

<u>Talented</u> though my wife is, she is a hopeless cook.

（我的老婆雖有才華，但她的廚藝真差。）

<u>Much</u> as I sympathize with you, I am not able to help you.

（我雖然同情你，但卻沒有能力幫你忙。）

<u>Try</u> as she may, she cannot bring him around.

（她雖然嘗試去做，卻無法使他回心轉意。）

3. $\left.\begin{array}{l}\text{Despite} \\ \text{In spite of} \\ \text{For/With all} \\ \text{Notwithstanding}\end{array}\right\}$ + $\begin{array}{l}① \text{ n} \\ ② \text{ v-ing}\end{array}$ … , S + V …

Despite John's repeated faults, I like him nevertheless.

（儘管約翰犯錯不斷，我還是一樣喜歡他。）

注意：

　1. though/although 不能搭配 but 引導子句。

　2. though 可置於句末（前須加一逗點）作副詞表『不過』。

1. _____ as your boyfriend looks, I believe he is an absolute liar.
   (A) Depending   (B) Dependent   (C) Dependable   (D) Dependence

2. Although he is a chef, Roberto _____ cooks his own meals. (94學測)
   (A) rarely   (B) bitterly   (C) naturally   (D) skillfully

3. _____ though it may sound, my idea is that we give up.
   (A) Strange   (B) Strangely   (C) Strangeness   (D) Stranger

4. Though Dr. Wang has been away from his hometown for over ten years, he can still _____ his old house clearly. (94指考)
   (A) nominate   (B) visualize   (C) prolong   (D) sprinkle

5. _____ the bumper-to-bumper traffic, we managed to make it to the meeting.
   (A) In place of   (B) In spite of   (C) In fear of   (D) In front of

6. Although stories about aliens have never been officially _____, their existence has been widely speculated upon. (93學測)
   (A) conformed   (B) confirmed   (C) concerned   (D) concerted

7. Expert as Mr. Osborne is, he is _____ reliable.
   (A) not necessary   (B) not entire   (C) not together   (D) not always

8. _____ she's just five years old, Cindy Smart speaks five languages. (93指考)
   (A) Even as   (B) Even so   (C) Even although (D) Even though

9. _____ as we may, we still cannot make both ends meet.
   (A) Economy   (B) Economic   (C) Economical   (D) Economize

10. Bangkok is incredibly urbanized, _____ beneath its modern appearance lies an unmistakable Thai-ness. (92指考)
    (A) however   (B) but   (C) when   (D) despite

Nowadays advertisements can be seen everywhere. They are appealing to people of all ages. Many of us try to ignore them, indeed. No one can avoid being influenced by advertisements, __1__. Much __2__ we may pride ourselves on our good taste, we are no longer free to choose the things we want, for advertisements have __3__ subtle influence on us. In __4__ efforts to persuade us to buy this or that, advertisers have made a close study of human nature and __5__ all our little weaknesses.

1. (A) though   (B) too   (C) besides   (D) well

2. (A) although   (B) more   (C) like   (D) as

3. (A) presented   (B) exerted   (C) rolled   (D) staged

4. (A) their   (B) our   (C) which   (D) whose

5. (A) classify   (B) classifying   (C) classified   (D) classic

翻譯造句

1. 雖然這一對雙胞胎長得很像，我還是能夠分辨他們。 (Much as)

   試譯：＿＿＿＿＿＿＿＿＿＿＿＿＿＿＿＿＿＿＿＿＿＿＿＿＿＿＿＿

2. 儘管年紀很大，我爺爺還是喜歡開玩笑。 (despite)

   試譯：＿＿＿＿＿＿＿＿＿＿＿＿＿＿＿＿＿＿＿＿＿＿＿＿＿＿＿＿

3. 我要自己作選擇，即使我父母不同意。 (even though)

   試譯：＿＿＿＿＿＿＿＿＿＿＿＿＿＿＿＿＿＿＿＿＿＿＿＿＿＿＿＿

4. 雖然老闆都已給她加薪，她仍在抱怨。 (although)

   試譯：＿＿＿＿＿＿＿＿＿＿＿＿＿＿＿＿＿＿＿＿＿＿＿＿＿＿＿＿

5. 儘管又高又壯，他其實是一個很害羞的人。 (but)

   試譯：＿＿＿＿＿＿＿＿＿＿＿＿＿＿＿＿＿＿＿＿＿＿＿＿＿＿＿＿

表『不論…』的句型

$$
\text{1.} \left.\begin{array}{l} \text{Whoever} \\ \text{Whatever} \\ \text{However} \\ \text{Whichever} \\ \text{Whenever} \\ \text{Wherever} \end{array}\right| + \text{S} + (\text{may}) + \text{V} \cdots, \text{S} + \text{V} \cdots \rightarrow 不論誰/什麼\cdots
$$

$$
= \text{No matter} \left|\begin{array}{l} \text{who} \\ \text{what} \\ \text{how} \\ \text{which} \\ \text{when} \\ \text{where} \end{array}\right| + \text{S} + (\text{may}) + \text{V} \cdots, \text{S} + \text{V} \cdots
$$

Whoever wins the election, it won't make any difference to me.

= No matter who wins the election, it won't make any difference to me.

（不論誰贏得這次選舉，對我來說都一樣。）

2. Whether … A or B, S + V …→不論是 A 或 B …

= A or B, S + V … （AB 兩項須詞性相同並可置於句末）

We cannot do without friends, (whether they are) new or old.

（不論是新的或舊的，我們不能沒有朋友。）

3. regardless/irrespective of + n →不論其…

We consider all qualified job applicants, regardless of sex or age.

（所有合乎條件的應徵者我們都考慮，不論其性別、年齡。）

注意：

1. whoever/whatever/whichever 有時作（複合）關係詞使用，宜詳加比較。

2. whether 引導副詞子句時不可用 if 代替。

1. _____ you call a meeting, remember to make it short and sweet.
(A) Whoever   (B) Whatever   (C) Whenever   (D) Whichever

2. Many researchers have been interested in _____ or not an individual's birth order has an effect on intelligence. (94指考)
(A) whatever   (B) whether   (C) why   (D) where

3. She feels she must get divorced, no matter _____ the consequence may be.
(A) how   (B) who   (C) what   (D) which

4. _____ the weather, the athletic meetings will be held on time. (93學測)
(A) Instead of   (B) In relation to   (C) On behalf of   (D) Regardless of

5. _____ you are, I won't make any exceptions.
(A) Whoever   (B) Whatever   (C) However   (D) Whenever

6. Believe it or _____, America's favorite snack food is the potato chip. (90推甄)
(A) no   (B) not   (C) none   (D) nothing

7. Rain or _____, I go jogging every morning.
(A) sun   (B) sunny   (C) shine   (D) shiny

8. _____ dropped the shoe must have been a brave and determined woman. Perhaps she was successful and made it to Alaska. (90推甄)
(A) Who   (B) No matter who   (C) Whoever   (D) It was who

9. Once formed, all habits are hard to _____, good or bad.
(A) kick   (B) push   (C) pull   (D) strike

10. The shirt comes in three sizes. _____ size you pick, I'll give you a 30% discount.
(A) Whatever   (B) What   (C) Whichever   (D) Which

Fiction writers have more freedom than nonfiction writers in several ways. As far as content is ___1___, fiction writers can write anything they want. In other words, ___2___ they are writing, they can give full rein to their imagination, __3__ of novels or short stories. In terms of language, fiction writers' choice is much wider, too. They are free to use the words they choose, __4__ they are from their native dialects, from their slang, or even from other languages, living or dead. Thus, fiction writers may draw on many sources when it __5__ to writing.

1. (A) concerned   (B) mentioned   (C) referred   (D) suggested

2. (A) what   (B) whatever   (C) who   (D) whoever

3. (A) disregard   (B) instead   (C) display   (D) irrespective

4. (A) if   (B) whether   (C) where   (D) which

5. (A) goes   (B) comes   (C) turns   (D) makes

Unit 6　　　　　時態

要點 1

現在簡單式→表現在的事實、狀態、習慣或真理

1. S + 現在式動詞…（主動）

   He works as a journalist.

   （他當記者。）

2. S + is/am/are + pp …（被動）

   It is finished at long last.

   （工作終於被完成了。）

現在進行式→強調現在正在進行的動作

1. S + is/am/are + V-ing …（主動）

   My mom is cooking dinner now.

   （我老媽正在煮晚餐。）

2. S + is/am/are being + pp …（被動）

   You are being watched.

   （你正被監視中。）

3. S + is/am/are being + adj …（強調一時的行為）

   Anne is being considerate today.

   （安妮今天倒體貼起來了。）

注意：

『知覺』動詞如 know, understand, see, believe, forget, remember 等和『好惡』動詞如 like, love, hate, mind 等一般不用進行式。

1. Newton found that the planets, including the earth, _____ around the sun by what he called the law of gravitation.
   (A) go   (B) goes   (C) went   (D) going

2. The gym is closed on Monday for routine _____ work. The facilities are kept in good condition by the regular checking and repairing. (94指考)
   (A) disturbance   (B) eloquence   (C) maintenance   (D) alliance

3. Normally, most snakes _____ unless they are offended.
   (A) won't be bitten   (B) are not bitten   (C) do not bite   (D) are not biting

4. Irene does not throw away used envelopes. She _____ them by using them for taking telephone messages. (94學測)
   (A) designs   (B) recycles   (C) disguises   (D) manufactures

5. A job applicant _____ at this moment.
   (A) is interviewing   (B) is being interviewed
   (C) has interviewed   (D) has been interviewing

6. The little boy is very _____: he is interested in a lot of different things and always wants to find out more about them. (93指考)
   (A) accurate   (B) inquisitive   (C) manageable   (D) contemporary

7. Typhoons often _____ Taiwan between July and September, bringing a huge amount of rain along.
   (A) blow   (B) hit   (C) shoot   (D) stay

8. Jessica is a very religious girl; she believes that she is always _____ supported by her god. (93學測)
   (A) spritually   (B) typically   (C) historically   (D) officially

9. Take it easy, John. I think you are _____ too nervous now.
   (A) been   (B) being   (C) to be   (D) having been

10. Fiction is the name we use for stories that _____ make-believe, such as *Harry Potter* or *Alice in the Wonderland*. (91指考)
    (A) are   (B) have   (C) do   (D) take

Sometimes the real world can be a confusing place. It is not always fair or kind. And in the real world there are not always happy endings. That is why, every once in a while, we like to escape into the world of fantasy — a place where things always ___1___ and there is always a happy ending.

We want to believe in fantastic creatures in ___2___ lands. We want to believe in magic powers, good friends, and the power of good to overcome evil. We all fantasize about being able to fly and lift buildings off the ground. And how good a magic sword would feel in our hands as we go off to kill a dragon or win ___3___ of a beautiful princess.

The amazing adventures of Superman, Peter Pan, and Harry Potter have charmed many people, children and adults ___4___. The main reason is that these stories offer us chances to get away from this real, frustrating world and allow us to find some magical solutions to our problems. For example, Superman always arrives in the nick of time to prevent a disaster from happening. Peter Pan can fly at will to tease the bad guy Captain Hook, and Harry Potter has his magic power to ___5___ his uncle, aunt and cousin, who always ill-treat him. (91學測改編)

1. (A) go smooth   (B) go astray   (C) go our way   (D) go to pot

2. (A) imaginative   (B) imaginary   (C) imaginable   (D) imagination

3. (A) the day   (B) the game   (C) the hand   (D) the name

4. (A) alike   (B) liking   (C) likely   (D) likewise

5. (A) take revenge on   (B) take pity on
   (C) take advantage of   (D) take note of

過去簡單式和現在完成（進行式）的句型

1. 過去簡單式→表過去（某一點或一段時間）的事實、狀態、習慣。

   S + 過去式 V. +（過去時間副詞）

   The accident <u>happened</u> right here a week ago.

   （這起意外就在一星期前發生在這裡。）

   I <u>worked</u> there from 2000 to 2003.

   （我在那裡工作的期間是自 2000 年至 2003 年。）

2. 現在完成式→表從過去（某一點間）到目前為止的動作狀態。

   S + have/has + pp. + | ① since…
   | ② for + 一段時間
   | ③ so far (= up to now = up to the present)
   | ④ recently (= lately = of late)
   | ⑤ once/twice/three times

   We <u>haven't heard</u> from him for a long time.

   （我們已經很久沒有他的音信了。）

3. 現在完成進行式 (have/has been + V-ing) →強調從過去到現在並將持續下去的動作。

   I'<u>ve been waiting</u> for her for two hours.

   （我等她都已經等了兩個小時了。）

注意：

as (of) yet 亦可搭配現在完成式使用，唯僅限於『否定句』，如：As (of) yet, no evidence has been found.（到目前為止沒有找到任何證據。）

1. We are planning to celebrate our parents' wedding anniversary. They _____ for almost 25 years.
   (A) get married
   (B) have got married
   (C) are married
   (D) have been married

2. Bam once _____ as a trading post on the Silk Road. In the 16th and 17th centuries, treasures from the Far East were carried along the road into the capital cities of Europe. (94學測)
   (A) blossomed
   (B) worked
   (C) disguised
   (D) pictured

3. You are two hours late ! Where _____?
   (A) do you come from
   (B) are you from
   (C) did you come from
   (D) have you from

4. So it should come as little surprise that the Internet _____ the top 25 innovations of the past quarter century. (94指考)
   (A) has headlined
   (B) has invented
   (C) has preserved
   (D) has received

5. George is going to make a tour around the island _____.
   (A) recently
   (B) shortly
   (C) nearly
   (D) formerly

6. The week-long rainfall has _____ landslides and flooding in the mountain areas. (93學測)
   (A) set about
   (B) brought about
   (C) come about
   (D) put about

7. There _____ some hurricanes in the United States in recent months.
   (A) has had
   (B) have had
   (C) has been
   (D) have been

8. The release of his new album _____ the pop singer a huge fortune as well as worldwide fame. (93指考)
   (A) has brought
   (B) has sought
   (C) has thought
   (D) has bought

9. It _____ for about three hours, and it still gives no signs of letting up.
   (A) is raining
   (B) was raining
   (C) has been rained
   (D) has been raining

10. The power workers _____ work around the clock to repair the power lines since the whole city was in the dark. (92學測)
    (A) must
    (B) had to
    (C) will
    (D) ought to

Stress has become a favorite subject of everyday conversation. It is not __1__ to hear friends and family members talk about the difficulty they have in __2__ the stress of everyday life and the efforts they make to control the events __3__ cause stress.

Most of us understand the results of not controlling our reactions __4__ stress. Forty-three percent of all adults suffer terrible health effects __5__ stress. Most physician office visits are for stress-related illnesses and complaints. Stress is linked to the six __6__ causes of death－heart disease, cancer, lung disease, accidents, liver disease, and suicide. Currently, health care costs account for __7__ twelve percent of the gross domestic product.

Yet, while stress may damage our health, it is sometimes necessary, __8__ desirable. Exciting or challenging events __9__ the birth of a child, completion of a major project at work, or moving to a new city generate __10__ much stress as does tragedy or disaster. And without stress, life would be dull. (92學測)

(A) about   (B) from   (C) even   (D) as

(E) managing   (F) like   (G) to   (H) that

(I) unusual   (J) leading

過去完成式的句型

1. 一般過去完成式（不單獨使用，需搭配另一個過去式子句或時間副詞片語）：兩個過去的動作對比時，先發生的用 had + pp，後發生的用過去簡單式。

S + had + pp. + | when/before/until + S + 過去式 V.
              | by/until + 過去時間

They <u>had lived</u> in New York for ten years before they <u>moved</u> here.

（在搬來這裡之前，他們已在紐約居住了10年。）

She <u>had been</u> very busy until yesterday.

（她一直忙碌到昨天為止。）

2. 特殊過去完成式（可單獨使用）：表過去未能實現的希望、意圖等。

S + had + | hoped/wished/expected/
          | meant/intended/thought/ | to + V …
          | planned/wanted/desired

= S + | hoped/wished/expected/
      | meant/intended/thought/ | to have + pp …
      | planned/wanted/desired

I had hoped to visit the Louvre last summer.

= I hoped to have visited the Louvre last summer.

（我原本希望在去年夏天參觀羅浮宮的。）

聯考題型

1. The kids loved to visit the zoo because they _____ wild animals before.
   (A) did not see   (B) have not seen   (C) would not see   (D) had not seen

2. _____ 1975 the red fire ant had colonized over 52 million hectares of the United States. (94學測)
   (A) In   (B) After   (C) By   (D) From

3. I had already gone to bed _____ the doorbell rang.

(A) when   (B) once   (C) than   (D) so

4. _____ age 21, he had already published 25 professional papers on that topic. (94指考)

(A) By   (B) In   (C) With   (D) On

5. Peter had intended to call on you yesterday _____ he didn't.

(A) and   (B) but   (C) if   (D) however

6. John had failed to pay his phone bills for months, so his telephone was _____ last week. (93學測)

(A) interrupted   (B) disconnected   (C) excluded   (D) discriminated

7. Her husband had died in a plane crash _____.

(A) three years ago   (B) three years later
(C) three years before   (D) three years since

8. Of all the students surveyed, 27 percent said they _____ the Net. (92指考)

(A) never use   (B) has never used (C) never using   (D) had never used

9. Quite a few refugees starved to death because they _____ anything for a long time.

(A) has not eaten   (B) did not eat   (C) had not eaten   (D) were not eating

10. The 70-year-old professor _____ the university for age discrimination, because his teaching contract had not been renewed. (92學測)

(A) sued   (B) praised   (C) retired   (D) dreaded

克漏字

When we returned home after a long vacation, we found our house was a complete mess. What on earth __1__ during our absence? To our great surprise, many of our valuable things had disappeared without a __2__. My son's desktop, my wife's jewelry, and two bottles of my vintage wine had all __3__. It was evident that some burglars had broken into our house and had __4__ away with our things. But what angered me most was that the thieves had also damaged some of our household equipment. A window had been broken, the wardrobe had been __5__, and even the mattress in my bedroom had been removed.

1. (A) would happen　(B) has happened　(C) had happened　(D) might happen

2. (A) trace　　　　　(B) trick　　　　　(C) trend　　　　　(D) trial

3. (A) finished　　　　(B) vanished　　　　(C) polished　　　　(D) relished

4. (A) taken　　　　　(B) moved　　　　　(C) walked　　　　　(D) carried

5. (A) packed　　　　(B) attacked　　　　(C) racked　　　　　(D) ransacked

---

要點 4

未來完成式的句型（表未來某時或某動作發生之前已經完成的動作或狀態）：

$$S + will/shall + have + pp \cdots + \begin{vmatrix} by/on + 未來時間 \\ when + S + 現在式\ V \end{vmatrix}$$

We <u>will have finished</u> it by next Monday.

（下週一之前我們將已完成該工作。）

Winter <u>will have come</u> when we meet again.

（我們再見面時，冬天將已經來臨。）

說明：

未來完成式除了表『在未來某時之前已經完成』的概念外，也往往強調其『過程』。
如：We will have finished it by next Monday. 即暗示說話者將持續工作以至完成的
『過程』。另外，We will finish it next Monday.（我們將於下週一完成工作）則僅
強調其『結果』。

1. I _____ for 5 years by 2010.
   (A) will be retired
   (B) have been retired
   (C) will have been retired
   (D) may have retired

2. Next Tuesday is our silver wedding, which means we _____ for 25 years.
   (A) are married
   (B) will be married
   (C) have been married
   (D) will have been married

3. By Christmas Eve the parcel _____.
   (A) will arrive
   (B) will have arrived
   (C) has arrived
   (D) has to arrive

4. The train _____ by the time you get to the station.
   (A) has left   (B) had left   (C) will have left   (D) will be leaving

5. I will have worked here for 8 years _____ the end of this month.
   (A) by   (B) at   (C) with   (D) in

要點 5

名詞/形容詞/副詞子句的時態配合

1. S + 現在式 V. + (that) + S + V（任何合理時態）

   She knows you <u>are/were/will be</u> a successful businessman.

   （她知道你目前/曾經/將會是個成功的生意人。）

2. S + 過去式 V. + that/when等 + S +
   ① 過去式 V. →同時
   ② had + pp. →較早
   ③ would/could + V →較晚
   ④ was/were + V-ing →進行較久
   ⑤ 現在式 V. →真理或不變的事實

   John said that he <u>was</u> a salesperson.（同時）

   （約翰說他是名推銷員。）

He said that he <u>had been</u> a soldier.（較早）

（他說他以前當過軍人。）

He promised that he <u>would come</u> on time.（較晚）

（他保證準時來到。）

He came while I <u>was talking</u> on the phone.（較久）

（他來時我正在講電話。）

He told me (that) he <u>is</u> still in love with Mary.（至今不變）

（他說他至今仍愛著瑪麗。）

3. 關代引導的形容詞子句可搭配任何合理時態。

I know the man who <u>teaches</u> math in your school.

（我認識目前在你們學校教數學的那位先生。）

I know the man who <u>taught</u> math in your school.

（我認識曾經在你們學校教數學的那位先生。）

I know the man who <u>will teach</u> math in your school.

（我認識將要到你們學校教數學的那位先生。）

I know the man who <u>has taught</u> math in your school for 15 years.

（我認識那位已經在你們學校教15年數學的先生。）

4. 時間/條件副詞子句的未來動作一律以現在式表之。其它的副詞子句與名詞、形容詞子句的未來動作仍以未來式表之。

When you <u>see</u> Jack tomorrow, remember me to him.（時間副詞子句）

（明天你見到傑克時，代我向他問候一聲。）

If he <u>comes</u> next Monday, I'll give him a surprise.（條件副詞子句）

（如果他下星期一來的話，我會給他一個驚喜。）

I'm not sure when he <u>will be</u> back tomorrow.（名詞子句）

（我無法確定他明天何時會回來。）

Tell me the exact date when it <u>will take</u> effect.（形容詞子句修飾 date）

（請告訴我正式生效的日期。）

1. Don't worry. If he said he _____ help you, I'm sure he will.
   (A) shall   (B) would   (C) ought   (D) need

2. On the night of his speech, Dr. Thompson was delighted to see that the meeting hall _____ full. (94指考)
   (A) is   (B) was   (C) has been   (D) will be

3. The candles went out while we _____ dinner.
   (A) have had   (B) had had   (C) are having   (D) were having

4. The drug dealer was _____ by the police while he was selling cocaine to a high school student. (94學測)
   (A) threatened   (B) endangered   (C) demonstrated   (D) arrested

5. The whole area was flooded because it _____ for two weeks.
   (A) has rained   (B) is raining
   (C) has been raining   (D) had been raining

6. John _____ to pay his phone bills for months, so his telephone was disconnected last week. (93學測)
   (A) had managed   (B) had failed   (C) had tried   (D) had avoided

7. A lumberjack _____ to the ground while he was felling a tree.
   (A) falls   (B) fell   (C) failed   (D) had fallen

8. Two years ago, when we just moved into town, my daughter Amy came to ask me whether she _____ a pet puppy. (92指考)
   (A) can keep   (B) could keep   (C) can have kept (D) could have kept

9. You must have misunderstood me because that's not what I _____.
   (A) mean   (B) meant   (C) meaning   (D) to mean

10. I bought a used car that _____ to a clergyman.
    (A) belonging   (B) belong   (C) belonged   (D) had belonged

Although stories about aliens have never been officially confirmed, their existence has been widely speculated upon.

Many people believe that __1__ from outer space have visited us for centuries. Some say that life on Earth __2__ "out there" and was seeded here. Others say that aliens have __3__ what happens on Earth, and are responsible for quite a few legends, and that the ancient Greek and Roman gods, __4__ the fairies and dwarfs in many classical tales, were in fact "space people" living here. Still __5__ say that aliens were responsible for the growth of highly evolved civilizations which have __6__ perished, including the Incan and Mayan civilizations and the legendary Atlantis.

A lot of ancient civilizations, __7__ the Egyptians, Hindus, Greeks, and Mayans, have left writings and __8__ which indicate contacts with superior beings "from the stars." Many believe that the aliens are here to help us, while others hold that the aliens intend us __9__ . Still others think that most aliens visit Earth to study us like our scientists study primitive natives and animals, and have no interest in helping us __10__ . It is difficult to comment conclusively on these theories in general, apart from saying that any and all of them might be possible. Maybe time will tell. (93學測)

(A) as well as   (B) beings   (C) drawings   (D) in any way

(E) kept an eye on   (F) like   (G) others   (H) originated

(I) since   (J) harm

1. 我先生跟我結婚將近一年了。

   試譯：＿＿＿＿＿＿＿＿＿＿＿＿＿＿＿＿＿＿＿＿＿＿＿＿＿＿＿

2. 我們結婚的前八個月可以說非常快樂。

   試譯：＿＿＿＿＿＿＿＿＿＿＿＿＿＿＿＿＿＿＿＿＿＿＿＿＿＿＿

3. 可是最近他似乎對他的工作比較有興趣。

   試譯：＿＿＿＿＿＿＿＿＿＿＿＿＿＿＿＿＿＿＿＿＿＿＿＿＿＿＿

4. 他幾乎每晚都在加班。

   試譯：＿＿＿＿＿＿＿＿＿＿＿＿＿＿＿＿＿＿＿＿＿＿＿＿＿＿＿

5. 我該如何才能讓他多花點時間陪我呢？

   試譯：＿＿＿＿＿＿＿＿＿＿＿＿＿＿＿＿＿＿＿＿＿＿＿＿＿＿＿

Unit 7 　　動名詞

要點 1

1. 動名詞（片語）相當於單數名詞，作主詞時限接單<u>數</u>動詞。
   <u>Smoking</u> is habit-forming.（動名詞作主詞）
   （吸菸是會上癮的。）

2. 動名詞（片語）作受詞
   I enjoy <u>smoking after a meal</u>.（動名詞片語作受詞）
   （我喜歡飯後一根菸。）

3. 動名詞（片語）作主詞補語
   One of my bad habits is <u>smoking</u>.（作補語）
   （我的壞習慣之一就是抽菸。）

4. being + adj = n.
   <u>Being poor</u> (= poverty) is nothing to be ashamed of.
   （貧窮並不可恥。）

說明：

動名詞因兼有名詞與動詞性格，其前可置 adj. 或所有格；其後可置受詞或副詞。另外，動名詞和現在分詞很容易混淆。要之，動名詞作名詞用，現在分詞作形容詞用。動名詞表『用途或目的』，現在分詞表『動作或狀態』。如：a <u>sleeping</u> car（有臥舖的車廂）和 a <u>walking</u> stick（走路用的拐杖）是動名詞。A <u>sleeping</u> baby（正在睡覺的嬰兒）和 a <u>walking</u> dictionary（一部活字典）則為現在分詞。

聯考題型

1. _____ is very much like playing baseball: to get "home" safely is what counts.
   (A) Driving　　　(B) To drive　　　(C) A driver　　　(D) Being driven

2. Perhaps our worst mistake is believing that _____ equals being loved, being special, and being cherished. (94學測)

(A) keep fit   (B) stay slim   (C) being thin   (D) underweight

3. As the saying goes, "Teaching others _____ yourself."

(A) teach   (B) teaches   (C) teaching   (D) to teach

4. This is reading for deeper understanding, _____ a thoughtful look at what lies beneath the surface. (93指考)

(A) take   (B) takes   (C) to take   (D) taking

5. Melissa cannot adopt the child because she has a _____ problem.

(A) drinking   (B) drunk   (C) drunken   (D) drinker

6. The successful candidate, usually aged two or three, was then removed from his family to Lhasa to begin _____ training for his future role as a Dalai Lama. (93學測)

(A) spirit   (B) spirited   (C) spiritual   (D) spiritually

7. Being educated is one thing; being _____ is another.

(A) sensed   (B) senseless   (C) sensible   (D) sensory

8. The best time to see kangaroos in action is the evening and early morning. They spend the daytime _____ in the shade. (92指考)

(A) snooze   (B) snoozing   (C) sneeze   (D) sneezing

9. _____ driving can cost drivers a lot of money and, sometimes, their lives, too.

(A) Drinking   (B) Drinker   (C) Drunk   (D) Drunken

10. _____ is the genetic process of producing copies of an individual. (91學測)

(A) Copying   (B) Imitating   (C) Mating   (D) Cloning

文意選填

Falling in love is always magical. It feels eternal as if love will last __1__. We naively believe that somehow we are __2__ from the problems our parents had. We are assured that we are destined to live happily ever after.

But as the magic fades and daily life __3__, it happens that men, forgetting that men and women are supposed to be different, continue to expect women to think and react the way men do; women, ___4___, expect men to feel and behave the way women do. ___5___ taking time to understand and respect each other, we become demanding, resentful, judgmental, and intolerant.

___6___, our relationships are filled with unnecessary disagreements and conflicts. Somehow, problems creep in, resentments build, and communication ___7___. Mistrust increases and rejection and repression surface. The magic of love is then lost.

Very ___8___ people are able to grow in love. Yet, it does happen. ___9___ men and women are able to respect and accept their differences, love has a chance to blossom. Love is, ___10___, magical, and it certainly can last if we remember our differences and respect each other. (94學測)

(A) breaks down   (B) Consequently   (C)similarly   (D) indeed

(E) few   (F) forever   (G) Instead of   (H) takes over

(I) free   (J) As long as

要點 2

動名詞的時態和主、被動

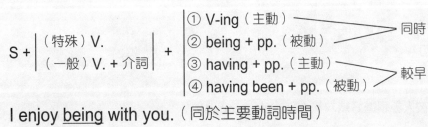

I enjoy being with you.（同於主要動詞時間）
（我喜歡跟你在一起。）

I was afraid of being recognized.（同於主要動詞時間）
（當時我害怕被人認出來。）

He denied <u>having been</u> a thief.（早於主要動詞時間）

（他否認曾經當過小偷。）

He remembered <u>having been framed</u> more than once.（早於主要動詞時間）

（他記得曾經不止一次被人設計陷害。）

聯考題型

1. I said I would stay and keep her company but she insisted on _____.
   (A) left alone
   (B) being left alone
   (C) having left alone
   (D) having been left alone

2. From a physiological standpoint, plants are completely different from animals. They cannot feel pain. Therefore, unlike animals' body parts, many fruits and vegetables can be harvested over and over again without _____. (94學測)
   (A) dying
   (B) dyeing
   (C) dieting
   (D) dating

3. My younger brother has been fined several times for _____.
   (A) speed
   (B) speeds
   (C) speedy
   (D) speeding

4. This is also one of the best areas of the Penghu Islands for bird _____. (94指考)
   (A) watch
   (B) watching
   (C) watcher
   (D) being watched

5. To be frank, I really don't like _____ "Fatty."
   (A) nickname
   (B) to nickname
   (C) nicknaming
   (D) being nicknamed

翻譯造句

1. 我承認曾經被人誣賴過好幾次。 (wrongly accuse)

   試譯：＿＿＿＿＿＿＿＿＿＿＿＿＿＿＿＿＿＿＿＿＿＿＿＿＿

2. 他以曾經當過軍人為榮。 (be proud of)

   試譯：＿＿＿＿＿＿＿＿＿＿＿＿＿＿＿＿＿＿＿＿＿＿＿＿＿

3. 我恥為人師。(be ashamed of)

試譯：_____

4. 她否認結過婚。(deny)

試譯：_____

5. 我有一種被騙的感覺。(have a feeling)

試譯：_____

要點 3

下列特殊動詞（片語）之後，限接動名詞（V-ing 或 being + pp）

admit（承認），anticipate（期望），appreciate（感激），avoid（避免），break/burst out（突然⋯起來），confess to（招認），consider（考慮），delay（延期），deny（否認），dread（害怕），enjoy（喜歡），escape（逃避），excuse（原諒），finish（完成），have done（完成），cannot help（無法避免），imagine（想像），keep（一直），be busy（忙於），loathe（厭惡），mean（意謂），mind（介意），miss（錯過），postpone（延期），practice（練習），quit（停止），recall（想起），resent（厭惡），resist（抗拒），risk（冒險），stand（忍受），suggest（建議）。

聯考題型

1. Nana and I are considering _____ snorkeling next weekend.
   (A) to   (B) to go   (C) going   (D) gone

2. Experts say that creativity by definition means _____ against the tradition and breaking the rules. (94學測)
   (A) go   (B) to go   (C) going   (D) to be going

3. Since there is a mechanical problem, I suggest _____ the manufacturer immediately.
   (A) contact   (B) contacting   (C) to contact   (D) contacted

4. The famous actress decided to sue the magazine for purposely _____ what she actually said and did at the party. (93指考)
(A) assigning　　(B) contributing　　(C) foreseeing　　(D) distorting

5. I anticipate _____ a few Japanese phrases while staying in Tokyo.
(A) picking up　　(B) to pick up　　(C) and pick up　　(D) but pick up

6. With the light produced by bacteria living there, they communicate with other flashlight fish to avoid _____ too close to each other. (93學測)
(A) getting　　　(B) to get　　　(C) got　　　(D) to be got

7. Many women cannot _____ spending money on anything which, they think, can make them look more beautiful or help them slim down.
(A) insist　　　(B) resist　　　(C) assist　　　(D) persist

8. History is nonfiction, too. Imagine _____ history about the 1989 San Francisco earthquake, or a report about a high school sports team. An old proverb says, "Truth is stranger than fiction." Do you think that's true? (91指考)
(A) writing　　　(B) written　　　(C) writer　　　(D) to write

9. I cannot stand passive _____, especially in places where ventilation is bad.
(A) smoke　　　(B) smoking　　　(C) smoker　　　(D) smoked

10. Sara enjoys amusing her friends by _____ stories. (90學測)
(A) speaking out　　(B) setting off　　(C) making up　　(D) giving away

---

克漏字

　　Now I can understand why some people should resort to stealing. About two weeks ago, while I was __1__ my shopping in a night market, I saw an old man limping along the busy street. He was in __2__, giving the impression that he was a beggar. He must have starved for quite a while, __3__ from the way he looked and walked. He looked very weak and walked unsteadily. Then he began to linger in front of a bakery, but he seemed unable to make up his mind whether to enter it or not. But the bread in there was so __4__ that he could not resist entering it. And I thought he went there to beg. But, to my surprise, the clumsy old man went in to steal ! I could not help __5__ about him. In the end, of course, he got caught and was sent to the police station. Even now, I sympathize with him.

1. (A) doing   (B) making   (C) going   (D) taking

2. (A) rag   (B) rags   (C) ragging   (D) ragged

3. (A) judge   (B) to judge   (C) judged   (D) judging

4. (A) enjoying   (B) exhausting   (C) inviting   (D) irritating

5. (A) worry   (B) worried   (C) to worry   (D) worrying

要點 4

一般介系詞（片語）+ V-ing/n

1. How/what about + V-ing/n …? →…如何？（表建議）

2. be not above + V-ing →不會不屑於…

3. be against + V-ing →禁止/反對…

4. besides + V-ing/n →除…之外（包含進來）
= in addition to + V-ing/n

5. between + V-ing … and V-ing … →因…又因…
= what with + V-ing … and V-ing …

6. be far from (being) …→絕非…

7. apart/aside from + V-ing/n. →除…之外
= except for + V-ing/n.（不包含）
= besides + V-ing/n.（包含）

8. in + V-ing … →在…之時

9. instead of + V-ing →不…（反而）…

10. (be) like + V-ing →像…
 = such as + V-ing（不帶 be 的 like 方等）

11. feel like + V-ing … →想要（做）…
 = would like to + V

12. look like + V-ing/n. →看起好像…

13. be past + V-ing →不再…

14. short of + V-ing →除…之外（不包括）

15. fall short of + V-ing/n. →未達到…

16. … never … without + V-ing →每…必…

17. be worth + V-ing/n. →值得…

聯考題型

1. Most of our students are highly motivated. Besides working hard, they are not _____ asking questions.
   (A) above   (B) over   (C) below   (D) beneath

2. _____ the list, the group singles out twenty-five non-medically related technological innovations that have become widely used since 1980. (94指考)
   (A) To create   (B) In creating   (C) With creation   (D) Over creation

3. _____ teaching and writing, my time was fully taken up.
   (A) Beside   (B) Besides   (C) Below   (D) Between

4. Boys were, however, clumsier than girls. They performed poorly at a detailed activity _____ arranging a row of beads. (93學測)
   (A) according to   (B) next to   (C) such as   (D) because of

5. There is a regulation _____ smoking in public places like restaurants, theaters and railway stations.

(A) against   (B) without   (C) above   (D) under

6. Fourteen percent of the respondents said they often turn to books for information _____ going online. (92指考)

(A) in search of   (B) in spite of   (C) instead of   (D) in terms of

7. You should look both ways before _____ the road.

(A) cross   (B) to cross   (C) crossing   (D) you crossing

8. To say that Bangkok is not Thailand is like _____ that New York is not America, Paris is not France, or London is not England. (92指考)

(A) to say   (B) saying   (C) being said   (D) said

9. I used to worry about her coming home late, but now I'm _____ caring.

(A) past   (B) worth   (C) like   (D) without

10. In fact, my life can be described as _____ of a series of "ups" and "downs." (92學測)

(A) consist   (B) consisting   (C) consisted   (D) to consist

文意選填

I had an extraordinary dream last night. In the dream the cloakroom attendant at a theater stopped me in the lobby and insisted on my __1__ my legs behind. I was not surprised, but I was __2__ annoyed. I said I had never heard of such a rule at a theater before. The man replied that he was very __3__ about it, but people often complained that other people's legs were always in the __4__. Therefore, it had been decided that people should leave their legs __5__. It seemed to me that the management had gone beyond their legal right in making this order. Under __6__ circumstances, I should have disputed it. However, I didn't want to __7__ a disturbance, so I sat down and prepared to obey the rule. I had never before known that the human leg could be taken off. I had always thought it was more __8__ fixed. But the man showed me how to undo them, and I found that they __9__ off quite easily. The discovery did not surprise me __10__ more than the original request that I should take them off. Nothing does surprise one in a dream. (90學測)

(A) sorry   (B) outside   (C) leaving   (D) securely

(E) any   (F) normal   (G) quite   (H) came

(I) make   (J) way

翻譯造句

1. 他除了是記者外，也是一位名小說家。 (besides)

   試譯：_____

2. 這結果絕非令人滿意。 (far from)

   試譯：_____

3. 我想要吃點冰淇淋。 (feel like)

   試譯：_____

4. 一起吃午餐如何？ (What/How about)

   試譯：_____

5. 她每次看電影必定買些爆米花。 (never … without)

   試譯：_____

下列常用片語的 "to" 皆為介系詞，需接 V-ing/n

1. be accustomed/used to →習慣於…

2. be addicted to →沈溺於…

3. adapt to →適應…

4. amount to →等於…

5. apply oneself to →致力於…
 = dedicate oneself/one's time to …
 = devote oneself/one's time to …

6. come close to →差一點就…
 = come near (to)

7. due/owing/thanks to →因為…

8. be equal to →（能）勝任…

9. in addition to →除…之外

10. look forward to →期盼…
 = anticipate

11. object to →反對…
 = be opposed to = oppose

12. prefer … to …→寧願…而不…；喜歡…甚於…

13. take to →（開始）喜歡…

14. What do you say to ⋯ ? → ⋯如何？
    = What/How about ⋯ ?

15. when it comes to →說到⋯
    = speaking of ⋯

16. with a view to →為了⋯
    = with an eye to

聯考題型

1. I'm already accustomed to _____ without the telephone and television.
   (A) live   (B) living   (C) alive   (D) lived

2. At age 15, he set out to devote his life to _____ a biological explanation of knowledge. (94指考)
   (A) develop   (B) developed   (C) developing   (D) development

3. Nowadays many kids are _____ to surfing the Net or playing computer games.
   (A) devoting   (B) adapted   (C) denied   (D) addicted

4. For example, an outbreak of avian influenza in the USA in 1983-1984 resulted in the destruction of more than 17 million birds _____ nearly US$ 65 million. (93指考)
   (A) with a view to   (B) in regard to   (C) at a cost of   (D) on account of

5. In addition to _____ his hair blue, Vincent was wearing a fancy shirt.
   (A) dying   (B) dyeing   (C) dye   (D) die

6. After retirement, Mr. Wang _____ ice skating, which he had always loved but had not had time for. (92學測)
   (A) appealed to   (B) took to   (C) related to   (D) saw to

7. You don't have to ask him again because his angry silence amouts to _____ "No."
   (A) saying   (B) say   (C) telling   (D) tell

8. After signing million-dollar contracts with recording companies, singers devote most of their time _____ their music perfect while companies are busy commercializing their products. (91指考)
   (A) in doing   (B) for singing   (C) to making   (D) at playing

9. What a near miss ! The truck came close to _____ my scooter.
   (A) hit   (B) hitting   (C) strike   (D) striking

10. Many students like to watch that talk show because the host is brilliant at _____ young people. (90聯招)
    (A) entertaining   (B) offending   (C) turning down   (D) laughing at

翻譯造句

1. 說到廚藝，她真是笨手笨腳。 (when it comes to)

   試譯：_____

2. 我反對被人如此對待。 (object to)

   試譯：_____

3. 經營這樣的一個企業，他無法勝任。 (be equal to)

   試譯：_____

4. 我寧可快走也不要慢跑。 (prefer … to …)

   試譯：_____

5. 大衛搬到鄉下就是為了要過比較純樸的生活。 (with a view to)

   試譯：_____

1. 下列動詞可接 V-ing 或 to V，意義相同

$$S + \begin{vmatrix} like, love, hate, begin, \\ start, cease, continue, \\ intend, prefer, can't bear \end{vmatrix} + \begin{vmatrix} ① \ V\text{-}ing \\ ② \ to \ V \end{vmatrix}$$

Joy likes <u>hanging</u> out with those gangsters.

= Joy likes <u>to hang</u> out with those gangsters.

（喬伊喜歡跟那些古惑仔廝混在一起。）

I can't bear <u>being</u> laughed at.

= I can't bear <u>to be</u> laughed at.

（我無法忍受被人譏笑。）

2. 下列動詞可接 V-ing 或 to V，但意義不同

① stop + $\begin{vmatrix} V\text{-}ing \to 停止該動作 \\ to \ V \to \ 停下來做另一動作 \end{vmatrix}$

② forget + $\begin{vmatrix} V\text{-}ing \to 忘記做過…（已做） \\ to \ V \to \ 忘了要做…（未做） \end{vmatrix}$

③ remember + $\begin{vmatrix} V\text{-}ing \to 記得做過…（已做） \\ to \ V \to \ 記得要做…（未做） \end{vmatrix}$

④ regret + $\begin{vmatrix} V\text{-}ing \to 後悔做過… \\ to \ V \to \ 遺憾要做… \end{vmatrix}$

⑤ try + $\begin{vmatrix} V\text{-}ing \to 試試看… \\ to \ V \to \ 設法去做… \end{vmatrix}$

⑥ mean + $\begin{vmatrix} V\text{-}ing \to 意謂… \\ to \ V \to 意圖… \end{vmatrix}$

⑦ go on + $\begin{vmatrix} V\text{-}ing \to 繼續做（同一件事） \\ to \ V \to 接著做（另一件事） \end{vmatrix}$

3. 下列動詞可接 V-ing 或 to be + pp，表被動意義

① S + | need / want / require | + | ① V-ing / ② to be + pp | →需要（被）…

② S + | deserve / merit | + | ① V-ing / ② to be + pp | →值得（被）…

聯考題型

1. When a man's heart _____ to beat, he dies.
   (A) stops   (B) ceases   (C) ends   (D) terminates

2. Last year, this company began _____ a lawn-mowing robot called the Robomower. (90聯招)
   (A) sell   (B) sold   (C) sale   (D) selling

3. The idea has ceased being _____. You'd better come up with a new one.
   (A) novel   (B) a novel   (C) novelist   (D) a novelist

4. I could not find my suit because I forgot _____ to the laundry.
   (A) to send it   (B) sending it   (C) to be sent   (D) being sent

5. I regret _____ so young. How I wish I could get back to school again.
   (A) got married   (B) to get married   (C) getting married   (D) I get married

6. We regret _____ you that your contract will not be renewed.
   (A) to inform   (B) in forming   (C) to be informed   (D) being informed

7. His face seems so familiar to me. Now I remember _____ to him sometime last year.
   (A) to introduce   (B) introducing
   (C) to be introduced   (D) being introduced

8. Every time I am in a bad mood, I try _____ a tune.
   (A) hatching   (B) hanging   (C) humming   (D) hugging

9. When you finish this, go on _____ that.
   (A) doing   (B) to do   (C) and do   (D) being done

10. Trying to persuade him out of it means _____ your breath.
    (A) waste   (B) wasting   (C) to waste   (D) wasted

11. Most house plants require regular _____.
    (A) water   (B) watering   (C) to water   (D) to be watered

12. Patients in the ICU need _____ good care of.
    (A) take   (B) to take   (C) taken   (D) taking

13. I work hard and I think I deserve _____.
    (A) a well pay   (B) a well paying
    (C) to be well paying   (D) to be well paid

14. Remember _____ in touch with your boss when you are abroad.
    (A) keeping   (B) to keep   (C) keep   (D) kept

15. Most women, regardless of their age, cannot _____ being sexually harassed.
    (A) bear   (B) beat   (C) deal   (D) delay

翻譯造句

1. 一名路人停下來撿起一枚硬幣。

    試譯：_____

2. 咱們繼續做昨天應該完成的工作吧。 (go on)

    試譯：_____

3. 被機車撞倒的那個男子試圖站起來，但徒勞。 (try)

    試譯：_____

4. 我記得曾經被一隻惡狗追著跑。 (remember)

    試譯：_____

5. 她值得好好獎賞一番。 (deserve)

    試譯：_____

其它搭配 V-ing 的句型

1. S + have + | fun / a good time | + V-ing … → …很愉快

   We had a good time singing at a karaoke bar.

   （我們在一家卡拉 OK 酒店歡唱。）

2. S + have + | difficulty/trouble / a hard time | + V-ing … → …有困難

   Three months after the accident, he still has difficulty walking.

   （發生事故三個月之後，他走路仍有困難。）

3. S + go + V-ing … → 從事…（活動）

   I'll go rock climbing tomorrow.

   （明天我要去攀岩。）

4. do + | the, some, a little, / much, little, one's | + V-ing … → 做…

   We did a lot of sightseeing recently.

   （最近我們參觀了很多景點。）

聯考題型

1. They had a pretty hard time _____ body and soul together.
   (A) keeping   (B) putting   (C) gathering   (D) getting

2. We had good fun _____ at our old pictures.
   (A) look   (B) to look   (C) looking   (D) looked

3. At that time I had difficulty _____ myself understood in Japanese.
   (A) making   (B) letting   (C) allowing   (D) causing

4. My wife is a career woman. Therefore, I sometimes _____.
   (A) do the cook   (B) do the cooking   (C) do a cook   (D) do a cooking

5. On hot days the kids would _____ swimming in the river.
   (A) do   (B) like   (C) go   (D) want

翻譯造句

1. 他們昨晚說笑話，過得很愉快。 (have a good time)

   試譯：_____

2. 我們毫無困難找到你的家。 (have no difficulty)

   試譯：_____

3. 彼德和他的女友這個週末要去泛舟。 (whitewater rafting)

   試譯：_____

4. 該輪到你燙衣服了。 (do the ironing)

   試譯：_____

5. 咱們今天下午去衝浪吧。

   試譯：_____

Unit 8　　　　　　不定詞

要點 1

不定詞（片語）作名詞用

1. 作主詞（限接單數 V.）

   <u>To marry a woman</u> like her is my dream.（主詞）

   （娶一個像她的女人為妻是我的夢想。）

   It's a great honor <u>to be invited</u>.（真主詞）

   （受到邀請是一種殊榮。）

2. 作受詞（通常接於表『意願』或『企圖』的動詞之後）

   S + | decide, desire, expect <br> hope, like, manage, <br> plan, wish, want | + to V

   I've decided <u>to accept the job</u>.（受詞）

   （我已決定接受那份工作。）

3. 作補語

   His last wish is <u>to see his grandson once more</u>.（主詞補語）

   （他的最後願望就是再見他的孫子一面。）

   We believe her <u>to be above suspicion</u>.（受詞補語）

   （我們認為她沒有嫌疑。）

聯考題型

1. To go abroad for further studies _____ my future goal.
   (A) is　　　　(B) are　　　　(C) has　　　　(D) have

2. The aim of the campaign is to _____ people of the damage the deadly weed does to their body. (94學測)
   (A) refer　　　(B) regard　　　(C) remind　　　(D) renovate

3. My grandfather makes it a rule _____ to bed before 10 p.m.
   (A) going　　　　(B) to go　　　　(C) of going　　　　(D) gone

4. Piaget _____ to establish a body of psychology all his life and became a very influential figure in educational psychology. (94指考)
   (A) forgot　　　(B) afforded　　　(C) sought　　　(D) tended

5. It's too dangerous for you _____ that fast.
   (A) driving　　　(B) to drive　　　(C) drive　　　(D) are driving

6. In order to write a report on stars, we decided to _____ the stars in the sky every night. (93學測)
   (A) design　　　(B) seize　　　(C) quote　　　(D) observe

7. The man said he was a taxi-driver, but I believed him _____ a cop.
   (A) is　　　　(B) was　　　　(C) being　　　　(D) to be

8. Jane usually buys things on impulse. Her purchases seem _____ by some sudden force or desire. (93學測)
   (A) to drive　　　(B) to be driving　　　(C) to be driven　　　(D) being driven

9. He knew he might lose all the money, but he chose _____ a chance.
   (A) to run　　　(B) running　　　(C) and run　　　(D) by running

10. One important purpose of the course is for the students _____ to make sound judgments so that they can differentiate between fact and opinion without difficulty. (93指考)
    (A) to learn　　　(B) who learn　　　(C) are learning　　　(D) are learned

---

克漏字

Most of us have learned to vary our language and our behavior to meet the needs of different circumstances. We may feel free to yell and __1__ at children when we are angry with them, but we are usually very careful about __2__ our voices to our bosses or to someone __3__. We may tease our friends or joke around with __4__, yet we tend to be more serious with strangers. __5__, we may accept hugs and __6__ from other members of our family, but many of us get __7__ when people we don't know very well touch us. Besides these obvious signals __8__ which we communicate familiarity, ___9___ are more subtle messages that we send to show whether other people are close friends or whether the relationship is more ___10___. The subtle changes may include slight differences in language, eye contact, and other forms of nonverbal behavior. (83聯招)

1. (A) hit   (B) look   (C) shout   (D) terrify

2. (A) raising   (B) softening   (C) lowering   (D) hardening

3. (A) anterior   (B) inferior   (C) superior   (D) posterior

4. (A) all   (B) each   (C) many   (D) them

5. (A) Anyway   (B) However   (C) Likewise   (D) Although

6. (A) food   (B) money   (C) kisses   (D) clothing

7. (A) moved   (B) uneasy   (C) pleased   (D) used

8. (A) by   (B) in   (C) for   (D) from

9. (A) thus   (B) they   (C) those   (D) there

10. (A) verbal   (B) distant   (C) obvious   (D) intimate

要點 2

不定詞（片語）作形容詞用（修飾其前的名詞）

1. S + V + n. + to Vt.

I have nothing more to say.

（我沒有其它的可說了。）

2. S + V + n. + to Vt + O.

He makes enough money to support a family of five.

（他賺的錢足以養活一家五口的人。）

3. S + V + n. + <u>to V + (O.)</u> + （固定）介系詞.

Your husband is a nice person <u>to work with</u>.

（你的老公是一個很不錯的共事對象。）

4. S + <u>be</u> + <u>to V</u>. →意謂、預定、義務、命令

To love others <u>is to love oneself</u>.（意謂）

（愛人即愛己。）

She and I <u>are to meet at the airport</u>.（預定）

（她和我預定在機場碰面。）

You <u>are to remain here until 5</u>.（義務）

（你應該繼續留在這裡直到5點。）

He <u>is to report to me at once</u>.（命令）

（他必須立刻向我報到。）

聯考題型

1. Because of the power failure, I lit a candle _____.
   (A) to read   (B) to read for   (C) to read by   (D) to read at

2. The rise of oil prices made scientists search for new energy resources to _____ oil. (94學測)
   (A) apply   (B) replace   (C) inform   (D) persuade

3. I think we need a kitchen _____.
   (A) to cook where   (B) to cook here   (C) there to cook   (D) to cook in

4. Here was the perfect opportunity _____ his knowledge of modern medicine. (94指考)
   (A) to show   (B) to showing   (C) in showing   (D) for show

5. She had no friend _____ for help, so I promised to help her.
   (A) to turn to   (B) to turn on   (C) to turn in   (D) to turn back

6. So he stopped going to the market for three days and tried to think of a way _____ the donkey a lesson. (91學測)
(A) to teach　　(B) to teaching　　(C) to be teaching　(D) of teaching

7. Give me a piece of paper to write something _____.
(A) down　　(B) with　　(C) for　　(D) about

8. His bad health has a lot _____ with his eating habits.
(A) to deal　　(B) to do　　(C) to dine　　(D) to diet

9. She lent me a novel to kill time _____.
(A) on　　(B) with　　(C) for　　(D) about

10. After the earthquake, many people had no house _____.
(A) to live on　　(B) to live in　　(C) to live with　　(D) to live for

翻譯造句

1. 他不是一個會食言的人。 (to break his word)

   試譯：_____

2. 不吃早餐並非減肥的好方法。 (to lose weight)

   試譯：_____

3. 感謝你給我這個機會演講。 (to make a speech)

   試譯：_____

4. 他們預定在下個月結婚。 (to get married)

   試譯：_____

5. 沒有什麼好擔心的。 (to worry about)

   試譯：_____

不定詞（片語）作副詞用：

1. 表目的

S + V + | to
         | in order to | + 原形動詞→為了…
         | so as to

I stayed in Japan to learn Japanese.

（我留在日本為了學日文。）

2. 表因果

S + | V + so + adj/adv
    | be + such | + as to + 原形動詞→如此…以致於…

She is so stupid as to believe him.

（她笨到居然相信他。）

His manner was such as to offend almost everyone.

（他的態度如此惡劣以致幾乎得罪了每個人。）

3. 表意外的結果

S + V …, only to + 原形動詞→結果卻…

The soldier survived the war, only to die on his way home.

（這個士兵戰後餘生，結果卻死於回家路上。）

4. 不定詞（片語）修飾其前的形容詞

S + be + adj + to + 原形動詞

I'm curious to hear the story.

（我很好奇想聽這個故事。）

不定詞除了修飾一般形容詞，也常修飾與『情緒』有關的形容詞，如：happy, glad, pleased,delighted,lucky,sad,sorry,disappointed,surprised,shocked,frightened, excited, eager, anxious, afraid, ashamed 等。

聯考題型

1. The Athletics Federation has introduced stricker regulations _____ prevent cheating.
   (A) such as to   (B) so as to   (C) so much to   (D) such how to

2. To gain more _____, some legislators would get into violent physical fights so that they may appear in TV news reports. (94學測)
   (A) publicity   (B) reputation   (C) significance   (D) communication

3. Her treatment of her employees is _____ as to cause great resentment.
   (A) such   (B) so   (C) thus   (D) that

4. In 1991 he unveiled the World Wide Web. Today, this No.1 invention has become _____ commonplace that it is almost taken for granted. (94指考)
   (A) such   (B) so   (C) very   (D) much

5. The driver swerved to avoid an oncoming van, _____ have his own car turn upside down.
   (A) in order to   (B) just to   (C) in addition to   (D) only to

6. _____ to this campaign and save three lives for only $5, send your donation to: American Assistance for Cambodia, P.O. Box 2716, GPO, New York, NY 10116. (93學測)
   (A) Contributing   (B) Contribute   (C) To contribute   (D) For contributing

7. I'm sorry _____ you waiting, but I'll treat you to a movie to make up for being late.
   (A) to keep   (B) to let   (C) in keeping   (D) in letting

8. A variety of preventive measures are now _____ in order to minimize the potential damage caused by the deadly disease. (93指考)
   (A) by birth   (B) at will   (C) in place   (D) on call

9. Every morning before I go to work, I manage to do some exercise _____ keeping fit.
   (A) so as to   (B) in order to   (C) with a view to   (D) with the aim to

10. Marketers recognize this fact and often use elements of youth culture _____ their products. (92學測)
    (A) to promote   (B) to recycle   (C) to control   (D) to manufacture

翻譯造句

1. 他急著想知道考試的結果。 (anxious)

   試譯：_____

2. 麥可這個人很容易相處。 (Michael …)

   試譯：_____

3. 我們十分願意跟警方合作。 (willing)

   試譯：_____

4. 我趕到車站，卻發現火車已經開走了。 (only to)

   試譯：_____

5. 她如此悲慘以致於使大家都掉淚。 (be such)

   試譯：_____

不定時的時態

$$S + V + (O) + \begin{cases} \text{to + 原形動詞（主動）} \\ \text{to be + pp（被動）} \\ \text{to be + V-ing（進行式）} \\ \text{to have + pp（主動）} \\ \text{to have been + pp（被動）} \end{cases}$$

同於或晚於主要 V 時間

早於主要 V 時間

They are planning <u>to have a barbecue</u> on the beach tomorrow.（較晚）

（他們目前在計劃明天到海邊烤肉。）

Mary seemed <u>to be very popular</u> with her colleagues at that time.（同時）

（瑪麗當時似乎在同事之間頗受歡迎。）

You are supposed <u>to have arrived</u> by now.（較早）

（你應該老早就到的。）

The child appeared <u>to have been abused</u>.（較早被動）

（這個孩子似乎被人虐待過。）

聯考題型

1. Yuki's grandfather is said _____ a samurai when he was young.
   (A) to be   (B) of being   (C) to have been   (D) to become

2. As a small child, he would pick up a broom and pretend _____ the guitar for the entertainment of family guests. (94學測)
   (A) to be playing   (B) to be played   (C) by playing   (D) he is playing

3. Nicole Kidman seems _____ a much sought-after actress at that time.
   (A) to be   (B) as if   (C) like   (D) to have been

4. On paper, the Dubai Tower looks something like a giant space shuttle about _____ into the clouds. (94指考)

(A) launching   (B) to launch   (C) being launched   (D) to be launched

5. When a company ventures into new markets, it will need _____ various problems.

(A) to face   (B) facing   (C) to be faced   (D) how to face

6. Many believe that the aliens are here _____ us, while others hold that the aliens intend us harm. (93學測)

(A) help   (B) helping   (C) to help   (D) helped

7. Mr. Wang's only child is missing and is reported _____ kidnapped.

(A) to have   (B) to be   (C) to have had   (D) to have been

8. The first American space toilet was Alan Shepard's space suit. His flight was supposed _____ only 15 minutes, so there was no provision made for him to relieve himself in the capsule. (92學測)

(A) to last   (B) to have lasted   (C) to be lasted   (D) to have been lasted

9. Judging from the old pictures, your family seems _____ better days.

(A) seeing   (B) having seen   (C) to see   (D) to have seen

10. Magic is believed _____ with the Egyptians, in 1700 B.C. A magician named Dedi of Dedsnefu was reported to have performed for the pharaoh, or the king. (92學測)

(A) to begin   (B) beginning   (C) to have begun   (D) having begun

克漏字

Dr. Thompson was pleased. Just three months after moving to the small Midwestern town, he had been invited __1__ an evening meeting of the Chamber of Commerce. Here was the perfect opportunity to show his knowledge of modern medicine and to get his practice off to a flourishing start. With this __2__, the doctor prepared carefully.

On the night of his speech, Dr. Thompson was __3__ to see that the meeting hall was full. After being introduced, he strode confidently to the lectern and announced his topic: "Recent Advances in Medicine." He began with a detailed discussion of Creutzfeldt-Jakob disease, a rare brain disorder that had recently __4__ in the *New England Journal of Medicine*. Next he outlined the progress that had been made in studying immune system disorders.

Just about this time, halfway through his speech, Dr. Thompson began to notice a certain restlessness in his audience. People were murmuring and shuffling their feet. Someone in the fourth row seemed to be __5__ at a newspaper. Nevertheless, Dr. Thompson plowed on. He had saved the best for last. He quoted extensively from an article in the *Lancet* about genetic research, __6__ sure his audience would be impressed by his familiarity with this prestigious British medical journal.

Then the speech was over. Dr. Thompson had expected __7__ by enthusiastic people, congratulating him and asking questions. Instead, he found himself standing __8__. Finally the president of the Chamber of Commerce came up to him. "Something tells me," said Dr. Thompson, "that my speech was not very successful. I can't understand it. I worked so hard to make it interesting." "Oh, it was a fine speech," replied the president. "But maybe it would have gone over better with a different __9__. Creutzfeldt-Jakob disease is not exactly a factor in these people's __10__ experience. You know, here we are in January. If you'd talked about ways to avoid getting the flu, you'd have had them on the edge of their seats !" (94指考改編)

1. (A) to address   (B) to speak   (C) to lecture   (D) to spend

2. (A) in heart   (B) in mind   (C) in head   (D) in view

3. (A) ashamed   (B) delighted   (C) pleasing   (D) exciting

4. (A) to cover   (B) covered   (C) been covered   (D) to be covering

5. (A) reading   (B) studying   (C) discussing   (D) glancing

6. (A) feeling   (B) felt   (C) to feel   (D) and feel

7. (A) surrounding   (B) being surrounded
   (C) to surround   (D) to be surrounded

8. (A) alone   (B) lonely   (C) lonesome   (D) along

9. (A) faculty   (B) staff   (C) audience   (D) team

10. (A) dairy   (B) everyday   (C) painful   (D) pleasant

不定詞（片語）搭配 too 的句型：

1. too … to + V →太…以致於不…
= too … for + n/V-ing
   The situation is too complicated to describe.
= The situation is too complicated for description.
   （這情形太複雜，無法描述。）

2. too … not to + V →太…不致於不…
= … enough to + V …
   He is too clever not to know what I want.
= He is clever enough to know what I want.
   （他太聰明了一定知道我想要什麼。）

3. not/never too … to + V →不致於太…而不…
= 反義字 + enough to + V
   A woman of 30 is not too old to get married.
= A woman of 30 is young enough to get married.
   （三十歲的女人結婚還不致於太晚。）

4. only too + | happy / glad / pleased | + to + V →非常高興/樂意…

   I'm only too glad to meet you there.
   （在那裡跟你會面我非常樂意。）

1. In terms of learning, there is really no age limit. We are _____ too old to learn.
   (A) ever   (B) never   (C) even   (D) but

2. Except for very large pieces _____ heavy to move, virtually all surviving Angkorian statues, wood carvings and artifacts have been replaced with copies. (94指考)
   (A) very   (B) so   (C) too   (D) much

3. Oh, no. I'm getting too old _____ romantic relationships.
   (A) to   (B) for   (C) with   (D) in

4. I'm sorry I didn't come to your party. I was too busy _____ for an oral report.
   (A) preparing   (B) to prepare   (C) prepared   (D) preparation

5. Human nature does not change, or let me put it this way, human history is too short for any change of it to be _____.
   (A) available   (B) perceptible   (C) manageable   (D) imaginable

翻譯造句

1. 戒煙永遠不嫌太遲。

   試譯：_____

2. 我太窮了買不起這些奢侈品。

   試譯：_____

3. 她太年輕了，還不懂愛情這回事。

   試譯：_____

4. 我弟弟非常高興能夠再次見到你。

   試譯：_____

5. 他太小心了，不會沒注意到那個錯誤。

   試譯：_____

需接原形動詞（或其它形式）之句型：

1. 感官動詞

$$S + \begin{vmatrix} \text{see, look at,} \\ \text{watch, hear,} \\ \text{listen to, feel} \end{vmatrix} + O. + \begin{vmatrix} ① \text{原形 V.（主動事實）} \\ ② \text{V-ing（主動進行）} \\ ③ \text{pp.（被動）} \end{vmatrix}$$

I saw her <u>enter/entering</u> the bank yesterday.

（我昨天看到她進入那家銀行。）

I heard my name <u>called</u> in my dream.

（在夢中我聽到有人叫我名字。）

2. 使役動詞

$$(1)\ S + \begin{vmatrix} \text{have} \\ \text{make} \end{vmatrix} + O. + \begin{vmatrix} ① \text{原形 V.（主動）} \\ ② \text{pp.（被動）} \end{vmatrix}$$

He will have someone <u>service</u> your car.

= He will have your car <u>serviced</u> (by someone).

= He will get someone <u>to service</u> your car.

（他會找人來維修你的車。）

$$(2)\ S + \text{let} + O. + \begin{vmatrix} ① \text{原形 V.（主動）} \\ ② \text{be + pp.（被動）} \end{vmatrix}$$

Let him <u>do</u> it.

（讓他做吧。）

Let it <u>be done</u> at once.

（馬上把事情做好。）

$$3.\ \text{All/What} + \begin{vmatrix} \text{you, we} \\ \text{they, I} \end{vmatrix} + \text{have to do is} + \text{原形 V.}$$

All you have to do is <u>say sorry</u>.

（你必須做的就是說聲抱歉而已。）

4. cannot (help) but + 原形 V.→（別無選擇）只好…

= have no choice but + to + 原形 V.

= cannot help + V-ing

He could not but <u>take</u> her advice.

（他只好聽她的勸。）

5. help + (O.) + $\begin{vmatrix} \text{to + 原形 V.} \\ \text{原形 V.} \end{vmatrix}$ →幫助…；有助於…

Regular exercise can help <u>(to) lower</u> your blood pressure.

（規律的運動有助於降低你的血壓。）

6. do nothing but + 原形 V. →除…之外，什麼也沒做

Babies do nothing but <u>eat and sleep</u> most of the time.

（大部分時間嬰兒只是在吃跟睡而已。）

7. Why (not) + 原形 V…？→為何要/何不…呢？

Why give him a hand?

（為何要幫他忙呢？）

注意：

1. desire nothing but + to + 原形 V. →只想要…

2. think of nothing but + V-ing →只想到…

1. All of a sudden, I felt something _____ up my leg.
   (A) crowd   (B) crawl   (C) cross   (D) cruise

2. European politicians are trying to get the UK government to make cigarette companies _____ photos on the packets. (94學測)
   (A) print   (B) printing   (C) printed   (D) to print

3. Yesterday while I was on my way to work, I saw a dog _____ over in the middle of the road.
   (A) run   (B) ran   (C) to run   (D) running

4. More importantly, if it's happiness that we want, why not _____ our energy there rather than on the size of our body? (94學測)
   (A) put   (B) to put   (C) putting   (D) we put

5. The Buddhist monk said he would help _____ my dream come true.
   (A) let   (B) make   (C) cause   (D) allow

6. Hotels and corporate offices now require guests to present a photo ID at check-ins and entrances. Airlines refuse to _____ passengers carry razor blades, scissors, or screwdrivers on flights. (92指考)
   (A) permit   (B) allow   (C) let   (D) approve

7. All you have to do now is _____ to her.
   (A) apologize   (B) apologizing   (C) apology   (D) apologies

8. There is a limitation to one's capacity, so one should not make oneself _____. (91學測)
   (A) overjoyed   (B) overtired   (C) overheard   (D) overcharged

9. Let that _____ a lesson to you not to play with fire.
   (A) be   (B) teach   (C) learn   (D) give

10. To tell you the truth, I desire nothing but _____ married and settle down.
    (A) get   (B) to get   (C) getting   (D) got

Alex was a classmate of mine in high school, and we've been great friends ever since. He is a nice guy, but his weakness is ___1___ too shy, especially when he is in the presence of girls. His parents, both over 60, had kept nagging him to get married and have children. He was deeply troubled by this and turned to me for help. Two months ago, I introduced a beautiful girl ___2___ Sarah to him at a fast-food restaurant. Earlier that day, I had told him ___3___ it easy. I even reminded him that all he would have to do was ___4___ at the girl and talk to her. However, he just could not help being nervous. He did talk to her during the meal, but I heard him stammering all the time. I'm afraid that Alex cannot but ___5___ single for the rest of his life.

1. (A) be   (B) to be   (C) been   (D) being

2. (A) name   (B) named   (C) naming   (D) to name

3. (A) taking   (B) making   (C) to take   (D) to make

4. (A) laugh   (B) laughing   (C) smile   (D) smiling

5. (A) keep   (B) continue   (C) maintain   (D) remain

獨立不定詞片語（可置於句首/末或插入句中）

1. to tell (you) the truth →坦白（跟你）說

2. to be honest (with you) →老實（跟你）說

3. to make matters worse →更糟的是

4. to make/cut a long story short →長話短說好了

5. to return to the subject →言歸正傳

6. to begin with →首先

7. to top it all →更有甚者

8. to do sb justice →為某人說句公道話
= to give sb his/her due

9. to use a common phrase →套句俗話說

10. to say the least →說最輕微的

11. sad/strange to say →說來悲哀/奇怪

12. not to say（常接 adj）→如果不說…的話

13. not to mention →更不必提…
= not to speak of
= to say nothing of
= let alone

14. to sum up →總而言之
= to conclude

15. to define it →要是給它下個定義

1. We cannot afford to buy an air-conditioner, _____ a house like that.
   (A) not to talk   (B) not to speak   (C) not to say   (D) let alone

2. _____, our manager has a heart of gold although he sometimes has a short temper.
   (A) To do him good   (B) To do him harm
   (C) To do him justice   (D) To do him a favor

3. To _____ a long story short, his wife has walked out on him, never to come back.
   (A) cut   (B) take   (C) tell   (D) let

4. The man has sticky fingers, to say the _____.
   (A) little   (B) less   (C) least   (D) last

5. _____ to say, many people, including men of all ages, are willing to spend a lot of money losing weight.
   (A) Strange   (B) Strangely   (C) Strangeness   (D) Stranger

Work and play are both an indispensable part of our life. Work, to define __1__, is the thing or things we have to do. Play, on the other hand, is __2__ we enjoy doing. Even reading, fishing, gardening or playing golf is work when we do it to make a __3__, though a literary critic may play golf to relax and a professional athlete may read for pleasure. To function normally, we all need work as we need food, sleep, or social contacts, Our aim, therefore, should not be to avoid work but to find __4__ that suits us best. The best way to relieve our stress is to select an environment (our neighborhood, friends, and even spouses) __5__ our preferences.

1. (A) this   (B) that   (C) it   (D) itself

2. (A) what   (B) how   (C) where   (D) when

3. (A) match (B) difference (C) living (D) fortune

4. (A) the one (B) the kind (C) the way (D) the time

5. (A) in line with (B) in love with (C) in favor of (D) in view of

要點 1

分詞（V-ing 和 pp. 兩種）主要作形容詞用：

1. 現在分詞（V-ing）表 ① 主動 ② 正在進行 ③ 令人感到…

2. 過去分詞（pp.）表 ① 被動 ② 已經完成 ③ 本身感到…

He gave a criticizing speech the other day.
（前幾天他發表了一篇批評性的演講。）
The next morning it became a criticized speech.
（隔天早晨它成為一篇備受批評的演講。）

Beware of falling stones when you drive.
（開車時要注意落石。）
The road was covered with a lot of fallen stones.
（路面上堆積著很多落石。）

It is an interesting party.
（這是一個令人覺得有趣的派對。）
The meeting will exclude any interested party.
（這個會議將排除任何有利害關係的人在外。）

　比較： Anyone interested can come to the party.
　　　　（任何有興趣的人都可以來參加這個派對。）

說明：

少數現在分詞可作副詞來修飾 cold, hot 這兩個形容詞，如 It's freezing/biting cold outside.（外頭現在冷得要命。）或 The bath water is boiling/scalding/steaming hot.（這洗澡水燙死人了。）

1. You must date her tonight because a _____ opportunity will never return.
   (A) losing   (B) lost   (C) loser's   (D) loose

2. One reason the earthquake caused such damage was that Bam's buildings were made mostly from _____ mud. (94學測)
   (A) bake   (B) baking   (C) baked   (D) baker's

3. Everyone else was getting bored with the speech. Only Adam kept listening with an _____ look.
   (A) interest   (B) interested   (C) interesting   (D) interestingly

4. Up to date, there is no agreement between these _____ views. And such a debate may continue for years to come. (94指考；按：up to date 為 to date 或 up to now 之誤)
   (A) opposing   (B) opposed   (C) oppose   (D) opposition

5. Calculus and physics are _____ courses in our department though they are both a headache to most students.
   (A) acquired   (B) acquiring   (C) required   (D) requiring

6. In the cross-lake swimming race, a boat will be _____ in case of an emergency. (93學測)
   (A) standing by   (B) turning on   (C) getting on   (D) running down

7. I'm tired of eating _____ food. I want a cooked meal.
   (A) can   (B) canned   (C) canning   (D) cannery

8. The major theme in the _____ issue of the best-selling monthly magazine will be "Love and Peace." (93指考)
   (A) forthcoming   (B) expensive   (C) brilliant   (D) ambitious

9. All the bedrooms have hot and cold _____ water.
   (A) running   (B) runny   (C) tape   (D) tapping

10. Today magicians try hard to find new ways to show their _____ skills. Magic is now entertainment for families all over the world. (92學測)
    (A) practice   (B) practiced   (C) practicing   (D) practical

It seems that more and more of our people are interested in both local and national politics. In recent years, with the spread of education and the __1__ freedom in our society, the desire to participate in political activities __2__ among our people. The authorities __3__ have time and again promised to liberalize our political system, so that people can __4__ their political ideals with less limitation. However, it is worth pointing out that no democracy can exist without national security and social stability. Despite our apparent affluence, our country is not completely __5__ from a few other worries.

1. (A) increased   (B) increasing   (C) added   (D) adding

2. (A) is growing   (B) is grown   (C) has growing   (D) has grown

3. (A) concern   (B) concerns   (C) concerning   (D) concerned

4. (A) pursue   (B) perform   (C) practice   (D) portray

5. (A) free   (B) freed   (C) freeing   (D) freedom

要點 2

分詞片語作（後位）形容詞片語和主/受詞補語：

1. 形容詞子句（化簡）→分詞片語（修飾其前的名詞）

n. +（主格）關代 + ① V ② be + V-ing ③ be + pp → n. + ① V-ing（主動） ② V-ing（主動進行） ③ pp（被動）

Who is the person <u>that won the prize</u>?

= Who is the person <u>winning the prize</u>?

（得獎的那個人是誰？）

The man <u>who is wearing a cap</u> is my dad.

= The man <u>wearing a cap</u> is my dad.

（頭戴棒球帽的那個人是我老爸。）

It is a novel <u>which was written by Dan Brown</u>.

= It is a novel <u>written by Dan Brown</u>.

（這是一本丹‧布朗寫的小說。）

2. 分詞片語作主詞補語

S + │ be, seem, come, go │ + │ ① V-ing
　　│ sit, stand, lie 　　│ 　 │ ② pp.

The meal is really <u>satisfying</u>.（令人…）

（這一餐真令人有飽足感。）

Everyone seems <u>satisfied</u>.（本身…）

（每個人似乎都感到滿意。）

He came <u>running toward us</u>.（主動）

（他朝我們這裡跑過來。）

She went away <u>unnoticed</u>.（被動）

（她離開時沒有人注意到。）

3. 分詞片語作受詞補語

S + │ find, keep, see, 　│ + O. + │ ① V-ing
　　│ notice, catch, 　 │ 　　　 │ ② pp
　　│ leave, send, set │

Mary now finds the music <u>soothing</u>.（令人）

（瑪麗現在發現這支曲子能緩和她的情緒。）

Tom left much homework <u>undone</u>.（被動）

（湯姆留下很多作業沒做。）

1. When I came back after a ten year's absence, I found the city greatly _____.
   (A) change   (B) changes   (C) changing   (D) changed

2. It has been very successful and has led to a 44% increase in smokers _____ to kick the habit. (94學測)
   (A) want   (B) wanting   (C) wanted   (D) to want

3. Sally caught her brother _____ her private letters several times.
   (A) read   (B) to read   (C) reading   (D) was reading

4. Like pearls _____ in the East Sea, the Penghu archipelago is situated in the southwest of the Taiwan Strait. (94指考)
   (A) scatter   (B) scattering   (C) to scatter   (D) scattered

5. Her remark left me _____ what she was driving at.
   (A) wonder   (B) wondering   (C) wondered   (D) to wonder

6. The book reads like a prayer, _____ specific beliefs about dying. (93學測)
   (A) express   (B) expresses   (C) expressing   (D) expressed

7. I once heard it _____ that every dog has its day.
   (A) said   (B) saying   (C) say   (D) to say.

8. He was concerned that so many of the young people _____ for positions with his firm knew absolutely nothing about the way a corporation is run. (93指考)
   (A) apply   (B) applied   (C) applying   (D) to apply

9. The two officials stood there _____ each other of taking bribes.
   (A) accusing   (B) accused   (C) accuse   (D) to accuse

10. Helen _____ with anger when she saw her boyfriend kissing an attractive girl. (92學測)
   (A) collided   (B) exploded   (C) relaxed   (D) defeated

11. On the lawn _____ a school teacher, surrounded by a group of children.
   (A) sat   (B) sitting   (C) seated   (D) to sit

12. Bangkok caters to diverse interests: there are temples, museums and other historic sites for those _____ in traditional Thai culture. (92指考)
   (A) interest   (B) interests   (C) interested   (D) interesting

13. In the afternoon, the old couple often sit on their rocking chairs, _____ in front of the television.
   (A) doze off (B) dozing off (C) dozed off (D) to doze off

14. I took him on a long drive, arbitrarily turning left and right and _____ U-turns. (92指考)
   (A) making (B) taking (C) going (D) giving

15. South America is a place of striking beauty and wonder. The heart of this continent is Amazon Rainforest, a vast paradise _____ by one of the world's greatest rivers. (91學測)
   (A) watered (B) organized (C) built (D) controlled

克漏字

Steven is a very famous movie director and he has won many awards. Most of the films he directed were __1__ entirely on location. One day while he was making a movie in a street, he suddenly __2__ on an idea for a realistic setting. Since the next shot called for a street brawl, he told the __3__ man:

"You see that guy __4__ along with his wife? Go ahead and insult her. And when her husband gets angry and makes an attack on you, then you guys over there with the camera, start to shoot."

So the actor went over to the couple, saying, "Excuse me, is she your wife?"

"Yes," answered the man. "So what?"

"Oh, I just think your wife is the ugliest and most horrible thing that I ever saw." And the actor prepared himself for the __5__ quarrel.

Instead, the man turned to his wife and said, "See? Didn't I tell you before?"

1. (A) shoot (B) shot (C) shooting (D) shooter

2. (A) hit (B) tried (C) looked (D) went

3. (A) lead   (B) leader   (C) leading   (D) led

4. (A) getting   (B) to get   (C) coming   (D) to come

5. (A) expect   (B) expecting   (C) expected   (D) expectation

要點 3

部分現在分詞作介系詞用：

1. including + n. →包含…
= inclusive of + n.
= n. + included

The price is $2,050, <u>including</u> tax.

= The price is $2,050, <u>inclusive of</u> tax.

= The price is $2,050, tax <u>included</u>.

（價格是2,050美元，含稅。）

2. excluding + n. →不包含…
= exclusive of + n.
= n. + excluded

The average cost is around $6,000 a year, <u>excluding</u> insurance.

= The average cost is around $6,000 a year, <u>exclusive of</u> insurance.

= The average cost is around $6,000 a year, insurance <u>excluded</u>.

（平均一年花費約6,000美元，不含保險。）

3. considering + n →要是考慮到

He looks very young, considering his age.

（要是考慮到他的年齡，他看起來算很年輕。）

4. | concerning, regarding / touching, respecting | + n →關於…

She refused to disclose information concerning/regarding the man's whereabouts.

（她拒絕透露有關這個男子的下落。）

5. barring + n. →除非…發生/存在

= unless … happens/exists

His knees were badly hurt and, <u>barring</u> a miracle, he won't be able to walk again.

（他的膝蓋嚴重受損，除非奇蹟出現，他無法走路了。）

6. failing this/that→如果這/那樣不行的話

You should get them to pay for the damage or, <u>failing</u> that, claim on the insurance.

（你應該要他們賠償損壞，或者如果那樣不行的話，就申請保險理賠。）

7. pending + n →等候…（處理）；靜候…

Sales of the drug have been stopped, pending further research.

（這種藥物已經停止販售，等候更進一步的研究。）

8. following + n. →在…之後

= after + n.

Following months of strong resistence, the guerrillas finally surrendered.

（經過幾個月的頑強抵抗之後，遊擊隊終於投降了。）

聯考題型

1. In many big cities, Taipei _____, garbage disposal has become a grave problem.
   (A) including   (B) included   (C) includes   (D) inclusive

2. The shocking pictures _____ images of smoke-damaged lungs and teeth, with reminders in large print that smokers die younger. (94學測)
(A) include (B) includes (C) inclusive (D) to include

3. The hardback costs $29.99 a copy, postage _____.
(A) exclude (B) excluding (C) exclusive (D) excluded

4. These indicators can provide vital information to the company _____ its marketing strategy. (94指考)
(A) regarding (B) relating (C) refunding (D) remaining

5. The defendant is free on bail, _____ an appeal to a higher court.
(A) waiting (B) pending (C) wasting (D) putting

6. _____ increasing calls for the return of artistic objects that were removed decades or centuries ago, some of the world's leading museums have signed a declaration that they will not hand back the ancient artifacts to their countries of origin. (93學測)
(A) Following (B) Followed (C) Follow (D) To follow

7. We will have a campfire tonight or, _____ that, we will stay indoors and play games.
(A) fail (B) failed (C) failure (D) failing

8. She can tell time and do simple math, _____ multiplication and division. (93指考)
(A) including (B) following (C) failing (D) regarding

9. _____ any further delays, we should be able to complete the project as scheduled.
(A) Unless (B) Barring (C) Until (D) Behind

10. Joyce brought up some questions _____ the danger of nuclear warfare.
(A) touch (B) touched (C) touching (D) to touch

克漏字

Fast food restaurants provide inexpensive food and quick service. They are so popular today that they have become a ___1___ phenomenon. Many of these restaurants serve such food as hamburgers, hot dogs, spaghetti, or fried chicken. Fast food restaurants come in a few types, ___2___ cafeterias, drive-ins, drive-throughs, and carry-out restaurants.

Cafeterias display food on a counter. Customers have to serve themselves while __3__ past the counter with a tray. They can choose __4__ a variety of dishes there. For those customers driving a car, drive-ins hire waiters or waitresses to bring food to them. Drive-throughs provide service through a special window. They don't even have to get out of their car. A carry-out restaurant resembles a drive-in, except that the customers do not eat there. They may take their food home, to a picnic area, or __5__ else.

1. (A) growing   (B) grown   (C) grew   (D) growth

2. (A) including   (B) included   (C) inclusive   (D) to include

3. (A) move   (B) moved   (C) moving   (D) to move

4. (A) on   (B) with   (C) at   (D) from

5. (A) any place   (B) anywhere   (C) any corner   (D) anyway

要點 4

分詞構句→化簡副詞子句（主要子句不動）

步驟：

1. 去掉 when/while/though/if 等『連接詞』（如會造成意思不清則保留為宜）。
2. 兩邊主詞相同時，去掉（原連接詞引導的）一個。
3. 兩邊主詞不同時需保留主詞，形成獨立分詞構句。
4. 將動詞化為分詞： ① 主動→ V-ing 或 having + pp
                      ② 被動→ being + pp 或 having been + pp.
5. 加一逗點與主要子句隔開（原句已有則免）。
6. being + pp 或 having been + pp 可再略為 pp，唯其前有 "not" 則否。
7. 分詞構句可置於句首，句中或句末，唯皆需有逗點與主要子句隔開，沒有逗點時則視為分詞片語作形容詞用。分詞構句形成的是副詞片語。

When he saw me, he came forward to give me a hug.

→ Seeing me, he came forward to give me a hug.

（看到我時，他就走向前來擁抱我一下。）

If it is seen from a different angle, that rock may look like a crouching tiger.

→ <u>Seen</u> from a different angle, that rock may look like a crouching tiger.

（從某個不同的角度來看，那塊岩石好像是一隻蹲坐的老虎。）

Because she was very busy, she didn't have time to call back.

→ <u>Being</u> very busy, she didn't have time to call back.

（因為很忙，她沒有時間回電。）

After he had said something to her, he mounted his bike and rode away.

→ <u>Having said</u> something to her, he mounted his bike and rode away.

（跟她說了幾句話後，他就跨上腳踏車騎走了。）

After the work had been done, Ling went out to grab a bite to eat.

→ The work <u>(having been) done</u>, Ling went out to grab a bite to eat.

（工作做好之後，阿玲就出去吃點東西。）

聯考題型

1. My mom did not notice the thief, _____ in the kitchen.
   (A) cooking   (B) cooked   (C) to cook   (D) being cooked

2. Red fire ants can cause a lot of problems. They construct their colonies on precious farmland, invading crops while _____ for insects underground. (94學測)
   (A) search   (B) searching   (C) searched   (D) to search

3. Weather _____, my friends and I will go bungee jumping tomorrow morning.
   (A) permit   (B) permitting   (C) permitted   (D) to permit

4. _____ his body into the taxi, he noticed the shiny interior and the smell of brand new leather. (94指考)
   (A) Squeeze   (B) Squeezed   (C) Squeezing   (D) To squeeze

5. _____ that day, my family made a tour around the small island.
   (A) It is fine   (B) It was fine   (C) It being fine   (D) It been fine

6. _____ the flashing code of her own species, a female signals back to the male, and he lands beside her. (93學測)
   (A) Recognizing   (B) Recognized   (C) Recognize   (D) To recognize

7. _____ with his term paper, I told the student to rewrite it.
   (A) Not been satisfied   (B) Been not satisfied
   (C) Not being satisfied   (D) Being not satisfied

8. _____ around 4,000 B.C., traditional Chinese brush painting has developed continuously over a period of more than six thousand years. (93指考)
   (A) Start   (B) To start   (C) Started   (D) Starting

9. _____, the weather is ideal for engaging in any kind of outdoor activity.
   (A) It is fine   (B) It being fine   (C) Being fine   (D) To be fine

10. Remember when Madonna hit the charts with her bra in full view while _____ about "virginity"？(92學測)
    (A) she sings   (B) to sing   (C) sung   (D) singing

11. There _____ no taxi to hail, we had no choice but to walk home.
    (A) was   (B) were   (C) being   (D) been

12. _____ upon its second aim, more international exchanges are encouraged and established. (91指考)
    (A) Base   (B) Basing   (C) Based   (D) To base

13. When _____ what to do, she just stood there with a silly smile.
    (A) ask   (B) asking   (C) asked   (D) to ask

14. _____ with this new situation, people have yet to find out how to deal with it. (91學測)
    (A) Face   (B) Faced   (C) Facing   (D) To face

15. _____ the way to take, the traveler went on his journey.
    (A) Told   (B) Telling   (C) To tell   (D) Been told

閱讀測驗

When a company ventures into new markets, it will need to face various problems. These problems can be broadly classified into several categories, including (1) cultural factors, (2) economic issues, (3) geographical factors, (4) political/legal issues, (5) religious factors, and (6) technological issues. Find an appropriate category for the problems discussed in each of the following paragraphs.

A company will face problems of this kind, as it is an alien when compared to the business climate of the country. Coca-Cola, for instance, was faced with such a problem in India, when it was given a choice of either to reveal its secret formula or leave the country. Coke chose to leave. But when it was welcomed back after several years, it was subjected to harassment and constant interference from the political activists.

1. The most appropriate category for the above paragraph is _____.
   (A) religious factors
   (B) economic issues
   (C) geographical factors
   (D) political/legal issues

Problems of this kind can make an impact on the properties of a product. This impact forces a company to adapt its products in order to meet the needs of the local market. To solve the problems, the level of economic development in a market should be assessed, for example, by the level of revenue, buying power of local consumers, and by the state of infrastructure in the foreign market. These indicators can provide vital information to the company regarding its marketing strategy.

2. The most appropriate category for the above paragraph is _____.
   (A) cultural factors
   (B) economic issues
   (C) geographical factors
   (D) technological issues

These problems are perhaps the biggest issue a researcher can come across while studying new markets. This is because markets that can be classified as similar on various grounds tend to be dissimilar when it comes to this particular aspect. There are differences even within the same country. Accordingly, travel advertising in Canada is divided between the English audience and the French audience. While pictures of travel advertisements show a wife alone for the English audience, a man and wife are shown for the French audience. This is done because the French are more bound by family ties.

3. The most appropriate category for the above paragraph is _____.
    (A) cultural factors   (B) economic issues
    (C) geographical factors   (D) political/legal issues

要點 5

準分詞與複合分詞（皆作形容詞用）

準分詞的形成

1. adj-n + ed → absent-minded（心不在焉的），bad-mannered（態度惡劣的），clear-headed（頭腦清晰的），double-edged（雙刃的），evil-minded（心地險惡的），far-sighted（眼光好的），good-tempered（脾氣好的），hard-hearted（心腸硬的），ill-timed（時機不對的），kind-hearted（心地善良的），light-fingered（有偷竊習慣的），open-handed（慷慨的），public-spirited（熱心公益的），quick-witted（急智的），red-handed（正在犯案的），simple-minded（頭腦簡單的），teen-aged（十幾歲的），warm-blooded（溫血的）。

2. 基數-n + ed → one-eyed（獨眼的），two-headed（雙頭的），three-legged（三雙腳的）

    例外：

    (1) 序數-n→first-rate（一流的），second-generation（第二代的），third-party（第三者的）

    (2) 基數-（度量衡或時間）n → one-week（一星期的），two-story（兩層樓的），three-meter（三公尺的）

    (3) blue-collar（藍領/勞動階級的），blue-ribbon（藍帶/高級的），red-carpet（隆重的），red-letter（紅字/特別重要的，指日子），pink-collar（粉領階級的），white-collar（白領階級的）

複合分詞的形成

1. n-V-ing→law-abiding（守法的），English-speaking（講英文的），face-saving（

顧面子的）、epoch-making（劃時代的）、record-breaking（破記錄的）、fault-finding（喜挑剔的）、time-consuming（費時的）、nerve-racking（令人緊張的）、heart-breaking（令人傷心的）、labor-saving（省勞力的）、mouth-watering（令人垂涎的）、trouble-making（喜惹事的）

2. n–pp.→hand-made（手工製的）、machine-made（機器製的）、self-taught（自學而成的）、heart-broken（傷心的）、candle-lit（燭光的）、weather-beaten（飽經風霜的）、bottle-fed（餵奶瓶的）、breast-fed（餵母奶的）、duty-bound（有責任在身的）、poverty-stricken（極為貧窮的）、war-torn（飽受戰爭的）

3. adj–V-ing → good-looking（好看的）、easy-going（隨和的）、bad-smelling（難聞的）、high-ranking（高階的）、close-fitting（緊身的）、high-sounding（唱高調的）

4. adj–pp. → ready-made（現成的）、high-born（出身高貴的）、clean-shaven（鬍子刮得很乾淨的）、full-fledged（羽毛長齊的）

5. adv–V-ing → far-reaching（影響深遠的）、hard-working（勤勉的）、never-ending（持續不停的）、off-putting（令人不悅/分心的）、well-meaning（善意的，通常指人）、fast-acting（效果迅速的）、long-lasting（長期的）、long-suffering（長期受苦的）、ill-fitting（不合身的）

6. adv–pp. → ill-founded（沒有根據的）、ill-favored（醜陋的）、ill-fed（吃不飽的）、well-known（知名的）、well-informed（消息靈通的）、well-meant（善意的，指言行）、low-cut（低胸的）、low-paid（薪資低的）、long-awaited（等候良久的）

聯考題型

1. He is a _____ worker. He doesn't belong to your blue-blooded class, mind you.
   (A) blue-color   (B) blue-colored   (C) blue-collar   (D) blue-collared

2. Due to the yearly bonus system, the 100 vacant positions in this _____ company have attracted many applicants from around the island. (94學測)
   (A) high-tech   (B) high-level   (C) high-ranking   (D) high-born

3. It is reported that the bandit was gunned down by a _____ soldier.
   (A) one-arm   (B) one-armed   (C) one-arming   (D) one-arms

4. Our chemistry teacher was on a _____ sick leave, so the principal had to find a teacher to substitute for her. (94指考)
   (A) one-month   (B) one-monthed   (C) one-monthing   (D) one-months

5. That boy is light-fingered. He has been caught _____ several times.
   (A) red-head   (B) red-headed   (C) red-hand   (D) red-handed

6. Each and every dollar you contribute will go toward the purchase of family-sized _____ mosquito nets costing $5 each. (93學測)
   (A) insecticide-treat   (B) insecticide-treated
   (C) insecticide-treating   (D) insecticide-treatment

7. Don't worry about that. I'm sure they will give your husband a _____ welcome.
   (A) red-light   (B) red-carpet   (C) red-tape   (D) red-hot

8. The _____ Cindy follows in the path of other breakthrough toys like Sony's barking Robot Aibo, which was the first to popularize voice command in the late 1990s. (93指考)
   (A) eagle-eye   (B) eagle-eyes   (C) eagle-eyed   (D) eagle-eyeing

9. The pair of lovers are planning to enjoy a _____ dinner together.
   (A) candlelight   (B) candlelights   (C) candlelighting   (D) candle-lit

10. Michael Jackson provoked new concerns for his children's welfare after he took them to the zoo covered in strange, _____ veils "to protect them from kidnappers." (92指考)
    (A) bright-color   (B) bright-colors   (C) bright-colored   (D) bright-coloring

11. I prefer movies that have been dubbed into English. Subtitles are so _____.
    (A) off-putting   (B) near-sighted   (C) on-coming   (D) far-fetched

12. In the early 1990s, many companies allowed their employees to wear casual clothes on Friday. This be came known as "_____ Friday" or "casual Friday." (91學測)
    (A) dress-down   (B) dressing-down   (C) dress-up   (D) dressing-up

13. Have you ever seen a _____ snake?
    (A) two-head   (B) two-heads   (C) two-headed   (D) two-heading

14. June 16 is a _____ day for us because we got married on the very day.
    (A) red-letter   (B) red-letters   (C) red-lettered   (D) red-lettering

15. A lot of problems are sometimes caused by _____ friends.
    (A) well-meaning   (B) well-meant   (C) well-mean   (D) well-means

獨立分詞片語

1. speaking/talking of … →說/提到…

   Speaking of religion, is your husband a very religious man?

   （說到宗教，你的先生是一個信仰很虔誠的人嗎？）

2. generally/strictly/comparatively speaking →一般/嚴格/比較而言

   Strickly speaking, you have no say in the matter.

   （嚴格而言，這件事情不容你置喙。）

3. judging from/by …→由…來判斷

   Judging by his face, he was angry.

   （由他的臉看來，他是生氣了。）

4. all things considered →全面考慮/檢討之後

   All things considered, I think we are sure to win the game.

   （全面檢討之後，我認為我們一定會贏這場比賽。）

聯考題型

1. _____ of money, I'm pretty hard up now.
   (A) Speaking   (B) Speak   (C) Spoken   (D) To speak

2. Generally speaking, our _____ clock is slightly disturbed if we just move into the next time zone. (94學測)
   (A) ecological   (B) biological   (C) psychological   (D) logical

3. "Look, here he comes." "Well, _____ of the devil !"
   (A) speak   (B) spoke   (C) speaking   (D) spoken

4. _____ from her accent, she must be an English woman.
   (A) Judge   (B) Judged   (C) Judging   (D) To judeg

5. We have decided to downsize our company, all things _____.
   (A) consider   (B) considered   (C) considering   (D) to consider

克漏字

People all have different lifespans. __1__ speaking, women live longer than men. Work and stress are the two __2__ factors. As __3__ , most men in the world are often stressed out both physically and mentally. Although the number of career women is steadily on the __4__ , it cannot be denied that, __5__ speaking, men have been exposed to more labor and danger.

1. (A) Broad   (B) Broadly   (C) Public   (D) Publicly

2. (A) lead   (B) led   (C) leading   (D) leader

3. (A) breadwinners   (B) pleasure-seekers
   (C) homemakers   (D) title-holders

4. (A) increasing   (B) increase   (C) growing   (D) growth

5. (A) comparable   (B) comparably   (C) comparative   (D) comparatively

Unit 10　助動詞

要點 1

shall 和 will 的用法

1. I/ We <u>shall</u> + 原形 V →純粹未來（主英式用法，在美式用法中，用 will 表所有人稱的純粹未來）

   I <u>shall/will</u> explain everything later.

   （待會兒我會把一切解釋清楚。）

2. You/I/He <u>will</u> + 原形 V →意願（＝be willing to）

   Who <u>will</u> help me in the kitchen?

   （誰願意到廚房來幫我？）

3. You/He/She/It <u>shall</u> + 原形 V →說話者的意志/願

   You <u>shall</u> have the money tomorrow.

   （明天你一定可以拿到錢。）

4. Shall I/we + 原V →詢問對方的意見/指示

   <u>Shall</u> we have lunch together?

   （要一塊用午餐嗎？）

5. Let's + 原形 V …, <u>Shall</u> <u>we</u>? →表建議

   Let's go fishing this afternoon, <u>shall</u> <u>we</u>?

   （咱們今天下午去釣魚，好嗎？）

翻譯造句

1. 你願意幫我放洗澡水嗎？ (run a bath)

   試譯：_____

2. 我的兒子絕不能受此待遇。 (shall)

試譯： _____

3. 我下個月就要成年了。 (come of age)

試譯： _____

4. 要不要我幫你洗碗？ (do the dishes)

試譯： _____

5. 我們吃點不一樣的好嗎？ (Let's …)

試譯： _____

要點 2

would 和 used to 的用法

1. would + 原形 V 的用法：
   (1) 表過去的『未來』

   He said that he <u>would</u> come over.

   （他說他要過來這裡。）

   (2) 表過去的『習慣』（偶有或時常）

   On winter evenings we <u>would</u> all sit around the fire.

   （在冬天的夜裡我們習慣圍著爐火坐著取暖。）

   (3) 表『客氣』的請求

   <u>Would</u> it be all right/okay if I used your cellphone?

   （手機借我用一下好嗎？）

   <u>Would</u> you mind waiting outside?

   （請在外面等候好嗎？）

   (4) 表『想要』做…

   I <u>would</u> like/love/prefer to see you alone.

（我想要單獨與你會面。）

2. used to + 原形 V 的用法：
　　(1) 表過去恆常的『習慣』（強調現已無此習慣）

　　I <u>used to</u> like gardening a lot, but I don't have time for it now.

　　（有一陣子我很喜歡園藝，可是現在沒有時間了。）

　　My dad <u>didn't use to</u> stay up late.

　　（我老爸過去並沒有熬夜的習慣。）

　　(2) 表『曾經⋯』

　　Mr. Zhao <u>used to</u> be a carpenter, but now he is a successful businessperson.

　　（趙先生曾經當過木匠，但現在他可是一位成功的生意人。）

注意：

1. be used to + V-ing/n. →習慣於⋯

　I am/was not used to <u>drinking</u> coffee.

　（我現在/過去並不習慣於喝咖啡。）

　Some people are not used to such <u>four-letter words</u>.

　（有些人並不習慣如此粗鄙的語言。）

2. be used to + 原形 V. →被用來⋯

　The machine is used to <u>monitor</u> the baby's breathing.

　（這個機器被用來監控這名嬰兒的呼吸狀況。）

　　　翻譯造句

1. 他們過去有時候會邀我們過去共度週末。(would)

　　試譯：＿＿＿＿＿＿＿＿＿＿＿＿＿＿＿＿＿＿＿＿＿＿

2. 她曾經常過演員，所以習慣這種場合。(used to; be used to)

　　試譯：＿＿＿＿＿＿＿＿＿＿＿＿＿＿＿＿＿＿＿＿＿＿

3. 現在很多手機可以被用來照相。 (be used to)

試譯：_____

4. 如果我現在就離開，好嗎？ (Would it be OK …)

試譯：_____

5. 我想要喝杯礦泉水。 (would like to)

試譯：_____

要點 3

should 的用法

1. should + 原形 V →表現在/未來『應該』…
= ought to + 原形 V
= be supposed to + 原形 V

We <u>should hope</u> for the best and prepare for the worst.

（我們應該抱持最佳的希望再做最壞的打算。）

The doctor <u>should be</u> here anytime now.

（醫生應該隨時會到。）

2. should have + pp. →表過去『應該』…但未…
= ought to have + pp
= be supposed to have + pp

You <u>should have taken</u> my advice.

（你本應該接受我的建言的。）

The police <u>should have arrived</u> by now.

（警方老早就應該到的。）

3. 表『竟/居然…』之錯愕、惋惜或歡欣的情緒

I'm shocked that Roger <u>should</u> descend to that level.

（令我震驚不已的是，羅傑竟然沉淪到那種地步。）

It's a miracle that you <u>should</u> have survived the disaster.

（你居然能夠逃過這一劫，真是奇蹟啊！）

4. should like to + 原形 V → 想要…（英式用法）
= would like to + 原形 V（美式用法）

I should like to take a day or two off.

（我想要休假一兩天。）

翻譯造句

1. 凡是違規停車者都應科以罰金。(fine)

   試譯：_____

2. 你做任何事情都不應半途而廢。(by halves)

   試譯：_____

3. 你們早就應該報警的。(call the police)

   試譯：_____

4. 遺憾的是她居然已經放棄希望。(give up hope)

   試譯：_____

5. 我想要跟你多見點面。(see more)

   試譯：_____

can 和 could 的用法

1. can + 原形 V →表（現在/未來的）能力/可能/許可/請求

   I'm so hungry that I <u>can</u> eat like a horse.（能力）

   （我現在很餓，所以我能吃得很多。）

   <u>Can</u> it be true that he is still alive?（可能）

   （聽說他還活著，這可能是真的嗎？）

   She is OK. You <u>can</u> go home now.（許可）

   （她沒事，你現在可以回家了。）

   <u>Can</u> you help me file this letter?（請求）

   （請你幫我將這封信存檔好嗎？）

2. could + 原形 V →表（過去的）能力；（現在/未來的）可能；（較客氣的）請求

   John <u>could</u> write poems when he was 6.（能力）

   （約翰 6 歲時就能寫詩。）

   In a situation like this, anything <u>could</u> happen.（可能）

   （在這種情況下，任何事都有可能發生。）

   <u>Could</u> you mail this letter for me?（請求）

   （麻煩您幫我寄這封信好嗎？）

3. can't have + pp + →推測『過去不可能…』

   He can't have forgotten about the wedding.

   （他不可能忘掉那場婚禮的。）

4. could have + pp →推測 ① 過去有可能…但不確定 ② 過去本可能…但未發生

   The explosion could have been caused by a gas leak, but I'm not sure.

   （當時的爆炸有可能漏油所引起的，可是我也不能確定。）

You could have married her, but you wouldn't.

（你原本可以把她娶回家的，可是你不願意。）

5. couldn't be + 比較級 adj →最/極為…

The two brothers couldn't be more different.

（這兩兄弟極為不同。）

翻譯造句

1. 父親漸漸老了。他不戴眼鏡就無法閱讀。 (can't)

    試譯：＿＿＿＿＿＿＿＿＿＿＿＿＿＿＿＿＿＿＿

2. 在他這個年齡的孩子有可能很叛逆。 (can)

    試譯：＿＿＿＿＿＿＿＿＿＿＿＿＿＿＿＿＿＿＿

3. 我爺爺年輕時能夠游過這條河。 (could)

    試譯：＿＿＿＿＿＿＿＿＿＿＿＿＿＿＿＿＿＿＿

4. 你能幫我洗衣服嗎？ (Can/Could …)

    試譯：＿＿＿＿＿＿＿＿＿＿＿＿＿＿＿＿＿＿＿

5. 當時只有湯姆在家。他總不可能把所有的食物都吃光吧。 (can't have + pp)

    試譯：＿＿＿＿＿＿＿＿＿＿＿＿＿＿＿＿＿＿＿

6. 是誰偷了我的車。有可能是我弟弟，但我不能確定。 (could have + pp)

    試譯：＿＿＿＿＿＿＿＿＿＿＿＿＿＿＿＿＿＿＿

7. 你原本有可能被解僱的。 (could have + pp)

    試譯：＿＿＿＿＿＿＿＿＿＿＿＿＿＿＿＿＿＿＿

8. 可否給我一點水喝？ (could)

    試譯：＿＿＿＿＿＿＿＿＿＿＿＿＿＿＿＿＿＿＿

9. 他們的生活方式極為不同。 (couldn't be more…)

試譯： _____

10. 我知道他極為富有。 (as…as can be)

試譯： _____

要點 5

may/might 的用法

1. 表或許/可能（might 的可能性較 may 更小）

   You <u>may/might</u> get into trouble again.

   （你或許會再度陷入麻煩。）

2. 表允許/請求（might 比 may 更為客氣）

   I wonder if I <u>may/might</u> use your telephone.

   （我不知道可否借用你的電話。）

   <u>May/Might</u> I ask Mr. President a question?

   （我可以請問總統先生一個問題嗎？）

3. may have + pp + →也許/可能已經…

   The injury <u>may have caused</u> brain damage.

   （這個外傷可能已經造成腦部受損。）

4. might have + pp → ① 也許/可能已經…（但不確定）
   ② 本來可能早已…但沒有發生

   I suppose he <u>might have missed</u> the flight.

   （我想他可能已錯過班機了，但不確定。）

   Cathy <u>might have been killed</u>！

   （凱西差點就喪生。）

5. may/might well + 原形 V →有足夠的理由（詢問/反應）

   You <u>may</u> <u>well</u> wonder why we need so much money.

   （你有足夠的理由想知道我們為何需要這麼多錢。）

6. may (very) well/easily + 原形 V →很可能/容易…
= might (very) well/easily + 原形 V

   The crisis <u>may/might</u> <u>very well</u> lead to war.

   （這個危機很可能會導致戰爭。）

7. may/might as well + 原形 V →不如/乾脆…算了

   Since there is nothing more to do, we <u>may/might as well</u> call it a day.

   （既然沒其它事可做，我們乾脆收工算了。）

   One <u>might</u> <u>as well</u> be hanged for a sheep <u>as</u> for a lamb.（諺語）

   （與其偷羔羊被吊死乾脆偷大羊算了/一不做二不休。）

翻譯造句

1. 既然時候不早了，我們乾脆回家算了。

   試譯：＿＿＿＿＿＿＿＿＿＿＿＿＿＿＿＿＿＿＿＿

2. 抱歉，他人還沒進來。可以幫你留言嗎？

   試譯：＿＿＿＿＿＿＿＿＿＿＿＿＿＿＿＿＿＿＿＿

3. 這個孩子也許已經迷路了。 (get lost)

   試譯：＿＿＿＿＿＿＿＿＿＿＿＿＿＿＿＿＿＿＿＿

4. 這是我們有十足理由擔憂的一個現象。 (might well)

   試譯：＿＿＿＿＿＿＿＿＿＿＿＿＿＿＿＿＿＿＿＿

5. 重感冒很容易導致一些併發症。 (complications)

   試譯：＿＿＿＿＿＿＿＿＿＿＿＿＿＿＿＿＿＿＿＿

need（兼有助動詞和本動詞形式）的用法

※ 助動詞 need 本身沒有字尾變化。本動詞 need 即一般動詞，有 needs/needed/needing 等變化。

助動詞 need 的句型：

1. need + 原形 V → （現在）需…（限用於否定句或疑問句）

You <u>need</u> not give me the exact number. Just give me a round figure.

（你無需給我精確的數字。給我一個整數就行了。）

<u>Need</u> I say more?

（已經夠清楚了，還需要我說什麼呢？）

2. need not have + pp → （過去）不需…但已做了

She need not have given the beggar so much money.

（她根本不需要給那名乞丐那麼多錢。）

3. need only + 原形 V …（to + 原形 V）→ 只需…（即可…）

You <u>need</u> <u>only</u> open the book to find the answer.

（你只需打開書本即可找到答案。）

本動詞 need 的句型：

1. need/needs/needed + | ① to + 原形 V → 需要…
　　　　　　　　　　　　　| ② V-ing/to be + pp. → 需要被…

My hair <u>needs</u> cutting.

= My hair <u>needs</u> to be cut.

（我的頭髮需要修剪了。）

2. don't/doesn't need to + 原形 V → （現在）不需要…

   You don't need <u>to see</u> a doctor right now.

   （你現在還不需要立刻去看醫生。）

3. didn't need to + 原形 V → （過去）不需要…也沒做

   I didn't need <u>to tell</u> him who I was because he already knew.

   （我當時沒有必要告訴他我是誰，因為他已經知道。）

4. 慣用語 if need be = if (it is) necessary 表『如有必要的話』。

翻譯造句

1. 有錢的人們不需為他們的三餐煩惱。 (need not)

   試譯：＿＿＿＿＿＿＿＿＿＿＿＿＿＿＿＿＿＿＿＿＿＿＿＿＿＿

2. 我當時根本不需寫好那封信，因為之後我便立即傳簡訊給她。 (text message)

   試譯：＿＿＿＿＿＿＿＿＿＿＿＿＿＿＿＿＿＿＿＿＿＿＿＿＿＿

3. 你只需在這裡簽名即可獲得一份免費的禮物。 (need only)

   試譯：＿＿＿＿＿＿＿＿＿＿＿＿＿＿＿＿＿＿＿＿＿＿＿＿＿＿

4. 我需要為這幾個孩子買票嗎？ (Do I …)

   試譯：＿＿＿＿＿＿＿＿＿＿＿＿＿＿＿＿＿＿＿＿＿＿＿＿＿＿

5. 大衛會加班的，如果有必要的話。 (if need be)

   試譯：＿＿＿＿＿＿＿＿＿＿＿＿＿＿＿＿＿＿＿＿＿＿＿＿＿＿

must 及其相關用法

1. must + 原形 V → ① （現在/未來）必須…
   ② （現在）一定/很可能…

   You <u>must</u> toe the line here. (= have to)

   = You <u>have (got) to</u> toe the line here

   （在這裡你必須遵守規定。）

   The Wangs <u>must</u> be better-off now. (≠ have to)

   （王家現在一定生活較寬裕了。）

2. had to + 原形 V → （過去）必須…

   Last Sunday Jane <u>had to</u> stay at home taking care of her baby sister.

   （上星期天阿珍必須待在家裡照顧小妹。）

3. must have + pp → （過去）一定/很可能…

   I <u>must have fallen</u> asleep then.

   （那時我一定是睡著了。）

4. 慣用語 a must-have/must-read/must-see + (n.) 表一件/本/個『必須擁有/閱讀/參觀』的某物。這種用法兼為名詞及形容詞。

   Nowadays an MP3 player is a must-have.

   （現今 MP3 機是人人必須擁有的東西。）

1. 所有機上的乘客都必須繫好安全帶。 (safety/seat belts)

   試譯：_____

2. 她的爺爺現在一定接近 90 歲了。 (nearly)

   試譯：_____

3. 昨天下午我必須早點離開去接小孩。 (pick up)

   試譯：_____

4. 我（現在）找不到我的小錢包。一定是被偷了。

   試譯：_____

5. 這是一部非看不可的電影。

   試譯：_____

要點 8

dare（兼有助動詞和本動詞）的用法

※ dare 作助動詞或本動詞時，其過去式均為 dared。

1. 作助動詞（限用於否定/疑問/條件句）接原形 V

   I <u>dare</u> not <u>tell</u> my mom the truth.

   （我不敢告訴我老媽真相。）

   <u>Dare</u> your friend <u>come</u> again?

   （你的朋友敢再來嗎？）

   Fight him if he <u>dare</u> <u>come</u>.

   （要是他敢來，就跟他打吧。）

2. 作本動詞 (Vi) 時接不定詞

S + dare/dares/dared + to + 原形 V

Larry <u>dares</u> <u>to argue</u> with the boss.

（賴瑞敢跟老闆爭吵。）

But Mary doesn't <u>dare</u> (to).

（可是瑪麗不敢。）

3. S + dare(s)/dared sb to do sth →激某人做…

Someone <u>dared</u> <u>him</u> to jump out of the 2nd-floor window.

（有人激他從二樓的窗戶跳下來。）

dare 的慣用語

1. Don't you dare + (do sth)！→諒你也不敢 (…)！

Don't you dare come near me again.

（諒你再也不敢靠近我！）

2. How dare you + (do sth)！→你竟敢 (…)！

How dare you enter my room without asking me.

（你竟敢沒問我一聲就進入我的房間！）

3. I dare say/daresay …→我敢說/認為…（主英式用法）

I dare say our economy will improve.

（我認為我們的經濟會好轉。）

翻譯造句

1. 我不敢洩漏秘密。 (dare not)

試譯：＿＿＿＿＿＿＿＿＿＿＿＿＿＿＿＿＿＿＿＿＿

2. 只有少數幾個學生敢回答老師的問題。 (dare to)

試譯：＿＿＿＿＿＿＿＿＿＿＿＿＿＿＿＿＿＿＿＿＿＿＿＿＿＿＿

3. 昨晚他們激我去超市偷一瓶威士忌。

試譯：＿＿＿＿＿＿＿＿＿＿＿＿＿＿＿＿＿＿＿＿＿＿＿＿＿＿＿

4. 諒你也不敢像那樣跟我說話。

試譯：＿＿＿＿＿＿＿＿＿＿＿＿＿＿＿＿＿＿＿＿＿＿＿＿＿＿＿

5. 你竟敢說我是賊！

試譯：＿＿＿＿＿＿＿＿＿＿＿＿＿＿＿＿＿＿＿＿＿＿＿＿＿＿＿

Unit 11　被動語態

要點 1

（一般）主動語態→被動語態（限 Vt）

S(A)　　+　　Vt　　+　　O(B)

S(B)　　+　　be+pp+by　　+　　O(A)

Watt invented the steam engine.

→ The steam engine was invented by watt.

（瓦特發明了蒸汽機。）

Mary is writing a letter.

→ A letter is being written by Mary.

（瑪麗正在寫一封信。）

The boss has fired Sam.

→ Sam has been fired (by the boss).

（老闆已經將山姆解僱了。）

說明：

1. 主動改為被動時需注意時態的一致。

2. 被動句的動詞單複數需與其（新）主詞一致。

3. by + 動作者，如果該動作者為籠統的 someone/people 或該動作者至為明顯或說話者不願提及，均可省略。

聯考題型

1. Hundreds of thousands of books _____ every year in our country.
   (A) are publishing
   (B) are published
   (C) are being published
   (D) have been published

2. The drug dealer was _____ by the police while he was selling cocaine to a high school student. (94學測)
   (A) threatened   (B) endangered   (C) demonstrated (D) arrested

3. At the present time many new roads and tall buildings _____ in this emergent country.
   (A) are built   (B) were built   (C) are being built (D) were being built

4. Thousands of people flooded into the city to join the demonstration; as a result, the city's transportation system was almost _____. (94指考)
   (A) testified   (B) paralyzed   (C) stablized   (D) dissatisfied

5. Your steak _____ and will be ready in a minute.
   (A) is been grilled   (B) is grilling   (C) has grilled   (D) is being grilled

6. Regardless of the weather, the athletic meetings will _____ on time. (93學測)
   (A) be held   (B) be holding   (C) have held   (D) hold

7. As a matter of fact, most people enjoy _____.
   (A) to be praised   (B) praising   (C) to be praising (D) being praised

8. Every September, students are _____ the opportunity to join Junior Achievement through the cooperation of local school systems. (93指考)
   (A) offered   (B) afforded   (C) opposed   (D) applied

9. The house _____ to be haunted will be torn down tomorrow morning.
   (A) which once believed   (B) once believed
   (C) which once believing   (D) once believing

10. The man was severely _____ in last weekend's tragic car accident and died shortly afterwards. (92學測)
    (A) wounded   (B) injured   (C) knocked   (D) crashed

不及物動詞的（特殊）被動：

1. 某些不及物動詞 + 介系詞　可視為及物動詞，因此可以有被動形式。

   Many people <u>laugh at</u> him.

   → He <u>is laughed at</u> by many people.

   （他被很多人嘲笑。）

   We cannot <u>count on</u> Aaron.

   → Aaron cannot <u>be counted on</u> (by us).

   （我們不能指望阿倫。）

2. 某些感官動詞 (look/smell/sound/feel/taste) 和聯綴動詞 (prove/keep) 接形容詞作補語，沒有被動形式但具被動意義。

   The roast duck <u>tastes</u> delicious.

   （這隻烤鴨吃起來很可口。）

   Their marketing strategy <u>proved</u> very successful.

   （他們的行銷策略證實非常成功。）

3. 某些不及物（用法）動詞 + 副詞也具被動意義。

   The novel <u>sells</u> <u>well</u>.

   （這本小說很暢銷。）

   Ripe bananas <u>peel</u> <u>easily</u>.

   （香蕉熟了容易去皮。）

1. A lot of old superstitions should be _____ away with.
   (A) done   (B) run   (C) walked   (D) made

2. Among the one hundred or so islands, only 20 are _____. (94指考)
   (A) lived   (B) living   (C) inhabited   (D) inhabiting

3. Being insulted this way is something that can't _____.
   (A) put up with   (B) be put up with   (C) put up with it   (D) be put up with it

4. Somehow, problems creep in, resements build, and communication _____. (94學測)
   (A) breaks down   (B) breaking down   (C) is broken down   (D) being broken down

5. Don't worry. Your pet will be _____.
   (A) taking care   (B) taking care of   (C) taken care   (D) taken care of

6. The book _____ like a prayer, expressing specific beliefs about dying. (93學測)
   (A) reads   (B) is read   (C) reading   (D) is reading

7. That God is _____ everywhere on earth only shows that people cannot do without religion.
   (A) believing   (B) believed   (C) believing in   (D) believed in

8. These days, even a walk in the woods can be transformed _____ an "extreme" sport. (93指考)
   (A) into   (B) for   (C) with   (D) at

9. I mean I have been taken advantage _____ for quite a long time.
   (A) by   (B) of   (C) with   (D) to

10. Since then Australia _____ from the rest of the world by vast oceans. The animals there no longer had contact with animals from other parts of the world. (92學測)
    (A) is isolated   (B) had isolated   (C) has isolated   (D) has been isolated

感官動詞與使役動詞的被動：

1. 感官動詞的被動

$$S + be + \begin{vmatrix} seen \\ heard \\ felt \end{vmatrix} + \begin{vmatrix} ① \ to + 原形 \ V \\ ② \ V\text{-ing} \end{vmatrix} + (by \cdots)$$

Someone saw him <u>enter/entering</u> a bar.

→ He was seen <u>to enter/entering</u> a bar (by someone).

（有人看到他進入一家酒吧。）

2. 使役動詞的被動

S + be made to + 原形 V + (by ⋯)

They made us <u>admit</u> defeat.

→ We were made <u>to admit</u> defeat (by them).

（我們被迫認輸。）

Let + O + be + pp + (by ⋯)

Let George <u>do</u> it.

→ Let it <u>be done</u> by George.

（讓喬治來做吧。）

聯考題型

1. We found the house _____. The furniture was all piled up and the chairs covered.
   (A) deserted　　(B) avoided　　(C) banished　　(D) painted

2. A young man was seen _____ out of the building after a gunshot.
   (A) leaving　　(B) receiving　　(C) hurrying　　(D) carrying

3. Jacob was never heard _____ ill of his friends or co-workers.
   (A) speak   (B) spoke   (C) spoken   (D) to speak

4. Ads _____ you believe that their product washes cleaner, lasts longer, protects you better, lets you have more free time, makes you more attractive, or impresses your friends.
   (A) have   (B) allow   (C) permit   (D) get

5. I was made _____ her story because she kept nagging me.
   (A) believe   (B) believing   (C) believed   (D) to believe

6. The pop star was pictured _____ through Berlin Zoo with his two elder children, Prince Michael, five, and Paris, four. (92指考)
   (A) walking   (B) walked   (C) walk   (D) by walking

7. Since this is a matter of urgency, let the letter _____ out loud to us.
   (A) read   (B) reading   (C) to read   (D) be read

8. Rosa didn't want to be heard _____ her own husband.
   (A) criticize   (B) to criticize   (C) critic   (D) criticism

9. She was heard _____ for help last night.
   (A) shout   (B) shouted   (C) shouting   (D) and shouted

10. The whole building was felt _____ violently when the earthquake happened.
   (A) to shake   (B) shake   (C) shook   (D) shaken

要點 4

疑問句的被動語態

1. Do/Did   +   S(A)   +   原形 V   +   O(B)?

   Be   +   S(B)   +   PP. + by   +   O(A)?

   Does George love Mary?

→ Is Mary loved by George?

（喬治愛瑪麗嗎？）

2. （其它） 助動詞 + S(A) +　　原形 V　　+ O(B)?

助動詞 + S(B) + be + pp + by + O(A)?

Can he fininish the work in time?

→ Can the work be finished in time by him?

（他能夠及時完成該工作嗎？）

3. 疑問字 (S)　　　　+ V　　 + O …?

By（或其它介系詞）+ 疑問字 (O) + be + S + pp?

Who broke the window?

→ By whom was the window broken?

（是誰打破了窗戶？）

句子改寫 / 填充

1. Have you seen the movie?

= _____　（被動）

2. What so surprise you?

= _____ _____ were you so surprised?

3. Who married your sister?

= _____ _____ was your sister married?

4. Which will satisfy you?

= _____ _____ will you be satisfied?

5. What interests your dad most?

= _____ _____ is your dad interested most?

在被動語態中，表『動作者』的介系詞需用 by。但有一些動詞的被動式則接其它介系詞（如 at, about, of, in, to, with 等）。下列一些易混淆且較重要的用法，宜熟記之。

1. be disappointed + | at/about/ with + 事物 | →對…感到失望
                       | in + 人

   I feel very disappointed <u>at</u> your decision.

   （我對你的決定感到相當失望。）

   Ruth is really disappointed <u>in</u> you.

   （露絲真的對你感到失望。）

2. be excited + | at/by + 消息/機會 | →對…感到興奮
                 | about + 一般事物

   We were all excited <u>at</u> the good news.

   （我們對這個好消息振奮不已。）

   A trip to Japan is nothing to get excited <u>about</u>.

   （去日本玩一趟沒什麼好值得興奮的。）

3. be frightened + | by … | →被…嚇到
                    | of … | →害怕…

   The child was frightened <u>by</u> a clap of thunder.

   （這個孩子被一聲雷響給嚇壞了。）

   Most people are frightened (= afraid) <u>of</u> snakes.

   （大多數的人都怕蛇。）

4. be engaged + | in + 事物→忙著（從事）…
                 | to + 人→與…訂婚

   The Cabinet members are currently engaged <u>in</u> making some foreign policies.

（內閣閣員目前正忙著制定一些外交政策。）

Milly is engaged <u>to</u> a man coming from Russia.

（米莉已跟一名俄羅斯籍的男子訂婚了。）

5. be covered + | with + 物→以…遮蓋/保護
               | in/with + 物→覆蓋（一層）…

His head is covered <u>with</u> a khaki turban.

（他的頭頂戴著一條卡其布料頭巾。）

All the furniture was covered <u>in/with</u> dust.

（所有的家俱都蒙上一層灰塵。）

6. be occupied + | by + 人→被佔領/使用
                 | with + 事物→忙著…

The island was once occupied <u>by</u> foreign troops.

（這座島曾經一度被外國軍隊佔領。）

George is still occupied <u>with</u> work.

（喬治仍舊忙著工作。）

7. be made + | of + 材料（不變）→由…做成
             | from + 材料（質變）
             | into + 成品→做成…

The shirt is made <u>of</u> silk.

（這件襯衫是絲織的。）

Red wine and white wine are both made <u>from</u> grapes.

（紅酒、白酒都是葡萄釀成的。）

Clay can be made <u>into</u> bricks.

（黏土可以製成磚塊。）

8. be known + | to + 對象 ─┐
              | for + 特色 ├→對/以…有名
              | as + 身分/場所 ┘
              | by + 方式   →以…方式被認知

It is a fact known <u>to</u> all.

（這是一個眾所周知的事實。）

He is known <u>for</u> his artistic achievements.

（他以在藝術方面的造詣有名。）

She was known <u>as</u> a feminist.

（她曾以女權運動者的身分有名。）

A man is known <u>by</u> the books he keeps.（諺語）

（觀其藏書知其為人。）

聯考題型

1. I am frightened _____ spiders. What about you?
   (A) of   (B) by   (C) with   (D) for

2. We are all very excited _____ the prospect of the party.
   (A) about   (B) at   (C) for   (D) with

3. Who will your sister be engaged _____?
   (A) to   (B) with   (C) in   (D) for

4. Both of Mike's shoes were covered _____ mud.
   (A) in   (B) by   (C) on   (D) for

5. The building is now occupied _____ its new owner.
   (A) with   (B) by   (C) to   (D) for

6. My mind is too occupied _____ moving to think about a vacation.
   (A) with   (B) by   (C) in   (D) for

7. Milk can be made _____ butter and cheese.
   (A) of   (B) from   (C) with   (D) into

8. A lot of housewives buy novels after they have been adapted _____ television.
   (A) from   (B) of   (C) for   (D) into

9. This place is known _____ a holiday resort.
   (A) as   (B) for   (C) to   (D) by

10. A man is known _____ the company he keeps.
   (A) as   (B) for   (C) to   (D) by

下列的動詞（片語）沒有被動的用法：

1. happen（發生）

2. occur（發生）

3. take place（舉行）

4. belong to（屬於）

5. consist of（由…組成）

6. look/taste/smell/sound/feel + adj

7. cost, take（花用）

8. resemble（像）= look like

9. last（持續）

說明注意：

1. take place = be held

2. consist of = be composed of = be made up of

聯考題型

1. These two moths _____ each other, but they are of different species.
   (A) resemble   (B) are resembled
   (C) seem resemble   (D) are resembling

2. The mayoral election will _____ on December 16.
   (A) hold   (B) be holding   (C) take place   (D) be taken place

3. The buffet lunch _____ several Japanese dishes and some Western foods.
   (A) consisted of   (B) was consisted of
   (C) composed of   (D) made up of

4. A bouquet of red roses like that _____ about 50 bucks now.
   (A) cost   (B) costs   (C) is costing   (D) is cost

5. Coffee without sugar _____ a little bitter.
   (A) tastes   (B) tasted   (C) is tasting   (D) is tasted

要點 1

1. 不變的事實/真理或恆真的命題之假設：

If + S + 現在式 V …, S + | 現在式 V / 現在進行式 | （if 接近 when）

If the engine <u>gets</u> too hot, it <u>starts</u> to smoke.

（如果引擎過熱，就會開始冒煙。）

If you <u>drive</u> without a driver's license, you <u>are breaking</u> the law.

（如果你無照駕駛，你就犯法了。）

2. 未來可能發生的情況之假設：

If + S + 現在式 V …, S + | shall / will / can / may | + 原形 V …

If it <u>rains</u> tomorrow, we'll <u>go</u> indoors.

（如果明天下雨，我們就改在室內。）

If you <u>are</u> late again, you <u>may lose</u> your job.

（如果你再遲到，你可能會丟了工作。）

說明：

恆真（命題）的假設，其中的 if 接近（但不等於）when。其中的差異即 when 表達的一定會發生，如：When the Queen dies, her son becomes king.（女王逝世時，她的兒子就成為國王。）這是事實。而 if 表達的終究帶有『不確定』的成分。

聯考題型

1. There is only one result when two people compete for a prize: if one wins, the other _____.

(A) lose　　　　(B) loses　　　　(C) would lose　　　　(D) is lost

---

2. Very few people are able to grow in love. Yet, it does happen _____ men and women are able to respect and accept their differences. (94學測)
   (A) unless   (B) until   (C) before   (D) if

3. If anyone _____ you where I am, tell them I'll be in the library.
   (A) ask   (B) asks   (C) asked   (D) will ask

4. If you _____ regularly, your blood circulation will be improved, and you will feel more energetic. (94指考)
   (A) exercise   (B) shall exercise (C) exercised   (D) will exercise

5. If somebody waves a red flag, it usually _____ danger.
   (A) mean   (B) meant   (C) means   (D) will mean

6. If people keep polluting the rivers, no fish there _____ in the long run. (93學測)
   (A) survive   (B) survived   (C) will survive   (D) would survive

7. If you _____ two aspirin tablets, you will soon feel better.
   (A) take   (B) eat   (C) chew   (D) swallow

8. Buried in her belly, Cindy's 16-bit microprocessor compares the text with her database of 700 words. If it's a match, "I love you," she _____. (93指考)
   (A) utter   (B) utters   (C) uttered   (D) would utter

9. If I go to bed late, I _____ bad in the morning.
   (A) am feeling   (B) would feel   (C) feel   (D) felt

10. If you feel depressed, going to a health spa _____ the right thing to make you feel better.
    (A) may be   (B) maybe
    (C) may have been   (D) has to be

與事實相反的假設

1. 與『現在事實』相反的假設

$$\text{If} + S + \begin{vmatrix} \text{過去式 V} \\ \text{were} \end{vmatrix} \cdots,\ S + \begin{vmatrix} \text{should} \\ \text{would} \\ \text{could} \\ \text{might} \end{vmatrix} + \text{原形 V}$$

If I <u>had</u> her e-mail address, I <u>would</u> <u>send</u> the manuscript to her.

（如果我有她的電子郵件地址，我就會將這手稿傳給她。）

If Peter <u>were</u> here, he <u>might help</u> us.

（如果彼德現正在這裡，他可能會幫助我們。）

2. 與『過去事實』相反的假設

$$\text{If} + S + \text{had} + \text{pp} \cdots,\ S + \begin{vmatrix} \text{should} \\ \text{would} \\ \text{could} \\ \text{might} \end{vmatrix} + \begin{vmatrix} \text{① have + pp.（純指過去）} \\ \text{② 原形 V（影響至現在）} \end{vmatrix}$$

If you had listened to me, you <u>wouldn't</u> <u>have been fired</u>.

（如果你當時聽我的話，你就不致於被解僱了。）

If you had listened to me, you <u>wouldn't</u> <u>be</u> out of work now.

（如果你當時聽我的話，你現在就不致於失業了。）

聯考題型

1. If you were in my position, you would do _____.
   (A) likely   (B) likewise   (C) likeness   (D) liking

2. If you'd talked about ways to avoid getting the flu, you _____ them on the edge of their seats. (94指考)
(A) are to have
(B) have had
(C) would have had
(D) had had

3. Listen to me. If you _____ such an expensive gift from him, you would be taking a bribe.
(A) receive
(B) received
(C) accept
(D) accepted

4. The ancient civilization would not be so deeply admired if these ancient artifacts _____ not so widely available to an international public in major museums throughout Europe and America. (93學測)
(A) were
(B) was
(C) did
(D) had

5. If I had worn warmer clothes, I _____.
(A) won't catch cold
(B) won't have caught cold
(C) wouldn't catch cold
(D) wouldn't have caught cold

6. You, of course, are real, and the moon is real, and many of the things that you could describe, such as the stars, the wind, and the pull of gravity, would be real. But your trip through space _____ be fiction. (91指考)
(A) can't
(B) shall
(C) would
(D) won't

7. If the boss _____ to be in here, you might have to face the music.
(A) occurs
(B) occurred
(C) happen
(D) happened

8. If I _____ the lottery, I would have bought a Ferrari.
(A) win
(B) won
(C) have won
(D) had won

9. If I _____ you, I'd have a talk with your parents. Better late than never, you know.
(A) am
(B) was
(C) were
(D) be

10. If it had poured all night, the whole area would _____ in danger of flooding now.
(A) be
(B) have been
(C) have
(D) have had

不確定的未來與絕不可能發生的未來假設

1. 不確定的未來：

If + S + should + 原形 V …, $\begin{vmatrix} ① 祈使句 \\ ② S + 助動詞… \end{vmatrix}$ →萬一…

If my mom <u>should</u> phone, tell her I'm out.

（萬一我老媽打電話來，告訴她我不在。）

<u>Should</u> you see him, please give him my regards.

（如果你見到他，代我問候一聲。）

2. 絕不可能或不太可能的情況：

If + S + were to + 原形 V …, S + $\begin{vmatrix} should \\ would \\ could \\ might \end{vmatrix}$ + 原形 V …

If Shakespeare <u>were to</u> return to the world, he would be amazed to find his plays being studied in schools.

（假如莎翁能再回到世上，他會很訝異他的劇本成為學校研習的教材。）

聯考題型

1. If all of us were _____ to the age of 200, we would have different life goals.
   (A) living   (B) alive   (C) lively   (D) to live

2. Should any problem _____, please feel free to let me know.
   (A) happen   (B) appear   (C) arise   (D) rise

3. If I were to be born again, I would _____ be a woman.
   (A) rather   (B) better   (C) prefer   (D) harder

4. Should there _____ any emergency, just press the red button.
   (A) be   (B) have   (C) come   (D) occur

5. Even if the sun _____ rise in the west, I would not marry such a man.
   (A) should   (B) might   (C) is to   (D) were to

6. If another world war _____ break out, it could be the end of the world.
   (A) should   (B) would   (C) could   (D) might

7. If Kirk _____ taller, he would have joined the police force.
   (A) is   (B) was   (C) were   (D) had been

8. Should the volcano _____ again, it could lead to a disaster of catastrophic proportions.
   (A) disrupt   (B) erupt   (C) corrupt   (D) interrupt

9. If you _____ die before your husband, who could take care of these five children?
   (A) would   (B) might   (C) are to   (D) were to

10. If you should fail to catch the school bus, _____ the MRT.
    (A) taking   (B) taken   (C) to take   (D) take

要點 4

直說法的條件句：

此類條件句非真正的假設。因為描述的內容就是事實或接近於事實，所以其動詞需『如實地』反映時間。

1. If + S + 現在式 V …, + 祈使句

   If you <u>are</u> afraid, <u>step</u> aside.

   （你如果害怕，就站到旁邊去。）

2. If + S + 過去式 V …, S + 過去式 V …

   If he <u>said</u> that yesterday, he <u>was</u> wrong.（接近事實）

   （要是他昨天說過那句話，他就不對了。）

比較：

If he <u>said</u> that now, he <u>would be</u> wrong.（假設）

If he <u>had said</u> that yesterday, he would have been wrong.（假設）

3. If + S + 過去式 V …, S + 現在/未來式 V …

If she <u>went</u> to elementary school in 1985, then she <u>is</u> older than me.

（如果她 1985 年上小學，那她的年紀比我大。）

4. If + S + will/won't …, S + will/won't … (will = be willing to)

If you <u>won't</u> tell, I <u>will</u>.

（你如果不願說，我來說好了。）

聯考題型

1. _____ errors, if there are any.
   (A) Correct   (B) Correcting   (C) To correct   (D) Corrected

2. If Luke said he would help you, I am sure he _____.
   (A) would   (B) could   (C) will   (D) shall

3. If she did not agree yesterday, still she _____ tomorrow.
   (A) won't   (B) wouldn't   (C) doesn't   (D) didn't

4. If you _____ cooperate, you'll get into trouble.
   (A) wouldn't   (B) shouldn't   (C) couldn't   (D) won't

5. If Peter was once your friend, why _____ he now?
   (A) doesn't   (B) isn't   (C) won't   (D) wasn't

表『若非…』之假設

1. 若非（現在）…

But for + (one's) + n
Without + (one's) + n
If it were not for + (one's) + n — , S + | should / would / could / might | + 原形 V

= S + | should / would / could / might | + 原形 V, but/only + S + 現在式 V

But for his illness, he would be laughing and talking now.

= He would be laughing and talking now, but he is ill.

（若非他今天生病，他就會談笑風生了。）

2. 若非（過去）…

But for + (one's) + n
Without + (one's) + n
If it had not been for + (one's) + n — , S + | should / would / could / might | have + pp

= S + | should / would / could / might | have + pp, but/only + S + 過去式 V

But for your assistance, I would have failed.

= I would have failed, only you assisted me.

（若非你的幫助，我早就失敗了。）

1. I would be a nervous wreck _____ your encouraging words.
   (A) but for   (B) except for   (C) only for   (D) even for

2. _____ the timely rain, all the crops might have died.
   (A) But   (B) Without   (C) Never   (D) Only

3. If it _____ for your early warning, our lives would have been in danger.
   (A) was not   (B) were not   (C) had not been   (D) had not had

4. Amy would have offered to babysit, _____ she had something else to do.
   (A) because   (B) until   (C) only   (D) for

5. But for his recent injury, Beckham _____ more points in the semifinal.
   (A) scored   (B) had scored   (C) would   (D) would have scored

翻譯造句

1. 要不是因為重感冒，我不會打電話請病假的。 (call in sick)

   試譯：＿＿＿＿＿＿＿＿＿＿＿＿＿＿＿＿＿＿＿＿＿＿＿＿＿＿

2. 若非颱風之故，夏令營的一切活動已如期舉行。 (as scheduled)

   試譯：＿＿＿＿＿＿＿＿＿＿＿＿＿＿＿＿＿＿＿＿＿＿＿＿＿＿

3. 要不是班機延誤，我們現在就在家裡了。 (a flight delay)

   試譯：＿＿＿＿＿＿＿＿＿＿＿＿＿＿＿＿＿＿＿＿＿＿＿＿＿＿

4. 若非有一些文法上的錯誤，這是一篇不錯的作文。

   試譯：＿＿＿＿＿＿＿＿＿＿＿＿＿＿＿＿＿＿＿＿＿＿＿＿＿＿

5. 要不是政府採取緊急措施，許多災民將已餓死。 (starve to death)

   試譯：＿＿＿＿＿＿＿＿＿＿＿＿＿＿＿＿＿＿＿＿＿＿＿＿＿＿

wish 的用法

1. S + wish + (that) + S +
   ① 過去式 V/were →現在
   ② had + pp →過去 （主觀認為無法實現）
   ③ could/would + 原形 V →未來

= If only + S +
   ① 過去式 V/were
   ② had + pp
   ③ could/would + 原形 V

= Would that + S +
   ① 過去式 V/were
   ② had + pp
   ③ could/would + 原形 V

I wish I <u>were/was</u> a billionaire.（was 為口語用法）

（但願我現在是一個億萬富翁。）

If only I <u>had won</u> the lottery.

（當時我要是有中樂透就好了。）

Would that I <u>could</u> travel around the world !

（真希望我有能力去環遊世界。）

2. 表可以實現的『祝福』

S + wish + <u>you/him/her</u> +
   (a) + n.
   well （受格）

= May <u>you/he/she</u> + 原形 V …!（主格）

We wish you a Merry Christmas and a Happy New Year !

= May you have a Merry Christmas and a Happy New Year !

（我們祝你們聖誕快樂、新年也快樂。）

注意：

hope 表可以實現的『希望』。

1. Sorry, I really don't like to go bowling. I wish I _____.
   (A) like   (B) liked   (C) do   (D) did

2. I hate being a cop. I wish I _____ a different career.
   (A) choose   (B) chose   (C) choosing   (D) had chosen

3. The incumbent president hopes to get re-elected, but it may be just _____ thinking.
   (A) hopeful   (B) wishful   (C) helpful   (D) handful

4. We wish the bride and the bridegroom _____.
   (A) very happy   (B) very happily
   (C) every happiness   (D) ever happy

5. Friends and relatives all wished the newlyweds _____ before they left for their honeymoon.
   (A) good   (B) well   (C) fine   (D) all right

6. I wish that I _____ afford such an expensive vacation.
   (A) could   (B) can   (C) would   (D) will

7. I wish my parents _____ treating me like a kid. I'm already 22 years old !
   (A) stop   (B) to stop   (C) should stop (D) would stop

8. A lot of people I know cannot face facts. A few of them sometimes even wish they _____.
   (A) were never born   (B) have never been born
   (C) would never be born   (D) had never been born

9. When Jeff saw me, he came up to me and wished me _____.
   (A) luck   (B) lucky   (C) luckily   (D) luckless

10. If only you _____ how hard I've been trying to please you.
    (A) know   (B) knew   (C) known   (D) have known

as if/though 的用法（表『好像…』）

1. 接假設法動詞，表與事實相反

$$S + V \cdots as\ if/though + S +\begin{cases}① \text{過去式 V/were} \to \text{現在/同時} \\ ② \text{had + pp} \to \text{過去} \\ ③ \text{would/ could + 原形 V} \to \text{未來}\end{cases}$$

He talks as if he <u>knew</u> our secret.

（他講話的口氣好像知道我們的秘密似的。）

He talks as if he <u>had known</u> our secret.

（他講話的口氣好像早已知道我們的秘密似的。）

He talks as if he <u>could uncover</u> our secret.

（他講話的口氣好像他能發現我們的秘密似的。）

2. 表接近事實的情況

S + V $\cdots$ as if/though + S + <u>直說法 V</u>

It looks as if it <u>is</u> going to rain.

（看起來好像快下雨了。）

It sounds as though she <u>has</u> really <u>been</u> ill.

（聽起來好像她真的病了一陣子。）

3. 感嘆句（As if + S + 假設法動詞！）

As if I <u>cared</u> ! (= I don't care.)

（好像我很在乎似的，才不呢！）

As if I <u>would</u> ! (= I won't.)

（好像我會去做似的，才不呢！）

4. 省略結構

$$S + V \cdots as\ if/though + \begin{cases} ① V\text{-ing} \to 主動/進行 \\ ② pp \to 被動/完成 \\ ③ to + 原形\ V \to 目的 \\ ④ 介系詞片語 \\ ⑤ 形容詞片語 \end{cases}$$

She kept smiling as if (she was) <u>enjoying</u> the speech.

（她一直保持微笑，好像很喜歡這個演講似的。）

He laughed heartily as though (he was) <u>sure of</u> success.

（他開懷大笑，好像對成功很有把握。）

聯考題型

1. Do not act as if you _____ a thousand years to live. Procrastination won't get you anywhere !
   (A) have　　　　(B) had　　　　(C) have had　　　(D) are having

2. Beware, the boss looks as though he _____ explode.
   (A) was going to　(B) were going to　(C) is going to　　(D) be going to

3. "George kept reminding me of the message he had left. As if it _____!"
   (A) matter　　　(B) mattered　　　(C) mattering　　　(D) to matter

4. The money just disappeared under my very nose as if _____.
   (A) like magic　　(B) like a magician　(C) by magic　　　(D) by a magician

5. I need some fresh air. You smell as though you _____ three packs of cigarettes a day.
   (A) smoke　　　(B) smoking　　　(C) have smoked　(D) are smoking

6. Bullshit ! You sound as if you _____ an authority on math.
   (A) was　　　　(B) were　　　　(C) to be　　　　(D) being

7. Whenever I do the skydiving, I feel _____ I'm floating on air.
   (A) as though　　(B) even though　(C) only if　　　(D) even if

8. Rex raised both hands as if _____.
   (A) surrendered　(B) to surrender　(C) has surrendered (D) had surrendered

9. This machine can pull up trees as if they _____ weeds. Quite amazing, isn't it?
   (A) are   (B) were   (C) have   (D) had

10. Every time she is at the wheel, she drives as if she _____ mad.
    (A) is   (B) were   (C) seems   (D) like

It's (about/high) time … 的句型：

1. It's (about/high) time + (that) + S + 過去式 V →該是某人做…的時候了（強調早就該做）

   It's (about) time you <u>had</u> your hair cut.

   （該是你去剪剪頭髮的時候了。）

   It's (high) time he <u>was taught</u> a lesson.

   （該是他被教訓的時候了。）

2. It's time (for sb) to do sth →該是（某人）做…的時候了（強調現在該做）

   It's time (for us) <u>to go</u> home.

   （該是我們現在回家的時候了。）

   比較：   It's time we <u>went</u> home.

   （在此之前我們就該回家了。）

聯考題型

1. It's about time you _____ to look after yourself.
   (A) learn   (B) learning   (C) learned   (D) to learn

2. Henry: I still don't have time to visit our clients.

   Nancy: It's time you _____.

   (A) have   (B) had   (C) do   (D) did

3. It's high time you _____ fooling around.
   (A) stop   (B) stopped   (C) to stop   (D) have stopped

4. It's time for your car _____.
   (A) maintained   (B) to maintain   (C) maintaining   (D) to be maintained

5. You are already 40. It's about time you _____ yourself a wife and settled down.
   (A) find   (B) found   (C) finding   (D) to find

要點 9

表『寧願…（而不願…）』的句型

    S + would rather/sooner … (than …)
= S + would as soon … (as …)

1. 表『寧願自己…』

S + would + | rather
sooner
as soon | + | ① 原形 V →現在/未來
② have + pp →過去 |

I would rather <u>be</u> a monk than <u>marry</u> her.

（我寧可當和尚也不要娶她。）

He would rather <u>have married</u> another woman.

（他寧願當時娶的是另外一個女人。）

2. 表『寧願他人…』（接 that 子句）

S + would + | rather
sooner
as soon | + (that) + sb/sth + | ① 過去式 V →現在/未來
② had + pp →過去 |

He would sooner you <u>went</u> alone.

（他寧願你一個人去。）

I'd rather he <u>hadn't told</u> me about that.

（我寧可他當時沒有告訴我那件事情。）

1. I would rather _____ about it anymore.
   (A) not talk   (B) not talking   (C) not to talk   (D) not having talked

2. Jenny doesn't want Tom to go to the party with her. Who do you think she'd rather _____ with her?
   (A) go   (B) going   (C) to go   (D) went

3. You must know that she'd rather you _____ smoking.
   (A) give up   (B) giving up   (C) to give up   (D) gave up

4. Most kids would _____ play as study.
   (A) rather   (B) soon   (C) as soon   (D) sooner

5. I would rather it _____ at once.
   (A) is done   (B) was done   (C) be done   (D) being done

翻譯造句

1. 他寧願去別家餐廳也不要站在這裡排隊等候。 (stand in line)

   試譯：_____

2. 我寧願你明天待在家裡。

   試譯：_____

3. 我有很多我寧可不說的話要說。

   試譯：_____

4. 她寧可保持沉默。

   試譯：_____

5. 這些士兵寧可犧牲性命也不投降。

   試譯：_____

1. S +
$\begin{cases} \text{suggest, propose, recommend} \\ \text{demand, require, request} \\ \text{order, command, decree} \\ \text{insist, maintain, urge} \end{cases}$ + (that) + S + (should) + 原形 V

2. It is
$\begin{cases} \text{necessary, essential,} \\ \text{urgent, imperative,} \\ \text{advisable, important,} \\ \text{desirable, recommendable} \end{cases}$ + (that) + S + (should) + 原形 V

3. It is
$\begin{cases} \text{funny, odd, strange,} \\ \text{unthinkable, incredible,} \\ \text{regrettable, a pity} \end{cases}$ + (that) + S + <u>should</u> + 原形 V
（竟然）

注意：

1. suggest 表『暗示』，insist 表『強調』時，其後的子句接直說法動詞。

2. 『建議/要求/命令/堅持』以名詞的形式出現（如 suggestion, insistence 等）時，仍適用原句型。

※ 3. It is necessary/essential/odd 等之後的子句亦可接『直說法』動詞。

聯考題型

1. Dan suggested that we _____ at some other place for a change.
   (A) eat   (B) ate   (C) eaten   (D) to eat

2. It is essential that our soldiers _____ the best training.
   (A) give   (B) giving   (C) be given   (D) be giving

3. It was her insistence that all rapists _____ to life.
   (A) should sentence   (B) would sentence
   (C) have sentenced   (D) be sentenced

4. Kim's pale look suggested that he _____ frightened.
   (A) was   (B) is   (C) would be   (D) be

5. We demand that all nations _____ equally.
   (A) are treated   (B) would be treated
   (C) be treated   (D) could be treated

6. Since a fire has broken out, it is urgent that the fire department _____.
   (A) should be notified   (B) would be notified
   (C) could be notified   (D) might be notified

7. The law I'm referring to requires that every motorist _____ accident insurance.
   (A) has   (B) had   (C) have   (D) to have

8. It's unthinkable that she _____ on sick leave all the time.
   (A) has   (B) take   (C) make   (D) is

9. Because I won the lottery, they insisted that I _____ everyone to a big dinner.
   (A) treat   (B) treated   (C) treating   (D) to treat

10. I wanted to skip breakfast, but my mom insisted I _____.
    (A) had it   (B) have it   (C) having it   (D) to have it

Unit 13   動詞與主詞的一致

要點 1

基本概念：動詞的單複數變化必須與主詞的人稱、單複數一致。

1. （單數）S +（單數）V.

The first step <u>is</u> always the hardest.

（萬事起頭難。）

2. $\begin{vmatrix} \text{V-ing} \cdots \\ \text{To + V} \cdots \\ \text{疑問字 + 不定詞} \cdots \\ \text{That/疑問字 + S + V} \cdots \end{vmatrix}$ + 單數 V …

Knowing <u>is</u> half the battle.

（知己知彼百戰百勝。）

How to solve these problems <u>is</u> up to you.

（如何解決這些問題由你來決定。）

3. $\begin{vmatrix} \text{Every} \\ \text{Each} \\ \text{No} \\ \text{Many a(n)} \end{vmatrix}$ + 單數 n   + 單數 V …

Every employee <u>has</u> his or her key to the building.

（每一名員工都有他/她自己的一把大樓鑰匙。）

Many a parent <u>is</u> worried about this situation.

（許多父母對這種情況都頗為憂心。）

4. （複數）S +（複數）V

Tigers <u>are</u> on the list of endangered species.

（老虎是瀕臨絕種的動物之一。）

5. 兩個名詞用 **and** 連接，一般接複數動詞，如表同一個人或同一件事物時接單數動詞。

Bread and butter are both necessities of life.

（麵包和牛奶兩項都是生活必需品。）

This island's bread and butter is tourism.

（這座小島主要的收入來源是觀光業。）

聯考題型

1. The technological development of computer hardware and software _____ changed people's ways of life a lot.
   (A) have   (B) has   (C) are   (D) is

2. Driving cars _____ full of excitement, but driving lessons are rather boring.
   (A) is   (B) are   (C) has   (D) have

3. In an assembly line, the products that are being manufactured _____, but the workers remain in the same place.
   (A) move   (B) moves   (C) moved   (D) moving

4. It is reported that many a spectator in the stadium _____ wounded because of the bombings.
   (A) was   (B) were   (C) had   (D) has

5. Bacon and eggs _____ my favorite breakfast.
   (A) was   (B) were   (C) use to be   (D) are

6. No signs of economic recovery _____ been shown up to the present time.
   (A) is   (B) are   (C) has   (D) have

7. Smiling every day _____ years to your life.
   (A) add   (B) adds   (C) adding   (D) to add

8. How to deal with the avian influenza _____ a great challenge to the government's wisdom.
   (A) pause   (B) pauses   (C) pose   (D) poses

9. To be a famous singer and dancer _____ always Judy's dream.
   (A) is   (B) are   (C) has been   (D) have been

10. Whether they are still alive after the tsunami _____ anybody's guess.
   (A) are   (B) is   (C) has   (D) have

易混淆名詞的單複數用法

1. 表「時間/距離/價值/重要」的名詞片語作主詞時，接單數 V。

   Twenty years <u>is</u> a long time to wait.

   （二十年的歲月等起來很漫長。）

   Twenty years <u>have</u> passed/elapsed since then.

   （自從那個時候以來二十年已經過去了。）

   註：一整段時間作主詞時用單數動詞。指其一天又一天，一年又一年的經過時，用複數動詞。

2. 複數形、單數意義的名詞作主詞，接單數動詞。

   這類名詞有：news（消息），mathematics（數學），statistics（統計學），ethics（倫理學），acoustics（音響學），physics（物理學），politics（政治學），economics（經濟學），phonetics（語音學），linguistics（語言學），falls（瀑布），crossroads（十字路口），measles（麻疹），mumps（腮腺炎），herpes（疱疹）。

   注意：

   statistics 表「統計數字」，ethics 表「道德原則」，acoustics 表「音響效果」，politics 表「政治理念」，economics 表「經濟運作」時，一律視為複數名詞。作主詞時需接複數 V。

3. The number of + 複數 n + 單數 V → …的數字…

4. A number of + 複數 n + 複數 V → 不止一些…

5. 集合名詞（如 family 表「家人」）作主詞時，可接單數 V（美式用法）或複數 V（英式用法）。

聯考題型

1. Quite a number of customers _____ standing in line outside of a McDonald's in order to get a Hello Kitty toy.

   (A) are   (B) is   (C) have   (D) has

2. The number of people who sign up for the voluntary work _____ increasing.
   (A) are   (B) is   (C) have   (D) has

3. My family _____ composed of my parents, my grandparents and me.
   (A) is   (B) are   (C) has   (D) have

4. Mathematics _____ the mother of all sciences.
   (A) is   (B) are   (C) has   (D) have

5. Fifty thousand dollars _____ too large a sum of money for me to pay.
   (A) are   (B) have   (C) is   (D) has

6. If economics can be defined as a problem of demand and supply, then politics _____ like a problem of vectors.
   (A) seems   (B) feels   (C) looks   (D) sounds

7. Statistics _____ a branch of mathematics.
   (A) is   (B) are   (C) has   (D) have

8. Statistics _____ sometimes a reliable index of economic growth or people's purchasing power.
   (A) is   (B) are   (C) has   (D) have

9. The police _____ called to put down the riot.
   (A) was   (B) were   (C) had   (D) have

10. A list of the company's top salespeople _____ posted on the bulletin board.
    (A) is   (B) are   (C) has   (D) have

11. Everybody knows that measles _____ a contagious disease.
    (A) is   (B) are   (C) has   (D) have

12. The acoustics in the National Theater _____ really excellent.
    (A) is   (B) are   (C) was   (D) being

13. This species of rose _____ very rare, so it is expensive.
    (A) is   (B) are   (C) has   (D) have

14. Some doctors are only busy making money. Their medical ethics _____ ignored by them.
    (A) is   (B) are   (C) has   (D) have

15. His politics _____ to become more and more conservative as he grows older.
    (A) seems   (B) seem   (C) likes   (D) like

1. There/Here + | 單數 V + 單數 S（限為名詞）
                | 複數 V + 複數 S（限為名詞）

Here <u>comes</u> the school bus.

（校車來了。）

There <u>are</u> only three cats in the house.

（這棟房子裡只有三隻貓。）

2.（表地方）介系詞片語 + | 單數 V + 單數 S（限為名詞）
                      | 複數 V + 複數 S（限為名詞）

On the table <u>lie</u> several dishes.

（餐桌上擺了好幾道菜。）

Under the pillow <u>was</u> <u>placed</u> a handgun.

（在枕頭底下有放著一把手槍。）

All
Most
Half
Part
Plenty
3. Some   + of + | 單數 n + 單數 V
The rest | 複數 n + 複數 V
A lot/Lots
The majority
分數/百分比

Half of the apple <u>is</u> rotten.

（這個蘋果爛了一半。）

Half of the apples <u>are</u> rotten.

（這堆蘋果爛掉一半了。）

1. In the wallet _____ two $100 bills and a few coins.
   (A) is   (B) are   (C) has   (D) have

2. You want the money now? OK, there _____.
   (A) you go   (B) go you   (C) you come   (D) come you

3. A lot of time _____ on those useless things.
   (A) are wasted   (B) were wasted
   (C) have been wasted   (D) has been wasted

4. Twenty percent of my salary _____ spent on amusement.
   (A) is   (B) has   (C) are   (D) have

5. The flight is sold out, so some of the passengers _____ on standby.
   (A) is   (B) are   (C) was   (D) were

6. A lot of damage _____ done by the earthquake so far.
   (A) was   (B) were   (C) has been   (D) have been

7. The damages you may have to pay _____ estimated at $6,000.
   (A) is   (B) are   (C) has   (D) have

8. Two-thirds of the crew on the ship _____ said to be under the weather.
   (A) is   (B) are   (C) has   (D) have

9. A large part of his speech _____ make any sense.
   (A) doesn't   (B) don't   (C) hasn't   (D) haven't

10. Among our guests _____ a famous host of a popular talk show, Mr. Whitehead, and his wife.
    (A) are   (B) is   (C) have   (D) has

1. A +
   - with（有）
   - along with（連同）
   - together with（連同）
   - as well as（以及）
   - rather than（而非）

   + B + V（單複數與 A 一致）

The new library with its tens of thousands of books and all kinds of journals <u>meets</u> everybody's needs.

（這座擁有數萬冊書籍和各種期刊的新圖書館迎合了大家的需求。）

Mr. Black rather than his children <u>is</u> to blame.

（該受責備的是布雷克先生而非他的孩子們。）

2. Not only A but (also) B + V（單複數與 B 一致）

Not only the players but also the coach <u>was</u> satisfied with the final result.

（不但是球員們而且連教練對最後之結果都很滿意。）

3.
   - A or B
   - either A or B
   - neither A nor B

   ：動詞與較接近的 A 或 B 一致

Either you or he <u>is</u> wrong.（靠近 he）

（不是你的錯就是他的錯。）

<u>Were</u> you or he on night duty then?（靠近 you）

（當時值夜班的人是你或是他？）

1. In the laboratory, he says, it is labor rather than oratory that _____.
   (A) count   (B) counts   (C) counting   (D) to count

2. Your friend as well as we _____ only too willing to help you out.
   (A) are   (B) is   (C) seem   (D) seeming

3. Neither the kittens nor the cat _____.
   (A) have been fed   (B) has been fed
   (C) have been feeding   (D) has been feeding

4. There _____ either a machine gun or other weapons in the log cabin.
   (A) is   (B) are   (C) has   (D) have

5. Not only the children but their mother _____ come down with the bird flu.
   (A) are   (B) is   (C) have   (D) has

6. There _____ neither tap water nor electricity in the house.
   (A) was   (B) were   (C) had   (D) has

7. That woman with her two young children tagging along _____ to need some help.
   (A) seem   (B) seems   (C) seeming   (D) to seem

8. The bat together with some mitts and balls _____. Someone must have taken them away.
   (A) have lost   (B) has lost   (C) are missing   (D) is missing

9. The captain as well as the crew _____ reported to have been held hostage.
   (A) is   (B) are   (C) has   (D) have

10. A drug lord along with a few addicts _____ arrested yesterday, according to a local news report.
    (A) were   (B) was   (C) had   (D) have

Unit 14　否定句型

要點 1

部分否定

1. $\begin{vmatrix} \text{Every} \cdots/\text{Everything} \\ \text{Both} \cdots \\ \text{All} \cdots \end{vmatrix}$ +（助）動詞 + not ⋯→並非⋯都⋯

= Not + $\begin{vmatrix} \text{every} \cdots/\text{everything} \\ \text{both} \cdots \\ \text{all} \cdots \end{vmatrix}$ +（助）動詞⋯

All of us do not like the idea.

= Not all of us like the idea.

（並非我們所有人都贊成這個構想。）

2. not always/necessarily→未必都一直/定⋯

The rich are not always happy.

（有錢人未必都一直很快樂。）

3. not entirely/wholly/altogether→不全⋯

The news source is not entirely reliable.

（這個消息的來源不完全可靠。）

注意：

Every/Both/All ⋯ not ⋯的句型有「歧義」性。如：All of us do not like the idea. 亦可解為 None of us like the idea.（即：我們所有人全都不贊成這個構想）。因此，除非是現成說法（如 All that glitters is not gold.）或前後文義夠明確，否則儘量少用這個句型。換言之，宜用意義明確的 Not every/both/all ⋯或 None/Neither ⋯之句型。

1. Not every man can be a hero, and the opportunity to become a hero is not _____ every day.
   (A) giving   (B) given   (C) to give   (D) being given

2. Just as good fortune is not all gain, so bad luck is not all _____.
   (A) lose   (B) lost   (C) losing   (D) loss

3. The fault is not entirely _____.
   (A) on me   (B) with me   (C) to me   (D) mine

4. This is a rare plant. It cannot be found _____.
   (A) anywhere   (B) nowhere   (C) everywhere   (D) wherever

5. _____ of the two brothers has come of age.
   (A) All   (B) Both   (C) None   (D) Neither

克漏字

In today's global village, interactivity between nations has become more and more frequent. As a matter of fact, no nation can live __1__ isolated from others. __2__ between nations never fails to bring about some influence on their languages. When two languages compete, the victory does not __3__ fall to the better one. Nor is it always the nation whose culture is superior that makes the nation of inferior culture __4__ its language. It seems that all languages, past and __5__, let nature take its course.

1. (A) entire   (B) entirely   (C) temporary   (D) temporarily

2. (A) Entry   (B) Encounter   (C) Contact   (D) Contract

3. (A) necessarily   (B) necessary   (C) evenly   (D) even

4. (A) adapt   (B) adopt   (C) abuse   (D) abide

5. (A) now   (B) new   (C) present   (D) pleasant

表「原因」的否定句

1. not … because …→ ① 因…而不… ② 不因…才…（此二義視前後文而定）

I did not buy the watch because it was too expensive.

（因為這隻手錶太貴了，所以我沒買。）

I did not buy the watch because it was cheap.

（我不是因為這隻手錶便宜才買的。）

2. not because … but because …→不因…而因…

I did not buy the watch because it was cheap, but because it had a new design.

= I bought the watch not because it was cheap, but because it had a new design.

（我買了這隻手錶，不是因為它便宜而是因為它有新造型。）

3. Just because + S + V … doesn't mean (that)…→光是因為…也未必代表…
= Just because + S + V …, it doesn't mean (that) …

Just because you've got a Ph.D. doesn't mean that I have to respect you.

（光是因為你得了博士學位也未必代表我必須尊敬你。）

4. Not that + S + V …, but that + S + V …→並非…而是…

Not that I like my teacher less, but that I like truth more. (Aristotle)

（吾愛吾師，但吾更愛真理。）

1. I did not go to the cocktail party because I was otherwise _____.
   (A) engaged   (B) engaging   (C) enforced   (D) enforcing

2. This is my wife's picture. She didn't marry me _____ I was rich and handsome then.
   (A) due to   (B) for   (C) owing to   (D) because

3. Not that I dislike this job, but that I'm not _____ it.
   (A) equal to   (B) opposed to   (C) subject to   (D) addicted to

4. _____ because you are my older sister doesn't mean I have to listen to you.
   (A) Only   (B) Merely   (C) Even   (D) Just

5. I enjoy mountain-climbing not because I want to exercise, _____ because I need to lose weight, but because it helps increase my appetite.
   (A) not   (B) either   (C) neither   (D) nor

引導寫作

1. 我們之所以吃香蕉，不是因為我們喜歡，而是因為香蕉比起其他水果，吃起來較不麻煩。蘋果，梨子去皮總是需要費點勁，可是香蕉幾乎是自己去好皮似的。

   We eat bananas, _____ because we like them, _____ because they give us _____ trouble than any other fruit. It always requires some _____ to peel an apple or a pear, but the banana almost peels _____.

2. 如果你習慣於寫文章謀生，便會瞭解有時候困難並不在於寫文章，而是在於選擇你喜歡的主題。主題並非很少，而是太多了，無從選起。

   If you are accustomed _____ writing articles for a living, you will know that sometimes difficulty does not _____ in writing the article but _____ choosing a subject you like. Not that subjects are few, _____ that they are too many to choose _____.

1. S + cannot + 原形 V … too …→再怎麼…也不為過

= S + cannot + 原形 V … enough.

= It is impossible for + O + to + 原形 V … too …

We <u>cannot</u> be <u>too</u> careful in the choice of company.

= We <u>cannot</u> be careful <u>enough</u> in the choice of company.

（選擇朋友時，我們要愈小心愈好。）

2. S（事物）+ cannot be overemphasized. →再怎麼強調也不為過

= S（事物）+ cannot be overestimated.

National security cannot be overemphasized.

（國家安全至為重要。）

3. S + cannot get enough of sth/sb →極為喜歡某物/人

He cannot get enough of Jolin's albums.

（他極為喜歡 Jolin 的唱片專輯。）

Many fans cannot get enough of the Korean actor.

（不少粉絲極為喜歡這位韓國男星。）

聯考題型

1. You are what you eat. In other words, you cannot be _____ careful in the choice of food.

   (A) very   (B) enough   (C) too   (D) so

2. Clothes cannot be too new; friends cannot be _____.

   (A) old too   (B) old either   (C) old enough   (D) enough old

3. A book may be compared to your neighbor. If it is good, it cannot last too long; if bad, you cannot get rid of it too _____.

   (A) late   (B) lately   (C) slowly   (D) quickly

4. Since knowing is half the battle, no people in trade can know _____ about the habits, tastes, and wants of their customers.

(A) too much   (B) as much   (C) so much   (D) very much

5. Good habits cannot be formed too _____.

(A) soon   (B) fast   (C) rapid   (D) quick

6. The importance of personal hygiene cannot be _____, especially in summer.

(A) overlooking   (B) overemphasized
(C) overhearing   (D) overcharged

7. Although money is the root of all evil, many people cannot get _____ of it.

(A) much   (B) most   (C) enough   (D) sufficient

8. I cannot thank you _____ for what you have done for me.

(A) very much   (B) too little   (C) so much   (D) enough

9. The importance of safeguarding the environment _____ be overestimated.

(A) shouldn't   (B) mustn't   (C) can't   (D) won't

10. It seems that a lot of people cannot get _____ of the *Harry Potter* series.

(A) sufficiency   (B) enough   (C) abundance   (D) plenty

要點 4

1. S + never + V + but + S + V. →不…則已，一…就…

= S + never + V + without + V-ing.

Ted <u>never</u> speaks <u>but</u> he stammers.

= Ted <u>never</u> speaks <u>without</u> stammering.

（泰德不說話則已，一說話就口吃。）

2. S + be + not $\begin{vmatrix} \text{so + adj} \\ \text{such a(n) + n} \end{vmatrix}$ + but + S + V …→沒有…到不能…之地步

She is <u>not</u> <u>so</u> ill <u>but</u> she can get out of bed.

（她還沒有病到不能下床的地步。）

He is not <u>such</u> a fool <u>but</u> he can distinguish between right and wrong.

（他並沒有笨到是非不分的地步。）

注意：

1. not so/such … but …屬「典雅」的用法，現代英文已少用。

2. 上述句型所使用的 never, not 可因句子結構需要，代之以其它的否定字，如 nobody, none, nothing 等。

聯考題型

1. She cannot stand her husband anymore. He never sleeps but _____.
   (A) snores   (B) snoring   (C) he snores   (D) his snoring

2. Nobody is _____ but he can learn something.
   (A) too old   (B) so old   (C) very old   (D) ever old

3. _____ is so hard but it becomes easy by practice.
   (A) Everything   (B) Something   (C) Anything   (D) Nothing

4. We never study the lives of great people _____ we notice that an apparent misfortune will end up being a very fortunate thing for them.
   (A) and   (B) or   (C) but   (D) if

5. George never goes to a bookstore but _____ some books.
   (A) buys   (B) buying   (C) to buy   (D) he buys

克漏字

Money is not everything, but without money people cannot do anything. Accordingly, few people are so foolish __1__ they want to always have some money at their disposal. However, there are quite a few people who never take any thought for their money __2__ they run out of it. On the other hand, many more people do the same __3__ how they use their time. They never come to understand that lost money can be __4__, but lost time is lost for ever. All people, therefore, should __5__ time since time is more precious than money.

1. (A) that　　　　(B) but　　　　(C) as　　　　(D) when

2. (A) if　　　　(B) lest　　　　(C) until　　　　(D) because

3. (A) regarding　　(B) remembering　(C) thinking　　(D) testing

4. (A) refunded　　(B) resisted　　(C) regained　　(D) repeated

5. (A) mark　　　(B) gain　　　(C) lose　　　(D) treasure

要點 5

1. none but + 人→只有…

   None but a math teacher can solve this problem.

   （只有數學老師才能解這道題。）

2. nothing but + 事物/身分→只是…

   I'm **nothing but** a math teacher.（指身分）

   （我只是一個數學老師而已。）

   His speech was **nothing but** hot air.

   （他講的只是空話而已。）

3. none other than + 人→不是別人，正是…

   The new arrival is **none other than** the prince himself.

   （剛抵達的不是別人，正是王子本人。）

4. anything but + | ① adj
   　　　　　　　 | ② n 　　→絕非…；一點也不…

= far from (being) … （接 n 時 being 不省略）

= not … at all

Our host was <u>anything but</u> friendly.

（我們的主人一點也不友善。）

Your friend is <u>anything but</u> a good guy.

（你的朋友絕非善類。）

5. all but + | ① 人/物 = all except …→除…之外，所有的…
         | ② adj/adv/v = almost …→幾乎…

<u>All but</u> the ancient mariner died.

（除了這名老水手之外，所有的人都死了。）

The ancient mariner <u>all but</u> died.

（這名老水手幾乎死掉。）

| 聯考題型

1. _____ a detective like Sherlock Holmes can solve such a grotesque crime.
   (A) All but   (B) Nothing but   (C) None but   (D) Anything but

2. _____ a handful of his henchmen hated the strongman.
   (A) All but   (B) Nothing but   (C) None but   (D) Anything but

3. The mystery guest turned out to be _____ Christie's ex-husband.
   (A) nothing but   (B) anything but
   (C) none other than   (D) any better than

4. We must admit the experiment is a total failure. The result is _____ satisfactory.
   (A) anything but   (B) nothing but   (C) all but   (D) none but

5. In business Nick is a "gambler" because he enjoys _____ taking risks when it comes to making any investment.
   (A) all but   (B) anything but   (C) none but   (D) nothing but

6. I'm not a great painter. I'm _____ a pavement artist in London, actually.
   (A) none but   (B) nothing but   (C) all but   (D) anything but

---

7. My boyfriend is _____ a coward. Don't ever judge a man by his looks.

(A) anything but   (B) all but   (C) none but   (D) far from

8. It was _____ impossible to recover the lost diamond. It was like looking for a needle in a haystack.

(A) anything but   (B) all but   (C) nothing but   (D) none but

9. _____ a genius can compose such a great piece of music!

(A) All but   (B) Nothing but   (C) Anything but   (D) None but

10. Don't ever believe him. Whatever he says is _____ reliable.

(A) all but   (B) nothing but   (C) anything but   (D) none but

要點 6

nothing 的重要慣用法

1. for nothing → ① 免費 (= for free)
   ② 毫無理由/目的

   I can get the tickets <u>for nothing</u>.

   （我可以免費取到門票。）

   Why did she cry <u>for nothing</u>?

   （她為什麼哭得莫名其妙？）

2. be nothing like … → 一點都不像…

   Her two daughters are nothing like each other.

   （她的兩個女兒彼此一點也不像。）

3. There is nothing like + n/V-ing … → （做）…最好

   There is nothing like having some ice cream on such a hot day.

   （在這種大熱天吃點冰淇淋是最好不過的事情。）

4. There is nothing in/to sth → 某事物非真/不可信

There is nothing in/to the report.

（這一則報導非真。）

5. nothing less than …→簡直…

It's nothing less than a fraud.

（這簡直是一樁詐欺案。）

6. There is nothing to it. →這太簡單了

= It's a piece of cake.

I did the crossword in five minutes. There is nothing to it.

（我五分鐘就把這個填字謎做好了。這太簡單了。）

7. have nothing on sb → ① （能力）不比某人好
② 沒有某人的把柄/犯罪證據

She has nothing on me when it comes to cooking.

（說到廚藝，她並沒有比我好。）

They could not arrest him because they had nothing on him.

（他們不能逮捕他，因為並沒有他犯罪的證據。）

聯考題型

1. Why call in a plumber when I can do it _____?
   (A) with nothing   (B) in nothing   (C) for free   (D) freely

2. You should beware of John's real motive. He did not help you _____.
   (A) for good   (B) for nothing   (C) for fun   (D) for fear

3. We have been rushed here and there by the tour guide. It's _____ taking a vacation.
   (A) nothing but   (B) nothing with   (C) nothing like   (D) nothing for

4. There is nothing _____ taking a nap in the afternoon after a busy morning.
   (A) like   (B) as   (C) alike   (D) but

5. There is nothing _____ the rumor that the President has been assassinated.
   (A) on   (B) for   (C) to   (D) with

6. You press the button first, see? There is nothing _____ it.
   (A) in   (B) for   (C) to   (D) with

7. We should celebrate because the release of your new CD is _____ a sensation.
   (A) no less than   (B) no more than
   (C) nothing short for   (D) nothing less than

8. He has nothing _____ you when it comes to playing chess.
   (A) in   (B) on   (C) to   (D) with

9. The police had nothing _____ Brad, so they let him loose.
   (A) with   (B) in   (C) on   (D) for

10. Kay: Thank you for giving me a ride.
    Ted: _____
    (A) Nothing doing.   (B) Nothing of the kind.
    (C) Nothing else.   (D) It's nothing.

要點 7

1. not so much A as B →與其說是 A 不如說是 B
   = not A but B
   = B rather than A
   = B but not A

   He is <u>not so much</u> an artist <u>as</u> an artisan.
   （與其說他是一位藝術家倒不如說是一名藝匠。）

   She is <u>not so much</u> poor <u>as</u> careless with money.
   （與其說她沒什麼錢倒不如說愛亂花錢。）

2. not so much that …, but that …→與其說…不如說…

It is <u>not so much that</u> the work is difficult, <u>but that</u> it is boring.

（這件工作與其說是困難，倒不如說是乏味的。）

3. do/did not so much as + 原形 V →甚至都不⋯

= do/did not even + 原形 V

= ⋯ without so much as + V-ing

They did not so much as <u>say</u> goodbye when they left.

= They left without so much as <u>saying</u> goobye.

（他們離開時甚至都不說再見。）

比較：

They never so much as <u>said</u> goodbye when they left.

（他們離開時從不說再見。）

| 聯考題型

1. Indeed, Mr. Pitt is a very learned man, but he is a pedant _____ a scholar.
   (A) not so   (B) not much   (C) other than   (D) rather than

2. The old woman is illiterate. She cannot so much as _____ her own name.
   (A) write   (B) wrote   (C) writing   (D) to write

3. The question is not so much _____ he looks as what he is.
   (A) what   (B) who   (C) how   (D) which

4. I did not so much as get a _____ of sleep last night.
   (A) blink   (B) pink   (C) sink   (D) wink

5. The real danger of our technological age is not so much that robots will begin to think like human beings, _____ human beings tend to depend on them all the time.
   (A) even that   (B) and that   (C) but that   (D) or that

In a modern city there are hostile microbes everywhere. These tiny enemies, such as bacteria and ___1___, are always trying every way to get into our bodies. Almost every day, We are exposed to a ___2___ number of them to make us infected with some disease. If we defeat them, it is not so much that we manage to avoid them, ___3___ that our bodies are equipped with a highly efficient defense system, which kills them by the million. If they get the upper ___4___, it is not because we have been accidentally exposed to them, but because we have, for some reason, lowered our defense. In our weakened condition, we easily fall ___5___ to those unfriendly microbes that fill the world around us.

1. (A) virtues   (B) viruses   (C) versions   (D) vessels

2. (A) sufficient   (B) enough   (C) adequate   (D) legal

3. (A) in   (B) seeing   (C) but   (D) so

4. (A) hand   (B) hold   (C) wind   (D) wing

5. (A) pray   (B) prey   (C) captive   (D) capital

要點 8

1. No + V-ing/n →禁止/反對…

No parking.

（禁止停車。）

No nukes.

（反對核武！）

2. There is no + V-ing …→不可能/無法…

= It is impossible + 不定詞

There is no <u>convincing</u> him.

= It is impossible <u>to convince</u> him.

（無法說服他。）

3. the last + (n) + $\begin{vmatrix} \text{(that) + S + V} \\ \text{to + 原形 V} \end{vmatrix}$ →最不（可能）…

She is the last woman that I'll want to marry.

（她是我最不可能想娶的對象。）

Your brother is the last person <u>to rely on</u>.

（你的哥哥是最不能信任的人。）

聯考題型

---

1. Did you see the sign which says, "＿＿＿＿＿ littering"?
   (A) Never   (B) No   (C) None   (D) Not

2. Many people believe whatever a fortune-teller says, but there is really ＿＿＿＿＿ knowing the future.
   (A) no   (B) not   (C) never   (D) none

3. There is no ＿＿＿＿＿ with such a stubborn person. Why not give up?
   (A) reason   (B) reasoned   (C) reasoning   (D) reasonable

4. A bad habit is often the ＿＿＿＿＿ thing we are afraid of. Therefore, it is hard to kick.
   (A) final   (B) last   (C) ultimate   (D) terminal

5. As your best friend, I'm the last person ＿＿＿＿＿ you. Take my word for it.
   (A) to betray   (B) betraying   (C) that betray   (D) but betray

6. Many demonstrators carried placards saying, "＿＿＿＿＿ Martial Law."
   (A) Never   (B) None   (C) No   (D) Not

7. There is no ＿＿＿＿＿ when they can be here today.
   (A) talking   (B) speaking   (C) telling   (D) shouting

8. There is no knowing _____ longer the old man can live.
   (A) how much   (B) so much   (C) too much   (D) very much

9. When I was young, the _____ thing I wanted to do was teach. I just can't understand how I became a career teacher later.
   (A) only   (B) first   (C) best   (D) last

10. Many a person I know believes in the power of science, but I would be _____ to say that science can explain everything.
   (A) the one   (B) the last   (C) the least   (D) the kind

克漏字

     Alex is an artist I've known for years. Although we are on first-name __1__, I have never really liked him. I always feel uncomfortable every time he __2__ in to see me. I'm quite sure that he looks upon me as a possible patron, __3__, as a matter of fact, I never buy paintings or any works of art. As a pragmatist, I don't want to __4__ money on those useless, expensive items. Even if I wanted to buy paintings, his would be __5__ to appeal to me.

1. (A) term   (B) terms   (C) turn   (D) turns

2. (A) drops   (B) gives   (C) checks   (D) participates

3. (A) when   (B) however   (C) while   (D) therefore

4. (A) collect   (B) fake   (C) store   (D) waste

5. (A) the last   (B) far from   (C) no longer   (D) even better

Unit 15　比較句型

要點 1

三級比較句型

1. 原級：S + V + as + $\begin{vmatrix} \text{adj} + (\text{a} + \text{n}) \\ \text{adv} \end{vmatrix}$ + as …→與…一樣…

其否定型式：not so/as … as …→不如…一樣…

Peter is <u>as</u> busy <u>as</u> a bee.

（彼德極為忙碌。）

The results were <u>not</u> <u>so</u> bad <u>as</u> I had expected.

（結果並沒有像我原先預期的那樣糟。）

2. 比較級：S + V + $\begin{vmatrix} \text{−er} \\ \text{more} \cdots \end{vmatrix}$ + than …→比…更…

其否定型式：less … than …→比…更/較不

I'm <u>taller</u> <u>than</u> my dad.

（我比我老爸更高。）

The new model uses <u>less</u> fuel <u>than</u> earlier ones.

（這款新車型比舊型更省油。）

3. 最高級：S + V + the + $\begin{vmatrix} \text{−est} \\ \text{most} \cdots \end{vmatrix}$ + $\begin{vmatrix} \text{of} + \text{複數 n.} \\ \text{among} + \text{複數 n.} \\ \text{in} + \text{單數（地方）n.} \end{vmatrix}$ 在…之中最…

其否定型式：the least … + $\begin{vmatrix} \text{of} \cdots \\ \text{among} \cdots \\ \text{in} \cdots \end{vmatrix}$ →在…之中最不…

His story is <u>the best of</u> all the stories told.

（在所有講過的故事當中，他說的最好。）

Playing computer games is now <u>the most</u> popular activity <u>among</u> teenagers.

（玩電腦遊戲是目前青少年最熱中的活動。）

Asia is <u>the largest</u> continent <u>in</u> the world.
（亞洲是全世界最大的洲。）

注意：

1. 比較級之前一般不加定冠詞 "the" ，但其後接 of the two(…) 時，則一定要加 "the" 於比較級之前，如：She is the better dancer of the two.（她是兩個舞者中較好的。）

2. 形容詞的最高級之前一般須加定冠詞 "the" ，但絕對最高級（即自身的比較時），則不加 "the" ，如：Dad is happiest when we are with him.（當我們陪著他時，老爸最高興。）

3. 副詞的最高級可省略 "the" ，也可保留，如：Which of the three do you like (the) best?（這三個你最喜歡哪一個？）

4. be best known/remembered for sth …表「以…最為有名/最令人懷念」，為固定用法。

5. 沒有比較/最高級形式的形容詞有：perfect, unique, round, square, dead 等。

聯考題型

1. Many people are now complaining that vegetables are not _____ cheap as they were last week.
   (A) more　　　　(B) less　　　　(C) so　　　　(D) such

2. Bam was _____ known for its 2000-year-old castle built out of mud, straw, and the trunk of palm trees. (94學測)
   (A) best　　　　(B) the best　　　(C) most　　　(D) the most

3. Jane is the most intelligent of _____ sisters.
   (A) both her　　(B) both the　　(C) all her　　(D) all the

4. The current tallest, at 101 floors, is the Taipei 101 in Taiwan, though Toronto's CN Tower is 180 feet _____, largely because of its huge antenna. (94指考)
   (A) high　　　　(B) higher　　　(C) highest　　(D) the highest

5. Most Chinese people believe the moon is _____ in mid-fall.
   (A) bright　　　(B) the brighter　(C) brightest　(D) the brightest

6. Girls were _____ more sensitive to sounds and more skillful at fine motor performance than boys. (93學測)
   (A) very   (B) both   (C) ever   (D) quite

7. George: "Men have greater strength than women."
   Mary: "Yes, but women live _____."
   (A) long   (B) longer   (C) longest   (D) the longest

8. As _____ to nature as one gets in New York, the park offered relief from the noise and congestion of the city. (93指考)
   (A) close   (B) closer   (C) closely   (D) more closely

9. Sitting in Jack's car, I worried a lot because he was _____ careful driver of all my friends.
   (A) more   (B) less   (C) the most   (D) the least

10. Today's teen consumer market is _____ profitable it has ever been. (92學測)
    (A) more   (B) the more   (C) most   (D) the most

翻譯造句

1. Tony 比他班上每一個人都高些。

   試譯：_____

2. 他看起來誠實，但實際上並不如此。 (not so … as)

   試譯：_____

3. 他並不像他弟弟是個用功的學生。 (not as … as)

   試譯：_____

4. 他的弟弟是兩人中比較可靠的。 (dependable)

   試譯：_____

5. 我喜歡他弟弟甚於Tony。 (less …)

   試譯：_____

原級比較的慣用法

1. as + adj + as …→與…一樣

= the same + n + as …

This bed is as <u>long</u> as that one.

= This bed is the same <u>length</u> as that one.

（這張床和那張床長度一樣。）

2. as … as possible/one can →儘可能…

Come here <u>as</u> soon <u>as</u> <u>possible</u>.

= Come here <u>as</u> soon <u>as</u> <u>you</u> <u>can</u>.

（儘可能快點來。）

3. as + adj + as can be →極為…

You are <u>as</u> wrong <u>as</u> <u>can</u> <u>be</u>.

（你大錯特錯。）

4. as … as ever →…一如往常；仍舊…

You are <u>as</u> hospitable <u>as</u> <u>ever</u>.

（你好客一如往常。）

5. as … as ever lived →有史以來最…

He is <u>as</u> great an athlete <u>as</u> <u>ever</u> <u>lived</u>.

（他是有史以來最偉大的運動員。）

6. as good as …→幾乎/簡直

= almost …

The used car looks <u>as</u> <u>good</u> <u>as</u> new.

（這部舊車看起來簡直是新的。）

7. as it is →
① 事實上（置於句首）= in fact
② 已經（置於句末）= already
③ 照現狀（置於句末）= as is

As it is, he's only halfway through the work.

（事實上，他的工作只完成一半。）

I have had enough trouble as it is.

（我的麻煩已經夠多了。）

They agree to buy the house as (it) is.

（他們同意照現狀買下這棟房子。）

8. as it was →照舊（現已罕用）

9. as it were →可以說是（插入句中）= so to speak

My husband is, as it were, a grown-up baby.

（我的先生可以說是像個永遠長不大的小孩。）

聯考題型

1. Since Leo is the same _____ as Max, I think they can get along.
   (A) old   (B) years   (C) age   (D) birth

2. The swimming coach asked us to stay underwater and hold our breath for as long as
   _____.
   (A) possible   (B) possibly   (C) it can   (D) it could

3. Don't think I'm a miserable old man because I'm retired. In fact, I am as happy
   _____.
   (A) as possible (B) as can be   (C) as it is   (D) as it were

4. I thought Richard might be angry at my words, but he was as polite and friendly as
   _____.
   (A) even   (B) ever   (C) normally   (D) usually

5. The manager in our company was kicked upstairs and became, as it were, a lame
_____.

(A) chicken   (B) duck   (C) goose   (D) swan

6. After the renovation, the office building was _____ new.
(A) as well as   (B) as long as   (C) as soon as   (D) as good as

7. He thought things would get better, but _____, they are going from bad to worse.
(A) as it is   (B) as follows   (C) as he wished   (D) as he knew

8. Would you shut up and get lost? I'm in enough trouble _____.
(A) as it was   (B) as it is   (C) as it were   (D) as it does

9. Mandela became, _____, the father of the nation because he loved his people as if
they were all his children.
(A) to speak so   (B) so to speak   (C) to speak such   (D) such to speak

10. He is as great a statesman as ever _____.
(A) live   (B) living   (C) lived   (D) to live

要點 3

1. (Just) as + S + V, so + $\begin{cases} \text{S + V} \cdots \\ \text{助 V./be + S} \cdots \end{cases}$ →正如…所以…

Just as you like to drink coffee, **so** I enjoy having tea.
（正如你喜歡喝咖啡，所以我喜歡喝茶。）

As you sow, **so** shall you reap.
（種瓜得瓜，種豆得豆。）

2. A is to B as/what C is to D. → A 之於 B 如同 C 之於 D
= As C is to D, so is A to B.
= What C is to D, that is A to B.
Air is to man **as** water is to the fish.
= **As** water is to the fish, **so** is air to man.
（空氣之於人就如同水之於魚一樣。）

1. As you make your own bed, _____ you must lie on it.
   (A) then   (B) so   (C) that   (D) soon

2. Just as the lion is the king of beasts, so the _____ is the king of birds.
   (A) eagle   (B) dove   (C) sparrow   (D) swallow

3. A nurse is to a _____ as a mother is to her child.
   (A) doctor   (B) patient   (C) volunteer   (D) visitor

4. Leaves are to a plant as _____ are to animals.
   (A) livers   (B) lungs   (C) kidneys   (D) spleens

5. As food can nourish all children, _____ reading can help their intellectual growth.
   (A) like   (B) such   (C) so   (D) for

克漏字

Most people have little difficulty distinguishing living things from non-living things. Just as we can easily recognize that a butterfly, a horse, and a tree are alive, __1__ we may readily tell a bike, a house, and a stone are not. We call a thing living if it is __2__ certain activities, such as growth and reproduction. Biologists, however, find it hard to define life, though they have __3__ knowledge of living things. They have difficulty locating the dividing line between animate beings and inanimate objects. For example, a virus is a lifeless particle __4__, but it becomes active and multiplies rapidly when inside a living cell. __5__ trying to define life precisely, biologists concentrate on deeping their understanding of life by studying living things.

1. (A) and   (B) or   (C) but   (D) so

2. (A) able to   (B) capable of   (C) able of   (D) capable to

3. (A) considerate   (B) considerable   (C) considered   (D) considering

4. (A) by itself   (B) of itself   (C) for itself   (D) to itself

5. (A) Rather than   (B) Better than   (C) Other than   (D) Worse than

比較級的重要句型

1. no more than + 數/量→只有…（表不滿意）
= only + 數/量

No more than five people applied for membership.

（只有五個人申請入會。）

2. not more than + 數/量→（大概）不到…；頂多…
= at (the) most + 數/量

There is not more than ten minutes left.

（剩下大概不到十分鐘。）

3. nothing/no/little more than + 人/物→不過（是）…
= nothing but + 人/物

My new boss is nothing more than a kid.

（我的新老闆不過是個小伙子而已。）

The interview is little more than a formality.

（這個面試只不過是一種形式而已。）

4. no more … than …→與…都不…
= neither … nor …

Jason is no more an expert than I am.

= Neither Jason nor I am an expert.

（傑生和我都不是專家。）

5. not more … than …→（可能）沒有比…更…
= probably less … than …

Don't worry. He's not more intelligent than you.

（放心好了。他又沒有比你更聰明。）

6. no less than + 數/量→（竟然）有…之多
= as many/much as …

 <u>No less than</u> 10,000 people attended the rally.

= <u>As many as</u> 10,000 people attended the rally.

= <u>No fewer than</u> 10,000 people attended the rally.

（居然有上萬人參加了這個造勢活動。）

 She spent <u>no less than</u> 50,000 dollars on clothes last month. (≠ no fewer than)

= She spent <u>as much as</u> 50,000 dollars on clothes last months.

（上個月她竟然花了五萬元買衣服。）

7. not less than + 數/量→至少…；不少於…
= at (the very) least

 The distance is <u>not less than</u> 500 miles.

（這段距離至少有 500 哩。）

8. no less … than …→與…一樣…
= as .. as

 Your older sister is <u>no less</u> fastidious <u>than</u> you mother.

= Your older sister is <u>as</u> fastidious <u>as</u> you mother.

（你的姊姊同你的媽媽一樣挑剔。）

9. not less … than …→（可能）比…更…
= probably more … than …

 You are not less talented as he.

（你可能比他更有才華。）

10. no better than …→無異於…（負面說法）

 That man is <u>no better than</u> a thief.

（那個人簡直就是小偷。）

1. 該政府不過是個傀儡政權而已。 (puppet regime)

   試譯：＿＿＿＿＿＿＿＿＿＿＿＿＿＿＿＿＿＿＿＿＿＿＿＿

2. 我既非富翁你也非慈善家。 (philanthropist)

   試譯：＿＿＿＿＿＿＿＿＿＿＿＿＿＿＿＿＿＿＿＿＿＿＿＿

3. 居然有十名登山客失蹤了。 (mountaineer)

   試譯：＿＿＿＿＿＿＿＿＿＿＿＿＿＿＿＿＿＿＿＿＿＿＿＿

4. 你似乎同她一樣嫉妒我。 (jealous)

   試譯：＿＿＿＿＿＿＿＿＿＿＿＿＿＿＿＿＿＿＿＿＿＿＿＿

5. 這簡直是勒索嘛。 (blackmail)

   試譯：＿＿＿＿＿＿＿＿＿＿＿＿＿＿＿＿＿＿＿＿＿＿＿＿

克漏字

All people in the world have one thing in common. That is , we all want ___1___ more than to live a happy life. However, this common goal is not easy to ___2___ since happiness is often hard to find and even harder to keep. Material things are necessary for us to lead a comfortable life, but they can never ___3___ us of happiness. There is no doubt that material things sometimes bring joy to us, but joy is never happiness. Happiness is much more than joy in that the latter cannot ___4___ long. Joy comes and goes like a flash in the pan. What on earth is happiness then? I think the key to happiness lies in our life attitude. As the Chinese saying goes, "Seek as much happiness as possible for yourself." It implies that we all need to make an effort to seek happiness, but we must also know that everything has its limitations. In a word, resignation is ___5___ essential than effort for living a happy life.

1. (A) everything　　(B) anything　　(C) nothing　　(D) something

2. (A) achieve　　(B) make　　(C) score　　(D) set

3. (A) insure　　(B) ensure　　(C) assure　　(D) reassure

4. (A) take　　(B) last　　(C) keep　　(D) remain

5. (A) no more　　(B) no less　　(C) not more　　(D) not less

要點 5

1. 否定字 ⋯ | −er ⋯ | → 最⋯
   | more ⋯ |
   = the best/most ⋯

　　As far as I know, <u>no</u> man is <u>more</u> cunning than he.

　= As far as I know, he is <u>the most</u> cunning man.

　（就我所知，沒有人比他更為狡滑。）

2. 否定字⋯ less ⋯→最不⋯
   = the least ⋯

　　<u>No</u> student is <u>less</u> diligent than Tom.

　= Tom is <u>the least</u> diligent student.

　（湯姆是最不用功的學生。）

3. none the wiser → （還是）不明白/知情
   = not any the wiser

　　After I read the directions, I was still none the wiser.

　（在我看了說明書之後，我還是不明白。）

4. know better than + 不定詞→不致於笨到⋯之地步

　　She knows better than <u>to lend</u> him money.

　（她不致於笨到借錢給他。）

1. Nothing is better than _____ a hot bath in winter.
   (A) taking   (B) washing   (C) running   (D) making

2. A more funny person than _____ I have never met.
   (A) he   (B) him   (C) who   (D) whom

3. You should consult Mr. Hopkins, than _____ there is no better adviser.
   (A) he   (B) him   (C) who   (D) whom

4. Nothing is more precious than time, yet nothing is _____ valued.
   (A) more   (B) less   (C) most   (D) least

5. Don't worry about that wise guy. As for his objection, I couldn't care _____.
   (A) more   (B) less   (C) most   (D) least

6. The mechanic gave a detailed explanation, but I was still _____ the wiser.
   (A) none   (B) not   (C) never   (D) nothing

7. Take a little money a day, and nobody will be _____ the wiser.
   (A) much   (B) any   (C) none   (D) all

8. You should know better than _____ all day.
   (A) fool around   (B) fooled around   (C) fooling around   (D) to fool around

9. You _____ have come at a more convenient time. I've just finished everything.
   (A) shouldn't   (B) wouldn't   (C) couldn't   (D) needn't

10. All of us are in the same boat. Nothing is more foolish than _____ holes in the boat we are in.
    (A) boring   (B) peeping   (C) bending   (D) picking

1. The + $\begin{vmatrix} -er \\ more/less \end{vmatrix}$ + S + V, the $\begin{vmatrix} -er \\ more/less \end{vmatrix}$ + $\begin{vmatrix} S + V \\ 助\ V/be + S \end{vmatrix}$ →愈…（就）愈…

The more money you make, the more you spend.

（你賺得越多，也花得越多。）

Sometimes the less I do, the more tired I feel.

（有時候我做得越少，就覺得越倦怠。）

2. $\begin{vmatrix} more\ and\ more\ \cdots \\ -er\ and\ -er \end{vmatrix}$ →愈來愈（多）…

More and more people are interested in yoga.

（愈來愈多的人對瑜伽感興趣。）

It's getting hotter and hotter day by day.

（天氣一天一天的逐漸炎熱了。）

3. less and less …→愈來愈不/少…

The tourist industry is growing less and less profitable.

（觀光業越來越無利可圖了。）

Less and less money is invested in this industry.

（投資在這個產業的資金越來越少了。）

4. more or less …→ ① 幾乎… ② 大約…

= ① almost …

② about …

I have more or less finished reading the book.

（這本書我幾乎快讀完了。）

It will take more or less an hour to cook the soup.

（這一道湯大約要熬一個鐘頭。）

5. more A than B →是 A 而非 B（兩項對稱）

= less B than A

= A rather than B

= not so much B as A

He is more <u>rich</u> than <u>generous</u>.（形容詞對稱）

（他有錢但不慷慨。）

My dad is more (of) <u>a poet</u> than <u>a novelist</u>.（名詞對稱）

（我老爸是詩人而非小說家。）

聯考題型

1. According to some doctors, the _____ you eat, the more healthy you'll become. Being overweight is always a burden.
   (A) more   (B) fewer   (C) less   (D) lesser

2. The more things you are interested in, the more colorful your life is and the _____ you are at the mercy of circumstances.
   (A) more   (B) less   (C) much   (D) little

3. Nowadays more and more people can afford to travel overseas because holidays flights are getting _____ expensive.
   (A) a lot more   (B) a bit more   (C) little by little   (D) less and less

4. We may have to hire a lawyer because the problem is _____ a moral issue than a legal one.
   (A) very much   (B) far from   (C) more   (D) less

5. An expert is not a know-it-all. An expert is a person who knows more and more about _____.
   (A) nothing   (B) little by little   (C) everything   (D) less and less

6. Her story did not scare me. Far from it! I was _____ amused than shocked by what she told me.
   (A) more   (B) less   (C) much   (D) little

7. To tell you the truth, our products are never subject to the business cycle. Our sales figures this year are _____ the same as last year's.
   (A) more and more (B) less and less (C) more or less (D) less or more

8. The old man is _____ than cautious. He has seen much of the world.
   (A) wiser   (B) more wise   (C) wisdom   (D) much wisdom

9. People are seldom satisfied with the things they have. In other words, the more they get, the _____ they want.
   (A) more   (B) less   (C) most   (D) least

10. More and more people are becoming vegetarians or even vegans for _____ reasons.
    (A) health   (B) healthy   (C) healthful   (D) healthier

翻譯造句

1. 濫用藥物的問題越來越嚴重了。

   試譯：_____

2. 我對政治愈來愈不感興趣了。

   試譯：_____

3. 在我們駛進那座森林後，天色就越來越暗了。

   試譯：_____

4. 你年紀愈大，記性就會愈差。

   試譯：_____

5. 與其說老闆吝嗇倒不如說是節儉。 (stingy; frugal)

   試譯：_____

1. be senior to …→比…（階級/地位）高

= be higher than … (in rank or position)

She is <u>senior</u> <u>to</u> me because she joined the company much earlier than me.（senior 為 adj.）

（她的職位比我高，因為她比我更早進公司。）

2. be one year/two years sb's senior →比…年長一/兩歲…

= be one year/two years older than sb

My hubby is three years <u>my</u> <u>senior</u>.（senior 為 n.）

= My hubby is my senior <u>by</u> three years.

= My hubby is three years older <u>than</u> me.

（我老公比我年長三歲。）

3. be junior to …→比…（階級/地位）低

= be lower than … (in rank or position)

There are only two officers <u>junior</u> <u>to</u> me.

（只有兩名軍官階級比我低。）

4. be one year/two years sb's junior →比…年輕一/兩歲

= be one year/two years younger than sb

His better half is 15 years <u>his</u> <u>junior</u>.

= His better half is his junior <u>by</u> 15 years.

= His better half is 15 years younger <u>than</u> him.

（他的老婆比他年輕 15 歲。）

5. be superior to …→優於…；高於…

= be better/higher than …

The sound quality is <u>superior</u> <u>to</u> that of a regular CD.

（這音質比一般 CD 的音質要好。）

A colonel is <u>superior</u> <u>to</u> a major.

（上校的階級比少校高。）

6. be inferior to …→劣於…；低於…

= be worse/lower than …

Their performance was <u>inferior</u> <u>to</u> that of the other team.

（他們的表現劣於另外一隊的表現。）

A corporal is <u>inferior</u> <u>to</u> a sergeant.

（下士的階級比中士低。）

7. prior to …→在…之前

= before …

They all left <u>prior</u> <u>to</u> my arrival.

（他們在我抵達前都離開了。）

注意：

依據現代英文的用法，senior 和 junior 作形容詞分別表「年長的」和「年輕的」時，只能置於名詞之前修飾該名詞，如：a senior/junior citizen 就是「一個年長/輕的市民」。

聯考題型

1. Frank was born in 1987 and I was born in 1990. He is _____ by three years.
   (A) senior to me　　(B) older to me　　(C) my elder　　(D) my senior

2. She will probably win the election because she is definitely _____ to the other candidates.
   (A) senior　　　　(B) better　　　　(C) superior　　　　(D) abler

3. My job is to supervise people who are _____ to me.
   (A) senior　　　　(B) junior　　　　(C) higher　　　　(D) lower

4. You may rest assured that all arrangements will be made _____ your departure.
   (A) prior to　　　(B) earier to　　　(C) senior to　　　(D) junior to

5. Our team is the best because the other teams are _____ us in many respects.
   (A) senior to   (B) junior to   (C) superior to   (D) inferior to

6. My wife is a little older than me. In fact, I'm her junior _____ two years.
   (A) by   (B) in   (C) for   (D) than

7. Please yield your seats to _____ citizens and the physically challenged. Thanks a lot!
   (A) superior   (B) inferior   (C) senior   (D) junior

8. There is nothing noble in beating others. As Hemingway said, "True nobility is in being _____ your previous self."
   (A) senior to   (B) junior to   (C) superior to   (D) inferior to

9. In our company there are only two positions that are senior to _____.
   (A) I   (B) me   (C) my   (D) mine

10. The plane must have caught fire a few minutes prior to _____.
    (A) take off   (B) it took off   (C) taking off   (D) being taken off

---

要點 8

倍數的句型

1. S + V + $\begin{vmatrix} \text{half/twice} \\ \text{three/four times} \end{vmatrix}$ + as + adj/adv + as …→…的幾倍

   My house is only <u>half</u> <u>as</u> <u>large</u> <u>as</u> yours.

   = Your house is <u>twice</u> <u>as</u> <u>large</u> <u>as</u> mine.

   （我的房子只有你的一半大。）

   The bullet train runs <u>three times</u> <u>as</u> <u>fast</u> <u>as</u> the regular train.

   （子彈列車行駛的速度是一般火車的三倍。）

2. S + V + three/four/five times + $\begin{vmatrix} \text{—er} \\ \text{more …} \end{vmatrix}$ + than …→…的幾倍

The bullet train runs <u>three times</u> <u>faster</u> <u>than</u> the regular train.

（子彈列車行駛的速度是一般火車的三倍。）

3. S + V + | half/twice / three/four times | + the + | age, size, amount, number | of …→…的幾倍

Your house is <u>twice</u> <u>the</u> <u>size</u> <u>of</u> mine.

= Your house is twice as large as mine.

（你的房子是我的兩倍大。）

說明：

1. half/twice　不接比較級，只接 as … as

2. half as … again as →…的一倍半

3. as … again as …→…的兩倍

4. twice … again as …→…的三倍

聯考題型

1. There are 1000 girls and 500 boys in our high school. In other words, girls are twice _____ of boys.
   (A) the many　　　(B) the much　　　(C) the number　　　(D) the amount

2. The brain of a chimpanzee has the same internal structure and on its surface the same pattern of folds as the human brain, which, however, is three times _____ of a chimpanzee's.
   (A) its large　　　(B) as large　　　(C) the size　　　(D) as size

3. Sound travels four times _____ in water than in air.
   (A) faster　　　(B) as fast　　　(C) so fast　　　(D) too fast

4. Mrs. Black is 24 years older than her daughter Amy. In two years, Mrs. Black will be 4 times older than her daughter will be at that time. Which of the following is true?
   (A) Mrs. Black is 32 years old now.
   (B) Amy will be 8 years old in a year.
   (C) Mrs. Black is now 5 times as old as Amy.
   (D) Amy is probably the youngest child.

5. If Africa is about three times the size of the United States, then the latter is about _____ as large as the former.
(A) three times　　(B) the third time　(C) one-third　　(D) two-thirds

Most of us know that doing exercise has a few advantages. First of all, it can make us healthier. If we exercise regularly, it will __1__ our blood circulation and speed up our metabolism. In this way, it helps us get rid of the toxins which __2__ in our body. Second, regular exercise can help us lose weight, thus making us stay slim and look younger. Third, getting some exercise on a daily basis can also __3__ to our mental health because it helps us relax. We always feel comfortable after a workout, don't we? Last but not least, doing exercise saves money, too. According to a study made on the medical costs of senior citizens, those who used to exercise at least 3 days a week spend only one-third as much for doctors and medicine __4__ those who never exercised. In a word, all people should be encouraged to do more exercise because who knows if it may __5__ a few more wonders?

1. (A) prove　　　(B) reprove　　(C) improve　　(D) disprove

2. (A) accumulate　(B) arise　　　(C) amount　　(D) appreciate

3. (A) attribute　　(B) contribute　(C) distribute　(D) tribute

4. (A) like　　　　(B) as　　　　(C) than　　　(D) for

5. (A) do　　　　(B) walk　　　(C) take　　　(D) make

Unit 16   倒裝句與附加問句

要點 1

否定副詞（片語）置於句子或子句之句首時須倒裝，但否定副詞（片語）修飾主詞時則不倒裝。

| Never, Little, Hardly, Rarely, Seldom, Scarcely, Nowhere, In vain, Much less, Not only, At no time, By no means, On no account, Under no circumstances | + | 助V
be | + S |

1. Lisa rarely wears makeup.
→ Rarely <u>does</u> Lisa wear makeup. (倒裝)
（麗莎很少化粧。）

2. I not only heard the noise but saw the car crash into a tree.
→ Not only <u>did</u> I hear the noise but I saw the car crash into a tree. (倒裝)
（我不但聽到那聲響，而且也目睹那輛汽車撞到那棵樹。）

3. Not only <u>John</u> but (also) <u>his wife</u> saw the accident. (修飾主詞不倒裝)
（不但約翰而且他老婆也看到這起意外事故。）

聯考題型

1. I picked a few numbers at random, and little _____ that I would win first prize.
   (A) thought I   (B) I thought   (C) I did think   (D) did I think

2. You won't do that; _____ is it possible for me to do it.
   (A) much more   (B) much less   (C) much better   (D) much worse

3. The police said that the escaped prisoner was extremely dangerous and that on no account _____.
   (A) he should approach anyone.
   (B) should he approach anyone.

(C) he should be approached by anyone.
(D) should he be approached by anyone.

4. Under no circumstances are you allowed to go out and play because you are _____.
   (A) grounded   (B) graduated   (C) graded   (D) granted

5. _____ is your boyfriend a good guy.
   (A) In no time   (B) By no means
   (C) On no way   (D) Under no circumstance

6. This species of cobra is native to this island. _____ else can it be seen.
   (A) Somewhere   (B) Anywhere   (C) Everywhere   (D) Nowhere

7. Hardly _____ we arrived at the camp site when it began to rain cats and dogs.
   (A) have   (B) had   (C) are   (D) were

8. Hardly a month _____ without another factory closing down.
   (A) goes by   (B) goes back   (C) goes ahead   (D) goes away

9. Not until she was 40 _____.
   (A) Jane married   (B) Jane was married
   (C) Married Jane   (D) was Jane married

10. Henry seems to have suffered much from his marriage life. _____ did he mention his wife.
    (A) At no time   (B) In no time   (C) For no time   (D) With no time

Only ＋ 副詞（片語、子句）置於句首（含子句）時，須倒裝

Only ＋ | adv
adv 片語
adv 子句 | ＋ | ① 助V
② be | ＋ S

1. Only recently <u>did</u> <u>I</u> find out the truth.
（就在最近我才發現真相。）

2. Only by working hard <u>can</u> <u>you</u> achieve success.
（只有靠努力你才能獲得成功。）

3. Only after we made the promise <u>was</u> <u>he</u> willing to cooperate with us.
（就在我們許下承諾後他才願意跟我們合作。）

聯考題型

1. I had been kept in the dark for quite a while, and _____ did I see the light.
   (A) only when   (B) when only   (C) only then   (D) then only

2. Only recently _____ clear that both sides are ready for peace talks.
   (A) it becomes   (B) does it become
   (C) it has become   (D) has it become

3. Only in a few Western countries _____ religion remain an important power in politics.
   (A) does   (B) do   (C) has   (D) have

4. Only by an installment plan _____ afford to buy a house like this. It has already been paid off, though.
   (A) we can   (B) can we   (C) we could   (D) could we

5. Only when you have your own children _____ aware that you owe your parents a lot.
   (A) you will   (B) will you   (C) you will be   (D) will you be

6. Only after I arrived at the airport _____ that I had forgotten my passport.
   (A) I discovered   (B) did I discover
   (C) I had discovered   (D) had I discovered

7. Only last week _____ that her husband had been cheating on her.
   (A) was she told   (B) has she told   (C) she was told   (D) she has told

8. Only on the eve of their wedding _____ the fact that they could not get along.
   (A) they were awake to   (B) were they awake to
   (C) they did awake   (D) did they awake

9. Only by adopting punitive measures can our government _____ those prevalent confidence games in our society.
   (A) crack down on   (B) lay emphasis on
   (C) make it to   (D) devote itself to

10. Only in the past 20 years or so _____ to understand that skin cancer has something to do with excessive exposure to the sun's rays.
    (A) we do begin   (B) do we begin
    (C) we have begun   (D) have we begun

要點 3

主詞和動詞直接互調（無需提出助動詞或 be 動詞）的倒裝句型

1. 地方／時間副詞（片語）：
   Here, There, Now,
   Away/Into/Out of...
   Before/After...
   At/In/On...
   $+ \begin{vmatrix} 一般V \\ be + pp \end{vmatrix} + \underline{S}$（限名詞）
   　　　　　　　　　　　↳ 代名詞不倒裝

   There <u>goes</u> <u>the school bus</u>.
   → There <u>it</u> <u>goes</u>.（代名詞不倒裝）
   （校車開走了。）

   After a storm <u>comes</u> <u>a calm</u>.（諺語）
   （雨過天晴；否極泰來。）

2. 主詞補語：

Adj/pp. | + be + S...
So.../Such |

Happy <u>is</u> <u>he</u> who is content.（諺語）

（知足常樂。）

So frightened <u>was</u> <u>she</u> that she went pale.

（她如此害怕，臉色都白了。）

| 聯考題型

1. Now _____ the best time to buy our products. You can enjoy a 30% discount if you pay in cash.
   (A) is   (B) are   (C) has   (D) have

2. In the palm of your hand _____ not just your own fortune but the future of the entire country.
   (A) lie   (B) lies   (C) lay   (D) lays

3. Blessed _____ the pure in heart, for they shall see God. (The Bible)
   (A) has   (B) have   (C) is   (D) are

4. On the table _____ several delicacies that would make anyone's mouth water.
   (A) was laid   (B) was lain   (C) were laid   (D) were lain

5. So humble was the master that he was not _____ keeping company with us.
   (A) about   (B) above   (C) beneath   (D) beyond

6. Interested not so much in his health as in his looks _____ the man who does strenuous exercise and sticks to a low-calorie diet.
   (A) is   (B) are   (C) has   (D) have

7. "Here _____," said Karen when handing me the first aid kit.
   (A) you go   (B) go you   (C) we are   (D) are you

8. Enclosed with the letter _____ several pictures she had taken when abroad.
   (A) had   (B) was   (C) were   (D) had been

9. _____ was their misery that we could not help shedding tears.

    (A) It   (B) Such   (C) So   (D) Which

10. I'm very happy to be back to my hometown, but _____ are those carefree days of my childhood.

    (A) gone   (B) went   (C) going   (D) to go

要點 4

1. 條件子句的倒裝

$$\text{If} + \text{S} + \begin{vmatrix} \text{were (to)...} \\ \text{should...} \\ \text{had} + \text{pp...} \end{vmatrix} \rightarrow \begin{vmatrix} \text{Were} \\ \text{Should} \\ \text{Had} \end{vmatrix} + \text{S...}$$

If I were a girl, I would marry you.

→ <u>Were</u> I a girl, I would marry you.

（如果我是女孩，我就嫁給你。）

If he should fail to come, cover for him.

→ <u>Should he</u> fail to come, cover for him.

（萬一他不能來，你代理他。）

If they had agreed, we would have taken action.

→ <u>Had they</u> agreed, we would have taken action.

（要是他們當時同意，我們就會採取行動。）

2. so, neither 引導的子句倒裝

$$\text{肯定句，and} + \text{S} + \begin{vmatrix} \text{be} \\ \text{do/can} \end{vmatrix}, \text{too.}$$

$$\rightarrow \quad \text{肯定句，and so} + \begin{vmatrix} \text{be} \\ \text{do/can} \end{vmatrix} + \text{S.}$$

You are a newcomer, and I am, too.

= You are a newcomer, and so <u>am</u> <u>I</u>.

（你是新來的，我也是。）

$$否定句，and + S + \begin{vmatrix} be + not \\ do/can + not \end{vmatrix} , either.$$

→ $否定句，and + neither + \begin{vmatrix} be \\ do/can \end{vmatrix} + S.（neither 為 adv.）$

→ $否定句，nor + \begin{vmatrix} be \\ do/can \end{vmatrix} + S.（nor 為 conj.）$

You don't like pickles, and I don't, either.

= You don't like pickles, and neither <u>do</u> <u>I</u>.（倒裝）

= You don't like pickles, nor <u>do</u> <u>I</u>.（倒裝）

（你不喜歡醃黃瓜，我也不喜歡。）

註：英式用法有……，and nor do/can + S 的句型。

聯考題型

1. _____ it not been for your help, I would still be homeless.
   (A) Should   (B) Would   (C) Had   (D) Were

2. _____ he change his mind and be willing to help, please give us a call.
   (A) Should   (B) Would   (C) Could   (D) Might

3. _____ the management acted sooner, the strike wouldn't have happened.
   (A) If   (B) Were   (C) Had   (D) Should

4. _____ it not been for the clue, they could not have solved the crime.
   (A) Had   (B) Should   (C) Were   (D) If

5. You have to work long hours, and I _____, too.
   (A) have   (B) do   (C) also   (D) am

6. Many people enjoy taking some time off, and _____.
   (A) so I do   (B) so do I   (C) so I am   (D) so am I

7. Money has never made any people truly happy, _____.
(A) neither will it
(B) neither will they
(C) nor will it
(D) nor will they

8. I haven't been to Las Vegas, and neither _____ my brother.
(A) is
(B) does
(C) goes
(D) has

9. That guy is really a headache to us. Being polite to him doesn't work, _____ do threatening words.
(A) neither
(B) either
(C) so
(D) nor

10. _____ you not listened to me then, you would be penniless now.
(A) Had
(B) If
(C) Should
(D) Were

要點 5

其他倒裝句型

1. O + S + Vt.（受詞部分太長或被強調時）

A better assistant than her I've never seen.

= I've never seen a better assistant than her.

（我從未見過比她更好的助理。）

2.

$$S + V... + \begin{vmatrix} as...as \\ -er/more...than \end{vmatrix} + \underline{be/助V} + S$$

↳ 不會造成意思不清時可省略

I understand him better than <u>does</u> anyone who is sitting in here.

= I understand him better than anyone who is sitting in here <u>does</u>.
(= understands him)

（我比在座任何一位更瞭解他。）

比較：

I understand him better than anyone who is sitting in here.（歧義）

（我比在座任何一位更瞭解他。或：我瞭解他甚於我瞭解在座諸位。）

1. The past we can know, but the future we can only _____.
   (A) preview   (B) prepare   (C) preserve   (D) predict

2. The joke he made about our dean really brought down the house. A more funny joke _____.
   (A) I have ever heard   (B) have I ever heard
   (C) I have never heard   (D) never have I heard

3. _____ they were asked to do in two weeks, they finished in three times as many.
   (A) What   (B) When   (C) How   (D) That

4. _____ advice or support I can give, I'll give you without hesitation.
   (A) Whoever   (B) However   (C) Whatever   (D) Wherever

5. Although David Wang had never studied English in America or England, he spoke English as well as _____ a native speaker.
   (A) has   (B) is   (C) does   (D) was

6. In fact, a lot of parents are as interested in playing computer games as _____ their teenaged kids.
   (A) if   (B) though   (C) are   (D) do

7. But what is actually impossible _____.
   (A) he considers possible   (B) he considers it possible
   (C) considers he possible   (D) considers him possible

8. Your Honor, I love the kids no less than _____ my wife, who is now accusing me of child ause.
   (A) does   (B) is   (C) love   (D) loves

9. What should have been a carefree childhood _____ in helping my dad scratch a living.
   (A) did I spend   (B) I spent   (C) spent me   (D) did it spend

10. This species of ape does not eat meat, as _____ a few other species.
    (A) is   (B) are   (C) does   (D) do

附加問句（即附加在主句之後的簡短問句）

形成原則：

(1) 時態不變。

(2) 主句肯定，附加問句否定，反之亦然。

(3) 附加問句的主詞限用代名詞。

(4) 附加問句的否定須用縮寫形式。

1. You don't mind, <u>do you</u>?

（你不介意，是嗎？）

2. Mary loves Peter, <u>doesn't she</u>?

（瑪麗愛彼德，是不是？）

注意：

1. 附加問句限用 it 代替 this/that，用 they 代替 these/those。

2. 主句中有 seldom, hardly, little, few, nothing 等字時，應視為否定句。因此，其附加問句須用肯定形式。

3. have/has to ＋原形V → 用 don't/doesn't 形成附加問句。

4. have/has + pp. → 用 haven't/hasn't 形成附加問句。

聯考題型

1. You seldom work on weekends, _____?
(A) is it   (B) isn't it   (C) do you   (D) don't you

2. I'm afraid you have made a mistake, _____?
(A) am I   (B) ain't I   (C) have you   (D) haven't you

3. Jenny has a crush on her PE teacher, _____?
(A) does she   (B) doesn't she   (C) has she   (D) hasn't she

4. There'll be a train strike, _____?
(A) will there   (B) won't there   (C) is it   (D) isn't it

5. There is nothing wrong with my new computer, _____?
   (A) is it　　　　　(B) isn't it　　　　　(C) is there　　　　　(D) isn't there

6. Buying things online is very convenient, _____?
   (A) are they　　　(B) aren't they　　(C) is it　　　　　　(D) isn't it

7. That is our new psychology teacher, Miss Hall, _____?
   (A) is that　　　　(B) isn't that　　　(C) is it　　　　　　(D) isn't it

8. Those are you neighbors, _____?
   (A) are those　　(B) aren't those　(C) are they　　　　(D) aren't they

9. The Smiths used to live in Liverpool, _____?
   (A) were they　　(B) weren't they　(C) did they　　　　(D) didn't they

10. I think Mr. Woods is to blame, _____?
    (A) do I　　　　　(B) don't I　　　　　(C) is he　　　　　　(D) isn't he

Unit 17　　名詞與冠詞

要點 1

可數名詞

1. 普通名詞（即一般具體的人事物名詞）：單數時其前須置 a(n)/the，複數時其後須加 s/es 或其它變化。

I'm not <u>the</u> master you are looking for. I'm only <u>an</u> apprentice.
（我並非你要找的大師。我只是個學徒而已。）

She would like to make <u>friends</u> with you.
（她想要跟你交個朋友。）

2. 集合名詞（即代表人事物的類／群）：
(1) 有複數形式的集合名詞（視為整體接單數V，個體接複數V）
audience（觀眾），body（團體），class（班級），club（俱樂部），committee（委員會），company（公司），congregation（會眾），council（議會），crew（全體船／機員），crowd（群眾），family（家庭），gang（一群／夥），government（政府），group（小組），jury（陪審團），mob（暴民），staff（員工），team（隊），union（聯盟）

The present government, which <u>hasn't been</u> in power very long, <u>is</u> <u>trying</u> to place a gag on the press.
（剛上台不久的現政府政設法箝制新聞自由。）

The government, who <u>were</u> conservative in every way, <u>are</u> now <u>trying</u> to improve their image.
（這批政府官員過去極為保守，現正設法提昇形象。）

Governments in all countries <u>are</u> trying to prevent any pandemic from happening.
（目前所有國家的政府都在設法防堵任何疫情發生。）

(2) 沒有複數形的集合名詞（可接單數或複數V）：
the aristocracy（貴族），the gentry（紳士），the proletariat（無產階級），the majority（多數），the minority（少數），the public（大眾）

The consuming public <u>is/are</u> becoming more and more reluctant to spend money.

（消費大眾愈來愈不願意花錢了。）

(3) 限接複數V的集合名詞（沒有複數形）：

cattle（牛），the clergy（教會人員），the military（軍方），people（人們），the police（警方），poultry（家禽），swine（豬），vermin（害蟲）等。

The police <u>have</u> blocked off the street.

（警方已經封鎖了這條街道。）

聯考題型

1. I come to seek your help because I had _____ the other day.
   (A) unusual experience
   (B) a unusual experience
   (C) experience unusual
   (D) an unusual experience

2. Your sister would be our first choice. I know she has _____ in fashion design.
   (A) many experiences
   (B) a lot of experiences
   (C) more experiences
   (D) more experience

3. If you are going to the zoo, be sure to change _____ at the next station.
   (A) a train
   (B) the train
   (C) trains
   (D) train

4. You cannot please everyone. Some people _____ never satisfied with whatever you do for them
   (A) are
   (B) is
   (C) have
   (D) has

5. Chaplin's movies captivated _____ throughout the world.
   (A) audience
   (B) an audience
   (C) many audience
   (D) audiences

6. The surviving crew _____ ferried ashore and sent to a nearby hospital.
   (A) was
   (B) were
   (C) has
   (D) have

7. Dukes, marquises, earls and so on are all members of the _____.
   (A) aristocracy
   (B) aristocracies
   (C) aristocrat
   (D) aristocrats

8. After the big fight, my older brother and I were not on speaking _____.
   (A) term
   (B) terms
   (C) time
   (D) times

9. What shocked them was all the cattle _____ either dead or dying.
   (A) was   (B) were   (C) is   (D) are

10. Vermin _____ everywhere in sewers, and diseases are spread through poor sanitary conditions.
    (A) are   (B) is   (C) have   (D) has

11. Don't forget to buy a few more _____ for our computers.
    (A) mouth   (B) mouths   (C) mouses   (D) mices

12. This species of orchid _____ very rare.
    (A) is   (B) are   (C) has   (D) have

13. My aunt is a witty woman, and her _____ are all like her in this respect.
    (A) sibling   (B) offspring   (C) kid   (D) child

14. The Halloween party was a real _____. We all had a great time in it.
    (A) treat   (B) taste   (C) trial   (D) tape

15. Mark is a man of his _____. That is, he never breaks his promises.
    (A) word   (B) words   (C) wording   (D) wordings

要點 2

不可數名詞

1. 物質名詞：純粹的物質名詞像air，barley，butter，coal，cotton，cloth，dust，fire，fur，glass，gold，hair，honey，ice，iron，jam，land，linen，meat，nylon，paper，snow，soil，tea，wood，wool 等為不可數名詞。若要數，則須加『單位』或『量詞』於其前。不過有一些物質名詞可轉成普通名詞使用，成為可數名詞。

Give me a piece of paper, please.

（請給我一張紙。）

Give me an evening paper, please.

（請給我一份晚報。）

Add some milk to your tea.

（在你的茶裡加些牛奶。）

I want one coffee and two teas to go.

（我要外帶一杯咖啡，兩杯茶。）

2. 抽象名詞：大多數的抽象名詞如 advice，behavior，caution，death，education，fiction，good，history，integrity，justice，knowledge，love 等為不可數的『概念』。不過有一些抽象名詞可轉成普通名詞使用，成為可數名詞。

Knowledge is power.

（知識即力量。）

He has a good knowledge of Chinese history.

（他對中國歷史的知識極豐。）

This country has become an economic power.

（該國已經成為一個經濟大國。）

3. 專用有名：特定的人名、地名、月份及星期名稱等為專有名詞，開頭字母須大寫，不可數，也不能加 a(n)/the 於其前（除非該專有名詞轉成普通名詞使用或其後接形容詞片語／子句）。

Helen and I are going to get married.

（海倫和我就快要結婚了。）

Is she the Helen (that) I met last year?

（是我去年見過的那位海倫嗎？）

聯考題型

1. Chicken is my favorite food. Sometimes when I'm really hungry, I can eat _____.
   (A) an all chicken   (B) all a chicken
   (C) a whole chicken   (D) whole chicken

2. This morning when I was looking for my glasses, I knocked over _____ and broke it.
   (A) glass   (B) a glass   (C) glasses   (D) the glasses

3. Sally had a boiled egg and _____ for breakfast this morning.
   (A) a toast
   (B) a slice of toast
   (C) some toasts
   (D) a toaster

4. Hundreds of students staged a sit-in and it left the college president with _____ on his face.
   (A) egg   (B) an egg   (C) eggs   (D) the eggs

5. Don't bother him now. He has _____ in the fire, you know.
   (A) much iron   (B) an iron   (C) several irons   (D) an irony

6. Before the dinner, the hostess served the guests with a _____ of oolong tea.
   (A) drop   (B) pot   (C) cup   (D) glass

7. My father can always give me _____ when I need it.
   (A) an advice   (B) some advices   (C) a bit of advice   (D) many advices

8. If I were you, I'd take whatever she says with _____.
   (A) a pinch of salt   (B) some salts   (C) a bag of salt   (D) more salts

9. To tell you the truth, I've been feeling a little under _____ this week.
   (A) a weather
   (B) the weather
   (C) some weather
   (D) all weathers

10. Lulu took out a cigarette and asked me, "Do you have _____?"
    (A) light   (B) lighter   (C) a light   (D) the light

11. The politician's sex scandal was brought to _____ by one of his bodyguards.
    (A) light   (B) news   (C) knowledge   (D) public

12. Because he still felt hungry, he asked for a second _____.
    (A) help   (B) helping   (C) serve   (D) service

13. Toyota is a very popular _____ of car in Taiwan, isn't it?
    (A) make   (B) making   (C) maker   (D) made

14. You need my help with that, right? No problem. It's _____.
    (A) a cake   (B) a pie   (C) a wind   (D) a breeze

15. As _____ would have it, a friend of mine gave me a lift.
    (A) luck   (B) the luck   (C) a luck   (D) lucks

單複數意義不同的名詞

1. air　　空氣／態勢；airs　　做作
2. arm　　手臂；arms　　手臂（複數）／武器
3. ash　　灰塵／燼；ashes　　骨灰
4. attention　　注意（力）；attentions　　獻殷勤；示愛
5. authority　　權威（人物）；authorities　　（主管）當局
6. brain　　腦部；brains　　腦力／最優秀的人才
7. cloth　　布；clothes　　衣服
8. color　　顏色；colors　　旗子；（真）面目
9. content　　（主題、故事）內容；contents　　內容物／目次
10. compass　　羅盤；compasses　　圓規
11. custom　　風俗；customs　　海關／關稅
12. damage　　破壞；damages　　（破壞）賠償金
13. depth　　深度；depths　　深處
14. duty　　責任／關稅；duties　　職／勤務
15. effect　　影響；effects　　（音響）效果
16. fact　　事實；facts　　難以面對的現實
17. force　　力量／軍種；forces　　（陸海空）三軍
18. future　　未來；futures　　期貨
19. glass　　玻璃；glasses　　玻璃杯／眼鏡
20. good　　好處／善行；goods　　貨物
21. green　　綠色；greens　　青綠色蔬菜
22. ground　　地面；grounds　　理由／園區
23. head　　頭部／數；heads　　硬幣的正面
24. height　　高處；heights　　高地／山崗
25. honor　　榮譽；honors　　最優異的成績／重要獎項
26. letter　　信／字母；letters　　文學
27. look　　表情；looks　　容貌／美貌
28. manner　　態度；manners　　禮貌
29. mean　　平均數／中庸；means　　手段／財力
30. pain　　痛；pains　　辛苦／努力

31. quarter 四分之一／十五分鐘；quarters 住處／宿舍
32. rag 破布；rags 破舊衣物
33. return 回來／利潤；returns 選舉結果
34. rank 階級；ranks （一群人的）行列
35. rating （民意）支持率；ratings 收視率
36. ruin 破壞／毀滅；ruins 廢墟
37. saving 儲蓄／節省；savings 儲金
38. spectacle 景象；spectacles 眼鏡
39. spirit 精神；spirits 心情／烈酒
40. sweat 汗水；sweats （運動）汗衫
41. sweet 餐後甜點（主英）；sweets 糖果／甜食
42. talk 交談；talks 重要會談
43. time 時間／段；times 時代
44. utility 使用／實用；utilities 水電瓦斯等設施
45. wood 木頭；woods 森林
46. work 工作；works 作品／工廠

聯考題型

1. 我討厭那些裝腔作勢的人。
   I hate those people who put on _____.

2. 英國的警察人員通常不攜帶武器。
   The British police do not usually carry _____.

3. 地板上滿是煙蒂和煙灰。
   The floor was littered with cigarette butts and _____.

4. 按照他的遺囑，這個老人的骨灰將被撒在大海裡。
   According to his will, the old man's _____ will be scattered over the sea.

5. 他不停的向她獻殷勤，使她備感困擾。
   She felt very embarrassed by his persistent _____.

6. 日本當局拒絕發給她簽證。
   The Japanese _____ refused to issue a visa to her.

7. 泰德是這一群人當中最優秀的人才。
   Ted is the best _____ of the group.

8. 為何不用一塊溼布來擦桌子呢？
   Why not use a wet _____ to wipe the table?

9. 直到她嫁給他之後他才露出他的真面目。
   He did not show his true _____ until she married him.

10. 這部電影的內容兒童不宜。
    The movie's _____ is not suitable for young kids.

11. 理查把他口袋裡的東西都掏出來放在桌上。
    Richard emptied out the _____ of his pockets onto the table.

12. 你帶那樣東西無法通過海關的。
    You won't be able to take that through _____.

13. 這些化學物質已經造成很多嚴重的環境破壞。
    These chemicals have caused a lot of environmental _____.

14. 漢克被要求付＄2000的賠償金。
    Hank was required to pay _____ of $2000.

15. 這座游泳池有多深？
    What is the _____ of the swimming pool?

16. 員警經常在出勤務的過程中受傷。
    Police officers are often injured in the course of their _____.

17. 任何生活方式的改變將會對你的健康有影響。
    Any change in lifestyle will have an _____ on your health.

18. 情節本身乏善可陳，不過其音響效果倒令人稱奇。
    The plot itself leaves much to be desired, but the _____ are amazing.

19. 那個年齡的小孩還分不清事實與虛構。
    Kids at that age still cannot tell the difference between _____ and fiction.

20. 我們不需那些溫馨的話，我們要的是嚴酷的事實。
    We don't need those soft words. We want hard _____.

21. 許多年輕人都希望擁有一個璀璨的未來。
    Many young people hope for a bright _____.

22. 現今越來越多人在做期貨交易。
    Nowadays more and more people are trading in _____.

23. 我想去海邊旅行一趟對我們有很多好處。
   I think a trip to the beach would do us a lot of _____.

24. 他們經營家俱和其他家用貨物。
   They deal in furniture and other household _____.

25. 穿綠色的那個女孩是我的前女友。
   The girl in _____ is my ex-girlfriend.

26. 多吃點青綠色蔬菜有助於降低你的膽固醇。
   Eating more _____ will help lower your cholesterol level.

27. 他以什麼理由指控你？
   On what _____ did he accuse you?

28. 這個農場有200頭牛。
   There are 200 _____ of cattle on the farm.

29. 我來丟銅板，你說正面或反面？
   I'll toss a coin, _____ or tails?

30. 我妹妹不敢座摩天輪，因為她懼高。
   My younger sister dare not ride the ferris wheel because she is afraid of _____.

31. 昆丁以最優異的成績畢業，所以他獲得該獎學金。
   Quentin graduated with _____, so he got the scholarship.

32. 不要以貌取人。
   Never judge people by their _____.

33. 喬治，你怎麼沒禮貌了呢？
   George, where are your _____?

34. 5，10，12的平均數是9。
   The _____ of 5, 10 and 12 is 9.

35. 我可以說是費盡心機要讓今晚的活動達到完美。
   I have taken great _____ to make the evening perfect.

36. 在那個國家大多數人都衣衫襤褸。
   In that country most people are dressed in _____.

37. 越來越多人加入了失業者的行列。
   More and more people have joined the _____ of the unemployed.

38. 人民對總統的支持率於選後開始下滑。
   The president's approval _____ began to fall after the election.

39. 這個綜藝節目從一開始收視率就很高。
The variety show had high _____ from the start.

40. 喝酒毀了他的一生。
Drinking was the _____ of him.

41. 這筆捐獻來自一個小孩子的儲金。
The donation came from a child's _____.

42. 我們在特價時買了這一台電視，讓我們省了5000元。
We got the television on sale, which made a _____ of 5,000 dollars.

43. 我不克前往，但精神上參加你的婚禮。
I cannot go to your wedding, but I will be there in _____.

44. 老爸今天的心情很好，是嗎？
Dad is in high _____ today, isn't he?

45. 傑夫的襯衫因流汗而溼透了。
Jeff's shirt is soaked in _____.

46. 吃太多甜食對你的健康有礙。
Eating too many _____ is bad for your health.

47. 約翰光說不練。
John is all _____.

48. 兩國很快將重啟和談。
Peace _____ between the two countries will resume soon.

49. 自從羅馬時代以來沒有一個國家如此強盛過。
Not since Roman _____ has a single nation been so powerful.

50. 你的租金有包括水電、瓦斯嗎？
Does your rent include _____?

冠詞的用法

1. 不定詞 a/an 的用法:

(1) 表一個（a/an = one）

I bought <u>a</u> new cell phone yesterday.

（我昨天買了一支新手機。）

強調數字對比時用 one 不用 a(n)，如:

I bought <u>one</u> new cell phone, not <u>two</u>.

(2) 表每一單位時間、數量（a/an = per）

They charge $25 <u>an</u> hour for their service.

（他們索取每小時25元的服務費。）

(3) 表全體同類（a/an = every）

<u>A</u> cat is a domestic animal.

（貓是一種家畜。）

(4) 表某一個（a/an = a certain）

<u>A</u> Mr. Wilson is waiting to see you.

（有一位威爾遜先生在等候與你見面。）

(5) 表相同的（a/an = the same）

Birds of <u>a</u> feather flock together.

（物以類聚。）

(6) 表像……的人（a/an = one like）

He wishes to become <u>a</u> Bill Gates.

（他想成為像比爾蓋滋這樣的人。）

2. 定冠詞 the 的用法:

(1) 第一次提到的單數可數名詞用 a(n)，第二次以後用 the

I looked up and saw <u>a</u> plane. <u>The</u> plane flew low over the field.

（我抬頭看見一架飛機。這架飛機低空飛過原野。）

(2) the + 比較級 adj + of the two

She is <u>the</u> more intelligent of the two.

（她是兩人當中智力較高的。）

(3) the + | 最高級 adj / first/second / only/same | + 名詞

Man is <u>the</u> only animal that can talk.

（人類是唯一會講話的動物。）

(4) the + 宇宙間獨一無二的事物

Whatever happens, <u>the</u> sun also rises.

（不論發生什麼，旭日照樣東昇。）

(5) the + 方位／向

They live in <u>the</u> east of the city.

（他們住在本市的東區。）

(6) play the + 樂器

She plays <u>the</u> piano and I play <u>the</u> violin.

（她彈鋼琴，我拉小提琴。）

(7) by the + 計量單位

Eggs are sold by <u>the</u> dozen.

（雞蛋按打出售。）

(8) the + 姓氏複數 → 這一家人

<u>The</u> Zhaos are all friendly.

（趙家這一家人都很友善。）

(9) the + 山脈／群島（但獨山孤島不加 the）

<u>the</u> Alps（阿爾卑斯山系）

<u>the</u> Bahamas（巴哈馬群島）

Mt. Everest（埃佛勒斯峰）

Easter Island（復活節島）

(10) the + 海洋／河流

<u>the</u> Pacific Ocean（太平洋）

<u>the</u> Nile（尼羅河）

3. 零冠詞
   (1) 零冠詞＋複數／不可數名詞　　表一般陳述

   Museums are closed on Mondays.

   （博物館每逢星期一休館。）

   Red is my favorite color.

   （紅色是我最喜歡的顏色。）

   (2) 零冠詞＋學科名詞（math，history 等）
   (3) 零冠詞＋稱呼／頭銜（Mr., Dr. 等）
   (4) 零冠詞＋日期／星期／月份／假日
   (5) by＋交通工具
   (6) 成對的人事物

   father and son（父子）

   husband and wife（夫妻）

   young and old（老少）

   light and dark（光明與黑暗）

   (7) 固定片語

   arm in arm（臂挽著臂）

   hand in hand（手拉著手）

   day after day（一天又一天）

   face to face（面對面）

   step by step（一步一步地）

   from door to door（挨家挨戶地）

   from start to finish（從開始到結束）

聯考題型

1. These two kids are _____, but they are not in the same grade.
   (A) at an age　　(B) at the age　　(C) of an age　　(D) of the age

2. All the workers here, except those working on a full-time basis, are paid _____.
   (A) by the hour　　(B) by an hour　　(C) on the hour　　(D) on an hour

3. Wait a minute! We ordered _____ coffee, not two.
   (A) a   (B) an   (C) one   (D) the

4. _____ knife cannot work. You need a screwdriver to do the job.
   (A) One   (B) A   (C) Such   (D) Even

5. How come you are here? What _____ surprise!
   (A) one   (B) the   (C) a   (D) may

6. I was in bed with _____ for an entire week.
   (A) a flu   (B) flus   (C) flu   (D) the flus

7. _____ you are looking for no longer lives here.
   (A) Mr. Thomson   (B) A Mr. Thomson
   (C) The Mr. Thomson   (D) Such Mr. Thomson

8. Something more serious could happen again. The recent riots are but _____ of the
   iceberg.
   (A) a tip   (B) the tip   (C) tips   (D) the tips

9. _____ is always a difficult day.
   (A) Monday   (B) A Monday   (C) The Monday   (D) Mondays

10. I would like to ask you a question, and I want _____.
    (A) a truth   (B) truths   (C) the truth   (D) a true one

11. _____ tourists came from Japan.
    (A) The Most   (B) Most of   (C) The most of   (D) Most of the

12. _____ twenty-seven can be divided by 3, 9, and 27.
    (A) Number   (B) A number   (C) The number   (D) Numbers

13. She hopes to get _____ or two in the Olympic Games.
    (A) a gold   (B) one gold   (C) the gold   (D) gold

14. I think education should be free. I did not receive _____ because we were too
    poor.
    (A) good education   (B) a good education
    (C) the good education   (D) so good education

15. The business has been run by _____ for over 20 years.
    (A) father and son   (B) the father and son
    (C) father and the son   (D) a father and son

16. Don't make _____ of yourself by making those faces.
    (A) fool   (B) a fool   (C) the fool   (D) fools

17. The news spread _____.
    (A) from mouth to mouth   (B) from mouths to mouths
    (C) from a mouth to mouth   (D) from the mouth to mouth

18. A young couple walked _____ into the park while I was waiting for my sweetheart.
    (A) arm in arm   (B) arm in arms
    (C) an arm in arm   (D) the arm in arm

19. _____ should be treated equally.
    (A) The rich and poor   (B) Rich and poor
    (C) Riches and poverty   (D) A rich and a poor.

20. Do you usually take a nap after _____?
    (A) lunch   (B) a lunch   (C) the lunch   (D) lunches

代名詞的用法

人稱代名詞：用於指人或物

1. 主格代名詞：I, you, he, she, we, they, it

   <u>You</u> must be tired.

   （你一定累了。）

   Your breakfast is ready. <u>It</u> is on the table.

   （你的早餐好了，就在桌上。）

2. 受格代名詞：me, you, him, her, us, them, it

   Fill <u>her</u> up, please.

   （請將油加滿。）

   If you see John, give <u>him</u> my regards.

   （你如果見到約翰，代我問候一下。）

3. 所有格形容詞：my, you, his, her, our, their, its

   She is <u>my</u> mother-in-law.

   （她是我的岳母。）

   He saved enough money to start <u>his</u> business.

   （他存了足夠的錢來開創自己的事業。）

4. 所有格代名詞：mine, yours, his, hers, ours, theirs, its

   I can't find my pen. Can you lend me <u>yours</u>?

   （我找不到我的筆。你的能借我嗎？）

   This is your cup. <u>Mine</u> is over there.

   （這是你的杯子。我的在那邊。）

5. 反身代名詞：myself, yourself, himself, herself, ourselves, yourselves, themselves, itself

   (1) 強調用法：反身代名詞可置於主詞之後或句尾。

I <u>myself</u> saw the accident.

= I saw the accident <u>myself</u>.

（我親眼看到這起事故。）

(2) 反身用法（作 Vt 的受詞）

You are cheating <u>yourself</u>.

（你是在欺騙自己。）

(3) 慣用法（oneself 須搭配主詞變化）

abandon oneself to → 耽溺於……

accommodate (oneself) to → 調整自己以適應……

avail oneself of → 利用……

behave (oneslef) → 守規矩

devote/dedicate oneself to → 致力於……

enjoy oneself → 玩得開心

excuse oneself → （暫時）告退／離席

help oneself to → 自行取用（食物等）

make oneself at home → 不拘束／謹

occupy oneself with → 使自己忙於……

rid oneself of → 除去／拋棄……

= get rid of...

between ourselves → 不告訴第三者

be/look oneself → （某人）身心正常

beside oneself → 像瘋了一樣

by oneself (= alone) → 獨自；不靠他人

in itself → （事情）本身

of oneself → 自動

to oneself → 給自己

1. Since I had little cash on me, I decided to charge _____.
   (A) it   (B) me   (C) mine   (D) myself

2. In that country, _____ have a lot of rain in June and July.
   (A) we   (B) you   (C) they   (D) all

3. "Rosa has been promoted to manager."
   "Lucky _____!"
   (A) she   (B) her   (C) hers   (D) her own

4. "Who's that?"
   "_____ our next-door neighbor, Mr. Burns."
   (A) His   (B) She's   (C) Its   (D) It's

5. Why buy a new car? _____ say oil prices will go up again soon.
   (A) They   (B) Persons   (C) We   (D) It

6. Don't use my comb. Use _____.
   (A) your   (B) your one   (C) your own   (D) your it

7. One thing you must remember is your dad is a rich merchant but _____ is a poor artist.
   (A) my   (B) me   (C) mine   (D) my one

8. The two bank clerks were very responsible because they blamed _____ for the mistake.
   (A) them   (B) themselves   (C) theirs   (D) each other

9. Strictly between _____, do you think he is the thief?
   (A) us   (B) ours   (C) ours own   (D) ourselves

10. Take a good rest. You do not look _____ today.
    (A) you   (B) it   (C) yourself   (D) itself

指示名詞

1. this/these（這個／這些）→ 指較近的人或物
   that/those（那個／那些）→ 指較遠的人或物

   <u>This</u> is your bike and <u>that</u> is mine.

   （這是你的腳踏車，那一部是我的。）

2. 在電話中可用 Is that/this Mr./Miss...? 來詢問對方是誰。但表明自己是誰時，限用：This is George/Mary/Mr... speaking. 另外，電視、收音機的播報人員常以 This is... reporting from... 來結束播報內容並表明身分。

3. 指對方所持／穿的東西、衣物用　that/those；指自己所持／穿的東西、衣物用　this/these。

   I like <u>that</u> jacket. It looks good on you.

   （我喜歡你穿的那件西裝外套。穿在你身上很好看。）

4. 比較時常用 that（＝the ＋單數n）或 those（＝the＋複數n）來代替同一句中提過的名詞，以避免重複。

   The climate of Taiwan is better than <u>that</u> of Japan.

   （台灣的氣候比日本的氣候好。）

5. 慣用法

   (1) and all that → （諸如此類）等等
   ＝ and so on

   (2) at that → 用於附加一句話後的強調

   She is a hair designer, and a very good one <u>at that</u>.

   （她是個髮型設計師，而且是很不錯的一個喔。）

   (3) That's it/That does it! → 我受夠了！
       另外：That's it! 也可用來嘉許別人（這就對了！）

   (4) That's a good boy/girl. → 這才乖。（讚美小孩或寵物）

   (5) What's all this? → 出了什麼狀況啊？

= What's the matter?

6. so/not 的用法
   (1) 肯定

   I think/believe/guess <u>so</u>.

   （我認為會如此。）

   I hope/am afraid <u>so</u>.

   （希望／恐怕會如此。）

   (2) 否定

   I don't think <u>so</u>. = I think <u>not</u>.

   （我不認為會如此。）

   I hope <u>not</u>/I am afraid <u>not</u>.

   （希望不會如此／恐怕不會如此。）

   注意：沒有 I don't hope so 和 I'm not afraid so 的說法。

聯考題型

1. Mary: _____ is Mary Smith. May I speak to John, please?
   John: Speaking.
   (A) It   (B) This   (C) That   (D) Now

2. (on TV): _____ is Kevin Benson reporting from New York.
   (A) This   (B) That   (C) It   (D) Then

3. I like _____ hat. It looks good on you.
   (A) this   (B) that   (C) these   (D) those

4. The voice was _____ of an elderly woman.
   (A) this   (B) that   (C) so   (D) such

5. In my opinion, the best wines are _____ from France.
   (A) this   (B) that   (C) these   (D) those

6. When I was younger, I was crazy about judo, karate, kung fu, and all _____.
   (A) that   (B) this   (C) those   (D) these

7. There are a number of problems we have to deal with, and fairly complicated ones at
   _____.
   (A) this   (B) that   (C) these   (D) those

8. _____! I'm not staying here to be insulted.
   (A) That's it   (B) It's that   (C) That all   (D) All that

9. Tommy, sit here and eat your breakfast. _____ a good boy.
   (A) It's   (B) This is   (C) That's   (D) To be

10. A: "Do you think the typhoon will come?"
    B: _____.
    (A) I don't hope so   (B) I am not afraid
    (C) I hope not   (D) So do I

要點 3

不定代名詞的用法

1. some 用於肯定句，any 用於否定、疑問或條件句表『一些』。另疑問句用 some 時，表期待對方肯定的回答。

   I would like to give you <u>some</u>, but I don't have <u>any</u> now.

   （我是想給你一些，但是我目前沒有。）

   We are having tea. Would you like <u>some</u>?

   （我們正在喝茶。你想喝點嗎？）

2. any 表三者或以上的『任一』可用於肯定句，either 表兩者的『任一』。

   <u>Any</u> of the three plans can work.

   （這三個方案的任何一個都可行。）

   <u>Either</u> of your parents can come with you.

   （你的父母任何一個都可以跟你一道來。）

3. 表『全部』，兩者用 both，三者或以上用 all。另外，all 亦可用來指不可數名詞的『全部』。表『全無』，兩者用 neither，三者或以上用 none。另外 none 亦可指不可數名詞的『全無』。

<u>None</u> of my friends has/have come.

（我的朋友沒有一個來。）

<u>Neither</u> of them will agree.

（他們兩個人都不會同意。）

4. 另一／其餘的表達

(1) one...the other → （兩者）一個……另一個

(2) one...another...the other → （三者）一個……一個……另一個

(3) one...the others → （三者或以上）一個……其餘的……

(4) others = other people → （自己以外的人）別人

5. such 的用法

(1) such as (= like) + n. → 像……（舉例）

Wild flowers <u>such as</u> orchids and primroses are becoming rare.

（像蘭花、櫻草花這些野花越來越稀少了。）

(2) as such → 如此

He is only a child and should be treated <u>as such</u>.

（他只是一個孩子，應該如此看待他。）

(3) Such...that... → 如此……以致於……

= ...such that...

Such was the damage that it would take a lot of time to repair.

（損壞到如此地步，需要很長的時間才能修好。）

1. I tried to get a ticket, but there weren't _____ left.
   (A) some　　　　(B) any　　　　(C) one　　　　(D) none

2. He looked everywhere for water but couldn't find _____.
   (A) any　　　　(B) some　　　　(C) none　　　　(D) little

3. You may choose _____ of the twin sisters as a flower girl on your wedding day.
   (A) any　　　　(B) some　　　　(C) either　　　　(D) both

4. _____ there will be 50 people coming to the party.
   (A) In all　　　　(B) All in　　　　(C) All tell　　　　(D) Telling all

5. Uncle Tom wants to give me advice, but I'll have _____ of it.
   (A) none　　　　(B) nothing　　　　(C) nobody　　　　(D) nowhere

6. There are trees on _____ side of the road.
   (A) every　　　　(B) both　　　　(C) all　　　　(D) either

7. Never speak ill of _____ behind their backs.
   (A) other　　　　(B) the other　　　　(C) others　　　　(D) another

8. Mr. Wilson is a man of integrity and should be respected _____.
   (A) like such　　　　(B) such like　　　　(C) as such　　　　(D) such as

9. The young couple used to work here. _____ left for a new company two weeks ago.
   (A) Both them　　　　(B) Both they　　　　(C) Them both　　　　(D) They both

10. Their relationship is _____ that they spend every possible minute together.
    (A) so　　　　(B) such　　　　(C) like　　　　(D) as

it 的句型

1. 作虛主詞

   (1)

   $$\text{It} + (\text{單數}) \text{V...} + \begin{vmatrix} \text{that} \\ \text{who} \\ \text{which} \\ \text{how} \\ \text{when} \\ \text{whether} \end{vmatrix} + \text{S} + \text{V...}$$

   It is not a bad thing that the future is unknown.

   （未來不可知並不是一件壞事。）

   It does not matter whether he'll agree.

   （他是否會同意並不重要。）

   (2)　It is + adj + for + O + to...（該 adj 指事物）

   It is impossible <u>for</u> him to believe you.

   （要他相信你的話是不可能的。）

   (3)　It is + adj + of + O + to...（該 adj 指人）

   It is unwise <u>of</u> him to have said so.

   （說出這種話他這個人真是不智。）

   (4)　It is... + V-ing/to + V...

   It is no use talking him out of it.

   （現在勸他退出也沒用了。）

2. 作虛受詞

   $$\text{S} + \text{Vt} + \text{it} + \text{O.C.} + \begin{vmatrix} \text{that} + \text{S} + \text{V...} \\ \text{to} + \text{V...} \end{vmatrix}$$

   She made it known that she had been a geisha.

   （她不諱言曾經當過藝妓。）

I think it better to say hello to him.

（我認為跟他打個招呼比較好。）

3. 強調用法

It is ＋強調部分＋ that ＋其餘部分

Tony will marry Lisa.（沒有強調）

→ It is Tony that will marry Lisa.（強調Tony）

→ It is Lisa that Tony will marry.（強調Lisa）

聯考題型

1. It goes without saying that happiness _____ good health.
   (A) supposes　　(B) presupposes　(C) imposes　　　(D) reposes

2. It does not matter to a great actor what part he plays. _____ matters is that he plays his part well.
   (A) It　　　　　(B) That　　　　(C) What　　　　(D) This

3. _____ that the casualties have amounted to 3,000.
   (A) It is report　(B) Report is it　(C) It has report　(D) Report has it

4. It _____ to me that she would get married soon.
   (A) happened　　(B) occurred　　(C) chanced　　　(D) struck

5. Judging from the evidence, it _____ that that guy is the murderer.
   (A) flows　　　　(B) flowing　　　(C) following　　(D) follows

6. It was careless _____ you not to lock your door when you went out.
   (A) of　　　　　(B) for　　　　　(C) with　　　　(D) to

7. It was last night _____ I found out about that.
   (A) then　　　　(B) which　　　　(C) that　　　　(D) what

8. You can't take _____ for granted small children will behave themselves.
   (A) it　　　　　(B) that　　　　(C) this　　　　(D) what

9. Technological progress has _____ the improvement of people's quality of life.
   (A) made it possible　　　　　　(B) made possible
   (C) made it possibly　　　　　　(D) made the possibility

10. It _____ us a small fortune to decorate the house we had bought.
   (A) charged   (B) spent   (C) paid   (D) cost

Unit 19 　　　形容詞與副詞

要點 1

形容詞的位置

1. 屬性形容詞 (attributive adjectives)：置於所修飾的名詞之前

   I prefer <u>red</u> wine when eating meat.

   （吃肉時我比較喜歡喝紅酒。）

   She enjoys listening to <u>popular</u> songs.

   （她喜歡聽流行歌曲。）

2. 敘述形容詞 (predicative adjectives)：置於 be 或 seem 等連綴動詞之後

   Look, the tea is <u>red</u> in color.

   （你看，這種茶是紅色的。）

   This hotel seems very <u>popular</u> with tourists.

   （這家飯店似乎很受觀光客的青睞。）

3. 大部分的形容詞兼有上述兩種用法，不過有些形容詞兩種用法的意思並不相同。

   He has been <u>ill</u> for two weeks.

   （他已經病了兩個星期了。）

   The clerk was fired because of her <u>ill</u> temper.

   （這名店員因為脾氣不好而遭解雇。）

4. 若干形容只有「屬性」用法

   (1) —— most: foremost, innermost, utmost

   　　Dr. Woods is the <u>foremost</u> authority on Egyptian culture.

   　　（伍茲博士是埃及文化的首席權威。）

   (2) —— er: elder, former, inner, latter, lesser, lower, other, outer, upper, utter

   　　She is the <u>former</u> mayor.

   　　（她是前任的市長。）

(3) —— en: brazen, drunken, earthen, golden, silken, wooden, woolen

The <u>drunken</u> man is her husband.

（那個醉漢是她的老公。）

注意：

Her husband is <u>drunk</u>. (not drunken)

（她的老公醉了。）

5. 「敘述」用法和「後置」形容詞（片語）

(1) 字首 a —— 開頭的形容詞：afraid, alike, alive, alone, ashamed, asleep, awake, aware

Ted was the only awake man at that time.（×）

Ted was the only man <u>awake</u> at that hime.（○）

（泰德是當時唯一清醒的人。）

(2)

| something/someone/somedody/somewhere |
| anything/anyone/anybody/anywhere |
| everything/everyone/everybody/everywhere | + adj.
| nothing/no one/nobody/nowhere |

Let's go somewhere <u>nice</u> for dinner.

（咱們找個好地方吃晚餐吧。）

(3) 固定慣用語

Asia <u>Minor</u>（小亞細亞）

body <u>politic</u>（全體國民；國家）

court <u>martial</u>（軍事法庭）

heir <u>apparent</u>（法定繼承人）

poet <u>laureate</u>（桂冠詩人）

聯考題型

1. They both look so _____ that it is very difficult to tell which is which.
   (A) like   (B) likely   (C) alike   (D) likewise

2. She enjoys watching the face of her _____ baby.
   (A) sleeping   (B) slept   (C) asleep   (D) sleep

3. William Faulkner is a highly _____ novelist in American literature.
   (A) imaginable   (B) imaginative   (C) image   (D) imaginary

4. These people are _____ to trust you.
   (A) hard   (B) impossible   (C) utmost   (D) unwilling

5. Money _____ cannot save their marriage. They have too many problems to solve.
   (A) alone   (B) lonely   (C) only   (D) mere

6. Out of the building on fire rushed _____.
   (A) an afraid man   (B) a frightened man
   (C) an astonish man   (D) a scare man

7. In spite of the _____ traffic, I managed to get to the airport in time.
   (A) heavy   (B) much   (C) crowded   (D) hard

8. Many _____ creatures in the sea are being affected by environmental pollution.
   (A) life   (B) live   (C) alive   (D) living

9. I'm going home to watch the _____ TV broadcast of the Olympics.
   (A) life   (B) live   (C) alive   (D) living

10. The child was found still _____ and kicking after being trapped under the rubble for two days.
    (A) life   (B) live   (C) alive   (D) living

11. She received a _____ sentence for murdering her husband.
    (A) life   (B) live   (C) alive   (D) living

12. It was very _____ of him not to take the bribe.
    (A) sensitive   (B) sensible   (C) sensory   (D) sensual

13. Most of the people in the country cannot read or write. Only about ten percent of the people are _____.
    (A) literal   (B) literary   (C) literate   (D) literature

14. In a democracy, we should be _____ of other people's opinions although we don't have to agree with them.
    (A) respectable   (B) respectful   (C) respective   (D) respecting

15. The good weather seems _____ for the test flight of the new model.
    (A) favored   (B) favorite   (C) favering   (D) favorable

16. The polluted lake is a _____ sight.
   (A) sick   (B) sickly   (C) sickening   (D) sickened

17. Tigers are now classified as a(n) _____ species. They need our protection.
   (A) dangerous   (B) danger   (C) endangering (D) endangered

18. Many countries in Africa are still not _____.
   (A) industrial   (B) industrialized (C) industrious   (D) industry

19. After the party we all went back to our _____ rooms.
   (A) respectable (B) respectful   (C) respecting   (D) respective

20. The president of our company had to resign because of some _____ problems.
   (A) health   (B) healthy   (C) healthful   (D) healing

21. Is King Arthur is a fictional character or a _____ figure?
   (A) history   (B) historian   (C) historic   (D) historical

22. We have saved a _____ amount of money in order to travel overseas.
   (A) considerable (B) considerate (C) considered   (D) considering

23. He is not a graduate of any university, but he has got many _____ degrees.
   (A) honorable   (B) honorary   (C) honored   (D) honoring

24. I have had enough of their _____ petty quarrels.
   (A) continuous   (B) continual   (C) continuing   (D) continue

25. Mrs. Lee has a _____ daughter, so she hopes that this young and rich man can be her son-in-law.
   (A) unmarried   (B) married   (C) marrying   (D) marriageable

1. 副詞的功用：

   (1) 修飾動詞

   I usually get up at 6 o'clock.

   （我通常六點鐘起床。）

   (2) 修飾形容詞

   Tom was too busy to keep me company.

   （湯姆太忙了，沒空陪我。）

   (3) 修飾其它副詞

   I tried very hard to remember his name.

   （我非常用力回想他的名字。）

   (4) 修飾介系詞片語

   You are entirely in the wrong.

   （你完全錯了。）

   (5) 修飾整句（可置於句首，句中或句末）

   Sadly, their business failed.

   （很不幸的是，他們的事業失敗了。）

2. 副詞的種類：

   (1) 程度副詞→ very, much, too, enough, almost, hardly, fairly, rather, so, badly, …

   (2) 狀態副詞→ angrily, carefully, curiously, gently, quietly, hard, slowly, suddenly, temporarily, …

   (3) 時間副詞→ now, then, today, yesterday, early, late, later, soon, …

(4) 頻率副詞→ always, usually, frequently, often, sometimes, seldom, never, …

(5) 地方副詞→ here, there, somewhere, anywhere, nowhere, home, abroad, indoors, outdoors, downstairs, upstairs, left, right, north, south, …

(6) 肯/否定副詞→ yes, no, sure, never, certainly, …

(7) 疑問副詞→ when, where, how, why（引導疑問句）

(8) 關係副詞→ when, where, how, why（引導名詞/形容詞子句）

聯考題型

1. Please lend me the money because I need it _____.
   (A) bad   (B) badly   (C) hard   (D) hardly

2. _____, she did not even thank me!.
   (A) Enough strange   (B) Strange enough
   (C) Enough strangely   (D) Strangely enough

3. I usually travel _____ because I hate packing and unpacking baggage.
   (A) light   (B) lightly   (C) lighten   (D) alight

4. Come _____ so that I can see you better.
   (A) closer   (B) more close   (C) closely   (D) more closely

5. Her mother asked her to send those packages _____.
   (A) express   (B) expressly   (C) expressive   (D) expressively

6. Why don't you go _____ to throw the boomerang? You need an open space to play the game.
   (A) indoor   (B) indoors   (C) outdoor   (D) outdoors

7. I need to take a good rest now because I'm _____ tired.
   (A) not a bit   (B) not that   (C) not a little   (D) not too

8. James was halfway through his explanation when Mary cut him _____.
   (A) short   (B) shortly   (C) shortness   (D) shortage

9. _____, the playboy is a very religious person.
   (A) Deeply   (B) Deep down   (C) Deeply down   (D) In depth

10. He left the office _____ after the meeting and no one knew where he was going.
    (A) direct   (B) directly   (C) rightly   (D) justly

11. Rachael stopped _____ in her tracks when she saw me with Jennifer.
    (A) dead   (B) deadly   (C) death   (D) deathly

12. When she saw him swallow the deadly poison, she went _____ pale.
    (A) dead   (B) deadly   (C) death   (D) deathly

13. Those who participated were _____ women.
    (A) most   (B) almost   (C) mostly   (D) most of

14. Peter was so nervous that he _____ forgot how to respond.
    (A) clean   (B) cleanly   (C) clear   (D) clearly

15. Lead-free gas is strongly recommended since it burns _____.
    (A) clean   (B) cleanly   (C) clear   (D) clearly

16. Their company has been in business for 20 years and is still going _____.
    (A) strong   (B) strongly   (C) strength   (D) strengthen

17. Julie's eyes were opening _____ when her husband took a big diamond out of his pocket.
    (A) wide   (B) widely   (C) widen   (D) width

18. Citizens aged 65 and over can travel _____ on the buses.
    (A) free   (B) freely   (C) freed   (D) freedom

19. Look, those birds are flying _____ in the sky.
    (A) high   (B) highly   (C) highness   (D) height

20. To do her justice, Linda is a _____ efficient secretary.
    (A) high   (B) highly   (C) highness   (D) height

要點 1

表「地方」的介系詞

1. at …
   (1) at + 社交/公共場所（視為會面、等候的地方）

   I'll meet you <u>at</u> the airport.

   （我會在機場與你會面。）

   (2) at home/work（在家/上班）

   (3) at breakfast/lunch/dinner（在用早/午/晚餐）

   (4) at + 地址

2. in …
   (1) in + 洲/國家/州/都市

   He was <u>in</u> Europe at that time.

   （他當時人在歐洲。）

   (2) in + 公共場所（強調在其範圍內）

   There are two or three banks <u>in</u> the airport.

   （機場裡有兩三家銀行。）

   (3) in the air/sky（在空中）

   (4) in the middle/center（在中間位置）

3. 其它介系詞
   (1) on …（在…的上面，有接觸）
   (2) over …（在…的正上方，沒有接觸）
   (3) above …（在…的上方，沒有接觸）
   (4) under …（在…的正下方，沒有接觸）
   (5) below …（在…的下方，沒有接觸）
   (6) by/beside …（在…的旁邊）
   (7) before …（在…之前）
   (8) behind …（在…之後）
   (9) between …（在兩者之間）

(10) among … （在三者或以上之中）

(11) around … （圍繞著…）

(12) across … （越過…）

(13) along … （沿著…）

(14) from … （從…）

(15) to … （到…）

(16) toward(s) … （朝…去）

(17) into … （進入…）

(18) out of… （自…出來）

(19) through … （穿過…）

(20) up … （向上）

(21) down … （向下）

(22) away from … （離開…）

(23) against … （倚靠著…）

(24) within … （在…裡面）

聯考題型

1. My grandparents live _____ 234 Park Road.
   (A) at   (B) in   (C) on   (D) along

2. Nancy is _____ the dentist's. She'll be back in about an hour.
   (A) at   (B) to   (C) on   (D) with

3. It was the astronauts' first experience living _____ space.
   (A) at   (B) on   (C) in   (D) for

4. The skyscraper is a new landmark _____ the center of the city.
   (A) at   (B) in   (C) on   (D) for

5. Tommy leaned over and kissed his mom _____ the cheek.
   (A) at   (B) on   (C) in   (D) above

6. We could see the Stars and Stripes flying _____ the American Embassy.
   (A) at   (B) in   (C) on   (D) over

7. Temperatures have been _____ average for several days.
   (A) over   (B) up   (C) above   (D) on

8. What are you kids doing _____ the table?
   (A) above   (B) over   (C) below   (D) under

9. We found a picnic area down _____ the river.
   (A) beside   (B) besides   (C) except   (D) except for

10. _____ the temple gate stands a bronze statue of Buddha.
   (A) After   (B) Before   (C) Among   (D) Between

11. Jimmy went out and shut the door _____ him.
   (A) after   (B) behind   (C) across   (D) below

12. _____ other things, Harry was accused of attempting to bribe a police officer.
   (A) At   (B) Between   (C) Among   (D) After

13. _____ you and me, our boss has an illegitimate son.
   (A) For   (B) Between   (C) Among   (D) As

14. Rescuers worked _____ the clock to free people trapped underground.
   (A) around   (B) across   (C) on   (D) behind

15. The congressman was assassinated, but it is still not clear who was _____ the murder.
   (A) below   (B) behind   (C) about   (D) across

16. In all, there are five bridges _____ the river.
   (A) across   (B) cross   (C) around   (D) round

17. How are you getting _____ with your Japanese?
   (A) around   (B) along   (C) away   (D) across

18. Josh had never liked any kind of music until he was _____ rock and roll two months ago.
   (A) in   (B) out of   (C) into   (D) toward

19. Much _____ our surprise, the millionaire's daughter has eloped with a young apprentice.
   (A) for   (B) in   (C) with   (D) to

20. I left my bike propped _____ a tree in front of the farm.
   (A) in   (B) away   (C) on   (D) against

表「時間」的介系詞

1. at + 某一點時間
   (1) at + 時刻
   (2) at rest/peace/war
   (3) at present/the moment
   (4) at night
   (5) at the age of …

2. in + 較長的時間
   (1) in the 21st century
   (2) in 2006
   (3) in (the) spring/summer/fall/winter
   (4) in January/March
   (5) in the morning/afternoon/evening

3. on + 特定的時間
   (1) on Monday/Tuesday
   (2) on weekends/the weekend
   (3) on the morning of April 23
   (4) on New Year's Day

4. by … →最遲不超過… = not later than …

5. from … to … → 從…到…

6. during …→ 在…期間

7. for + 一段時間 → 有…之久

8. since … → 自…到目前為止

9. till/until … → 直到…

10. through … → 從（某時間）一直到（某時間）

11. throughout … → 自始至終

12. toward →將近…

13. before/after … →在…之前/後

14. around/about … →大約…

聯考題型

1. It was _____ midnight when we finally arrived at the camping site.
   (A) in   (B) on   (C) until   (D) toward

2. My older brother is a bookworm. He's never been good _____ sports.
   (A) at   (B) on   (C) to   (D) with

3. _____ night temperatures will often drop to ten degrees below zero.
   (A) At   (B) In   (C) On   (D) For

4. I'll be back with you _____ a minute or two.
   (A) at   (B) for   (C) in   (D) to

5. All our employees are paid _____ the week.
   (A) in   (B) on   (C) for   (D) by

6. We should not spend all the money. We must save some _____ a rainy day.
   (A) in   (B) at   (C) for   (D) by

7. She married a Japanese businessman _____ the age of 18.
   (A) in   (B) at   (C) on   (D) for

8. My birthday is _____ the 15th of June.
   (A) in   (B) on   (C) at   (D) for

9. _____ the time she was 20, Mary had given birth to three children.
   (A) In   (B) With   (C) At   (D) By

10. It is dangerous to go into the park _____ dark.
    (A) at   (B) after   (C) through   (D) in

11. Most birds leave their nests _____ dawn.
    (A) at   (B) in   (C) on   (D) to

12. Nocturnal animals hunt _____ night.
    (A) by   (B) for   (C) in   (D) on

13. The child woke up three times _____ the night.
    (A) at   (B) in   (C) for   (D) by

14. It's now a quarter _____ 6, so I think we will be ready by 6:30.
    (A) of   (B) after   (C) at   (D) on

15. I have run out of my allowance _____ last week.
    (A) in   (B) on   (C) from   (D) since

16. Our store is open Monday _____ Friday.
    (A) to   (B) from   (C) until   (D) through

17. My grandfather was devoted to creative writing _____ his life.
    (A) at   (B) throughout   (C) to   (D) from

18. It was not _____ 1945 that World War II came to an end.
    (A) around   (B) through   (C) until   (D) in

19. It is _____ time that you kids went to bed.
    (A) around   (B) about   (C) until   (D) during

20. Last night we got back home _____ 11 o'clock.
    (A) around   (B) across   (C) during   (D) till

介系詞的其它用法

1. 表「材料」

(1) be made + $\begin{cases} \text{of + 材料（性質不變）} \\ \text{from + 材料（性質改變）} \\ \text{into + 成品} \end{cases}$

The bowl is made of wood.

（這個碗是木頭製的。）

Wood can be made into a statue.

（木頭可以製成雕像。）

注意：be made of 和 be made from 在現代英文中已逐漸沒有區別。

2. 表「原因」

(1) die of/from →死於疾病/外傷

Every year many people die of cancer.

（每年很多人死於癌症。）

(2) be dying for →很想得到⋯

I'm dying for a cup of coffee.

（我很想喝杯咖啡。）

(3) out of curiosity/habit/interest →由於好奇/習慣/興趣

I gave them food out of pity.

（我因同情而給他們食物。）

(4) with + 情緒/病痛

David's face was red with anger/fever.

（大衛因生氣/發燒而滿臉通紅。）

3. 表「方位」

(1) in the east/west of ⋯ →在⋯的東/西部（在內）

(2) on the east/west of ⋯ →在⋯的東/西邊（緊鄰）

(3) to the east/west of ⋯ →在⋯的東/西方（在外）

4. 表「目的」

(1) look/search/hunt for →尋找…

I've been hunting <u>for</u> the book all day.

（這本書我已找了一整天。）

(2) be/go after →追求/逐…

He is <u>after</u> fame and wealth.

（他追求名利。）

(3) be aimed at (doing) sth →目的為…

Traffic regulations are aimed <u>at</u> prevention of accidents, too.

（交通規則目的也在防止車禍發生。）

5. 表「價格」

(1) at + 價格（單價）

Tickets now sell <u>at</u> $15 apiece.

（門票現在每張 15 美元。）

(2) for + 價格（總價）

These paintings can be sold for millions of dollars.

（這些畫可以賣數百萬元。）

6. 表「除…之外」

(1) except/but … →除…之外（不包含）

I have everything <u>except</u> fame.

（除了名以外，我什麼都有了。）

(2) besides … →除…之外（包含）

She collects many other things <u>besides</u> stamps.

（除了集郵外，她也收集許多其它東西。）

7. 表「附帶狀況」

with (one's) + n + | 一般 adj/介詞（片語）
| V-ing（主動）
| pp（被動）

> Dad was reading a newspaper, with the television <u>on</u>.
>
> （老爸在看報，電視機開著。）
>
> Mom sat in front of the TV, with her eyes <u>closed</u>.
>
> （老媽坐在電視機前，眼睛是閉著的。）

聯考題型

1. I think this story can be made _____ a good movie.
   (A) of   (B) from   (C) into   (D) with

2. On such a hot day, I'm dying _____ a can of cold beer.
   (A) from   (B) of   (C) to   (D) for

3. George took a peep into the box _____ curiosity.
   (A) by   (B) in   (C) on   (D) out of

4. Cleopatra died _____ her own hand.
   (A) by   (B) from   (C) of   (D) for

5. Because of the cold spell, many employees came down _____ flu.
   (A) to   (B) with   (C) by   (D) for

6. Canada lies _____ the north of the United States.
   (A) on   (B) to   (C) in   (D) at

7. Kaohsiung is _____ the south of Taiwan.
   (A) on   (B) to   (C) in   (D) at

8. My hometown is about 50 miles _____ the west of Chicago.
   (A) on   (B) to   (C) in   (D) at

9. John runs _____ every pretty girl he meets.
   (A) after   (B) along   (C) around   (D) about

10. The plan is aimed _____ reducing our dependence on fossil fuels.
    (A) on   (B) for   (C) at   (D) with

11. All household goods are being sold _____ half price.
    (A) at   (B) in   (C) on   (D) for

12. Out superintendent stood over there _____ his arms crossed.
    (A) with   (B) by   (C) for   (D) as

13. Who's _____ charge here?
    (A) at   (B) in   (C) with   (D) on

14. _____ present circumstances, I feel I have no option but to resign.
    (A) Below   (B) Under   (C) Above   (D) Over

15. He was sentenced _____ life for the murder.
    (A) for   (B) to   (C) in   (D) with

16. _____ the way, have you heard from him lately?
    (A) In   (B) On   (C) At   (D) By

17. Your remarks are always _____ the point.
    (A) to   (B) on   (C) with   (D) at

18. You can get everything here _____ free.
    (A) in   (B) for   (C) at   (D) by

19. Stress can bring _____ some health problems.
    (A) in   (B) up   (C) out   (D) on

20. We are seriously understaffed. We have to take _____ more people.
    (A) up   (B) on   (C) into   (D) down

21. You have to teach your kids to put their toys _____.
    (A) off   (B) aside   (C) away   (D) up

22. A man is giving _____ leaflets at the entrance hall.
    (A) up   (B) in   (C) off   (D) out

23. Don't be too hard _____ her. She is a mere child after all.
    (A) on   (B) with   (C) at   (D) about

24. I think I met her in 2002, but I can't say _____ certain.
    (A) to   (B) with   (C) at   (D) for

25. When I wanted to say something to him, he had already got _____ a taxi.
    (A) on   (B) to   (C) with   (D) into

26. I couldn't believe Jane would hang up _____ me.
    (A) on   (B) to   (C) for   (D) at

27. Our boss looks stern, but he is a kind man _____ heart.
    (A) in   (B) at   (C) by   (D) with

28. Never count _____ Jack to give you a hand. He is too selfish.
   (A) in   (B) for   (C) on   (D) to

29. It might take a week or two to get _____ a bad cold.
   (A) through   (B) away   (C) over   (D) up

30. Many cars ground _____ a halt because of the accident a few miles ahead.
   (A) to   (B) in   (C) for   (D) with

解答篇

Unit 1

要點 1

聯考題型

1. (B) Money talks.（諺語），意為「錢能通神」。
2. (D) substitute for sb = take the place of sb（替代某人）。
3. (C) Old habits die hard.（諺語），意為「積習難改」。
4. (A) let go (of sth/sb) 表「放開（某物/人）」。
5. (A) Either will do.表「兩者任一皆可」。
6. (A) perish = die，尤指「慘遭橫禍而死」。
7. (B) pass as/for sb/sth 表「可以權充某人/物」。
8. (B) explode 本為「爆炸」。explode with anger 表「氣炸了」。
9. (D) fade away 表（人物）「逐漸凋零」。
10. (A) blush 表因羞愧或尷尬而「臉紅」。
11. (A) sell like hot cakes 表（某物）「極為暢銷」。
12. (D) ability to adapt 表「適應的能力」。
13. (A) It happened/chanced that … 表「恰好…」。
14. (B) don't hesitate to + V = feel free to + V（不要猶豫…）
15. (A) what remains = what is left 表「剩下來的東西」。

翻譯造句

1. "A barking dog seldom bites," as the saying goes.
2. If you persist/persevere, you will succeed.
3. Do you believe his idea can work?
4. That traffic cop happened to be my cousin.
5. lives to be 100 or more.

聯考題型

1. (C) sb is to blame 表「某人該受譴責或負責」。
2. (B) paralyzed 作形容詞，表交通系統「癱瘓掉」或「停滯」。
3. (C) It looks like rain.（看起來好像下雨了。）固定說法。
4. (D) available 指物時表「可以取得的」；指人時表「有空的」。
5. (A) fall asleep = drop off（睡著）。feel sleepy（想睡）。
6. (D) landmark = landmass（地標），指明顯的建築物。
7. (A) sound like … 表「聽起來像…」。
8. (B) be envious of sb 表「羨慕某人」。
9. (D) drop dead (of sth) 表（因某疾病）而「猝死」。
10. (C) be cancelled = be called off（被取消）
11. (A) turn +（零冠詞）+ informant/killer 表「變成告密者/殺手」。
12. (A) look athletic 表（某人）「看起來很會運動的樣子」。
13. (B) turn turtle = turn upside down 指船隻「翻覆」。
14. (C) be highly motivated 表「情緒激昂」或「士氣高昂」。
15. (A) smell of sth 表「聞起來有…之味道」，smell like sth 表「聞起來像…」。

翻譯造句

1. The curio proved to be a fake.
2. I hope (that) your dream will come true.
3. Be sure to keep in touch (with me).
4. Many teenagers fall victim to drugs.
5. To stay slim, she has only a meal a day.

1. (A) mean business/it 表某人的態度是「認真」的。
2. (B) recycle sth 是將某物「回收」再利用之意。
3. (B) have your say 表「有機會說出你想說的話」。這裡的 "say" 是名詞。
4. (B) visualize sth 表「在心裡形成某物的畫面」。
5. (C) toss/flip a coin 表「丟銅板（決定勝負/順序等）」。
6. (D) inspire sb = encourage sb 表「激勵某人」。
7. (B) bear washing 表（衣服/質料）而「耐洗」。
8. (C) postpone = delay = put off（延期）。
9. (C) carry weight 表（說話）「有份量」。
10. (D) download sth 表「下載某物」。
11. (B) call the roll（點名），這裡的 roll 表「名冊」。
12. (B) wave good-bye to sb（向某人揮手道別）。
13. (D) devote oneself/one's life to sth（專注/致力於某物）。
14. (B) analyze 表「分析」。
15. (B) 置於句首表「是否」限用 whether，不用 if。

翻譯造句

1. I am still hungry. May I have another helping?
2. Peter does not only the cooking but (also) the laundry.
3. If you don't mean her, then who on earth do you mean?
4. I won't take any chances from now on.
5. Mary has several phone calls to make.

1. (A) deny treatment to sb 表「不給某人治療」。
2. (D) a written apology（一封道歉函）。
3. (C) you owe sb a favor 意為「某人曾經幫過你，你欠他一個人情」。
4. (B) lend sth to sth 表「給某物增添某種性質/風味」。
5. (A) grant sth to sb 表「正式地給與某人某物」。
6. (C) save sth for sb 表「為某人省/留下某物」。
7. (B) deliver your order to your door（將你訂的貨送到家）。
8. (C) show your pass（亮出你的通行證）。
9. (B) need + V-ing = need to be + pp 表「需要被…」之意。
10. (D) bear sb no grudge（對某人沒有怨尤）。
11. (A) offer a reward（提供一個獎賞）。
12. (A) get sb a job（為某人弄到一個工作）。
13. (C) leave a message/note with sb（留信息/字條給某人轉交）。
14. (A) leave sth to sb（留財物給某人）。
15. (B) leave sth for sb（留食物/飲料給某人）。

翻譯造句

1. Mom has baked a big cake for us.
2. A can of coke won't do any harm to your health.
3. Pass the pepper to me, will you?
4. The department store is offering special discounts for New Year.
5. A police officer showed her the way to the airport.

1. (D) drive sb nuts/crazy 比喻「把某人逼瘋」。
2. (C) (be) foreign to sb 表「對某人而言很陌生」。
3. (B) make oneself understood（使自己的意思被人瞭解）。
4. (A) make sth possible = make possible sth（使某物成為可能）。
5. (D) see sb/sth + pp 表「看到某人/物被…」。
6. (C) have sth enlarged（將某物放大）。
7. (B) get sb to do sth（請/找某人做某事）。
8. (A) have something/nothing in common（有一些/沒有任何相同之處）。
9. (B) set a dog loose = unleash a dog（解開狗鏈）。
10. (B) close 作形容詞時表「接/親近的」，作動詞時表「關閉」。
11. (C) leave sb + V-ing/pp. V-ing 表「主動」義，pp 表「被動」義。
12. (A) nice and + adj. = very + adj. 表「非常…」之意。
13. (A) appoint sb (as) sth（任命某人為…）。
14. (A) beat sb black and blue（將某人毆打至淤青）。
15. (B) find sb + V-ing/pp, V-ing 表「主動」義，pp 表「被動」義。

翻譯造句

1. I found myself dancing to the music.
2. You should have your blood pressure taken/checked.
3. Many failures have made what I am today.
4. Let me help you (to) do the housework.
5. The mayor left several questions unanswered.

Unit 2

聯考題型

1. (A) there + be 表「有」…（be 動詞須搭配主詞單複數變化）。
2. (B) produce 作「農產品」解時為不可數名詞。product 可數。
3. (C) his = his parents。he 須接 remains。
4. (A) fall in love（陷入戀情）為固定說法。
5. (B) 原句亦可寫成：To err is human; to forgive is divine.
6. (A) 主詞是 the Taipei 101，搭配單數動詞 is。
7. (B) whether 接不定詞片語表「是否要…」。
8. (B) that 引導的子句作主詞 = the fact that …
9. (A) stage 在此表「上演」。
10. (C) what matters = the thing which matters 表「重要的事」。
11. (B) 動名詞片語作主詞（接單數 V）。
12. (A) 不定詞片語作主詞（接單數 V）。
13. (B) the + adj. 指人時為複數名詞，須接複數 V。
14. (A) a power failure 表「一次停電」。
15. (A) what one is（一個人的品德）作主詞接單數動詞 is。

翻譯造句

1. Whoever says that is a liar.
2. Falling in love is one thing; getting married is another.
3. to go on living is to suffer more.
4. Your encouragement means a lot to me.
5. The house is deserted, with garbage scattered all over the floor.

1. (D) How come you didn't …? = Why didn't you …?
2. (A) the answer is no/negative/yes/affirmative（回答是否/肯定的）。
3. (D) What do you do (for a living)? 用來問對方職業。
4. (A) 用過去式 did 搭配後一句的 meant。
5. (C) How often …? 問「頻率」。
6. (C) Are you someone who …? 問「你是這樣的一個人嗎？」
7. (A) 參閱(要點2)第4句型。
8. (A) why we like … 為名詞子句，作主詞補語。
9. (C) seldom 為否定副詞，附加問句須用肯定（主詞一律用代名詞）。
10. (D) Would you like A or B? 須回答 A 或 B。
11. (A) Let's …, shall we? 為固定用法。
12. (D) 回答 Yes 表「介意」，回答 No 表「不介意」，(B) 項顯然矛盾，應選 (D)。
13. (D) Do you have the time? 詢問時刻。
14. (A) How do you find A? 表「你認為 A 如何？」
15. (D) have/has to 的否定用 don't/doesn't 形成。

1. Did you tell me what she wanted?
2. What did you tell me she wanted?
3. How soon will the boss come back?
4. Who on earth do you mean?
5. How long is he going to stay here?

1. (A) What a(n) + adj. + n + S + V！
2. (C) work 表「可行/用」。
3. (B) How + adj. + S + be/look！
4. (D) Good/Gracious heavens！表驚嘆，如中文說「天哪！」。
5. (A) What + adj. + 不可數 n. + S + V！
6. (A) Well-done 表「做得好」。
7. (B) What + adj. + 複數 n. + S + V！
8. (A) Guess what? 表說話者要告訴對方一件可喜的事情或秘密。
9. (A) What + adj. + 不可數 n. + S + V！
10. (B) How + adv. + S + V … ！

翻譯造句

1. What a coincidence！I'm going shopping, too.
2. Look, how gracefully she is walking！
3. What a genius your younger brother is！
4. Listen, how hard it is raining！
5. What a pleasant surprise to meet you here！

1. (B) 祈使句用原形 V 開頭。
2. (A) Don't (you) ever + 原形 V … 表「千萬不要…」。
3. (A) 祈使句，and + S + V …
4. (B) Take sth, for example. 為固定用法。
5. (A) make + O. + O.C.
6. (C) 應該說 read … carefully 或 follow … closely。
7. (D) 諺語，意為「勿貪多而嚼不爛」。
8. (A) hang on to 表「堅持/守…」。
9. (A) say (you are) sorry（說聲抱歉）為固定說法。
10. (B) See if … 表「看看是否…」
11. (A) be sure to + 原形 V 或 make sure + S + V …
12. (B) go Dutch 表「各自付帳」。
13. (A) One more/Another + n, and + S + V …（再一…，就…）
14. (A) May + S + 原形 V …→祈願句。
15. (C) be ashamed of + n/V-ing 或 be ashamed to + 原形 V。

翻譯造句

1. Take it or leave it.
2. Don't make a fool of yourself.
3. One more effort, and you will succeed.
4. Be seated, please.
5. May those in love become life partners.

Unit 3

要點 1

聯考題型

1. (C) whether/if...(or not) 表「是否⋯」。
2. (B) how 表「如何（程度）」。(C) where 若原文強調「受損的部位」時亦可。
3. (B) be sure (that) ⋯ 表「確信/定⋯」。
4. (A) what = the thing(s) which
5. (C) whoever = anyone who
6. (D) that 引導名詞子句作主詞補語。
7. (A) who he is（他是誰）為名詞子句作主詞，接單數動詞 is。
8. (C) what 為複合關代，可作名詞子句中的主詞或受詞。
9. (A) That 引導名詞子句作主詞等於 The fact that ⋯。
10. (A) have no doubt that ⋯（對⋯有把握）。

要點 2

翻譯造句

1. It doesn't matter which she will choose.
2. Tell me whose turn it is.
3. Why he resigned is still a mystery to us.
4. I wonder whether/if they will get married.
5. Do you know how David makes a living?

1. One problem is that I don't have enough cash.
2. His opinion is that you should delay going abroad.
3. Her parents have made what she is today.
4. The idea that men are superior to women is wrong.
5. I'm confident that you will get the scholarship.

1. I'm ashamed that I made the mistake.
2. Are you aware that you should be responsible for this?
3. I'm convinced that we are doing right this time.
4. We are delighted that the final exam is over.
5. Are you sure (that) you did not forget anything?

聯考題型

1. (C) whose + n 作為該形容詞子句的主詞。
2. (C) of which many are … = many of which are …
3. (A) 此處 requiring 為 which requires 之略。
4. (B) 此處 caused 為 which is caused 之略。
5. (A) I thought 為「插入語」，who 作 was 之主詞。
6. (C) which 指 the university 作介系詞 to 的受詞。
7. (A) who 的先行詞是 He。本句為諺語：「初生之犢不畏虎」。
8. (A) who 作 exercises 的主詞，引導形容詞子句。
9. (D) for whom I've been waiting = whom I've been waiting for。
10. (B) 有連接詞 and 故選 it。沒有 and 須選 which。
11. (B) pay for sth（付錢買某物）。
12. (C) 沒有連接詞故選 which。
13. (D) whose + n 作為該形容詞子句 understand 的受詞。
14. (A) 此處的 run 是過去分詞，為 who was run 之略。
15. (C) 先行詞有人有（動）物時，關代用 that。

翻譯造句

1. The house whose windows are broken seems to be haunted.
2. The old man who has a long beard is my grandfather.
3. Is she the girl (whom) you mentioned?
4. He is the very person (that) the police are looking for.
5. There were few passengers, who escaped without injuries.

1. (C) whoever = anyone who，作主詞。
2. (A) what = the thing which
3. (A) what 引導名詞子句作主詞。
4. (C) whatever = anything which，作受詞。
5. (D) whichever = any one of those (ties) that

聯考題型

翻譯造句

1. Now he is not what he was/used to be.
2. Whatever is yours is mine.
3. Give this booklet to whoever wants it.
4. You may choose whichever suits you best.
5. They are not interested in what I suggested.

1. (D) during which time = and during that time
2. (B) what few/little … 表「僅有的一些…」。
3. (B) 同上。
4. (C) whichever + n 表（一些選擇當中的）任一…
5. (B) whatever price 表「不論什麼價格」。

翻譯造句

1. I'm ready to accept whatever help I can get.
2. He did not say much, but what little he said was full of wisdom.
3. They wanted me to quit smoking, which advice I did not take.
4. You may choose whichever method suits you best.
5. I gave that beggar what little money I had with me.

要點 4

聯考題型

1. (B) 先行詞為時間用 when。
2. (D) the way … 表「…的方式」。
3. (A) 先行詞為時間用 when。
4. (B) 先行詞為地方用 where。
5. (B) 非限定用法作補述用。
6. (B) 同上。
7. (D) 先行詞為地方用 where。
8. (D) what you/I like about sb/sth（你/我喜歡某人/物的一點）。
9. (A) 先行詞為地方用 where。
10. (D) the way … 表「…的方式」。

翻譯造句

1. He was born on the day when his grandmother died.
2. It is a small island where I have never been.
3. Tell me the reason why you would rather live alone.
4. This is how/the way I have slimmed down.

5. I don't like the way he looks at me.

要點 5

聯考題型

1. (B) there is no + 單數 n. + but + 單數 V.
2. (A) 先行詞 people 為複數，接複數 V.
3. (C) the same … as … 表「相似的…」。
4. (C) as … as ever + 過去式 V（有史以來最…的…）。
5. (D) such … 搭配準關代 as。
6. (A) but = that … not
7. (D) as … as … 為固定句型。
8. (C) 可以說 than they need 或 than is needed.
9. (A) the same … that … 表「同一個/件…」。
10. (A) such … 搭配準關代 as。

翻譯造句

1. There is none of us but supports you.
2. There are few people but enjoy being praised.
3. Beware of such people as will flatter you.
4. This is the same problem as we had last year.
5. She earns far more money than I earn.

1. (C) as 的先行詞是 He married the girl。
2. (B) the girl 為先行詞,用 whom 作 had scarcely known 的受詞。
3. (C) as 的先行詞是 She invited us to dinner。
4. (C) as 的先行詞是 He is a southerner。
5. (A) 置於句首時用 as。
6. (D) which 的先行詞是 She won a gold medal。
7. (B) which 的先行詞是 George said nothing …。
8. (D) 表身分用 which。
9. (D) 同上。
10. (D) which 的先行詞是 He wanted to be a policeman。

Unit 5

要點 1

聯考題型

1. (A) 表時間的一點用 when。
2. (D) 本句中 As a small child 為 As he was a small child 之略。
3. (A) while playing … 為 while she was playing …之略。
4. (B) 本句的 while = although。
5. (A) 表時間的一點用 when。
6. (C) whenever = every time when
7. (A) 本句用 as 相當於 while。
8. (C) 本句用 while 相當於 although。
9. (B) 本句用 while 相當於 whereas，表「對照」。
10. (A) just as … 表「正當…之時」。

克漏字

1. (C) do = change
2. (D) Unless (they are) made …
3. (D) As = When
4. (B) the time will come when … 為固定語法。
5. (A) 表一段時間用 while。

1. (B) since + S + 過去式 V.
2. (A) since + 過去的時間。
3. (D) since 當副詞用。
4. (A) 同上。
5. (B) long since 表「老早就…」。
6. (D) 副詞子句含 since（自從）時，其主要子句搭配現在完成式。
7. (C) 本句 since 表「因為」。
8. (B) 同上。
9. (B) now that = seeing that = since（因為）。
10. (B) since when 表「從何時開始…」。

1. (B) not … until …（直到…才…）。
2. (D) Not until … + 倒裝。
3. (A) It was not until … that … 固定句型。
4. (B) until 可搭配 hardly/scarcely 等否定副詞。
5. (B) till = until（直到…）

1. (B) your own 為 your own icebox 之略。
2. (A) own 作動詞時表「擁有」。
3. (C) not … until …（直到…才…）。
4. (B) likewise 是副詞，表「同樣地」。
5. (D) absorbed（被吸收）呼應前面的 digested（被消化）。

翻譯造句

1. On Sundays I usually sleep till noon.
2. You will not get homesick until you are away from home for a long time.
3. Nothing happened until the next morning.
4. Not until people lose their freedom will they know its value.
5. It was not until he was 25 years old that he was independent of his parents.

要點 4

聯考題型

1. (C) as soon as（一…就…）。
2. (A) once …（一旦…）。
3. (B) the minute/moment/instant … = as soon as …
4. (D) a written apology（書面的道歉）。
5. (A) no sooner 搭配 than。
6. (C) break up（分手）。
7. (D) hardly 搭配 when/before。
8. (A) once …（一旦…）。
9. (B) 同第3題。

10. (A) 時間副詞子句用現在式 V 表未來的動作。

克漏字

1. (A) the moment … = as soon as …
2. (D) 此處 ones = beings。
3. (A) that society 表「那一個特殊的社會」。
4. (B) 此處 as 為關代，指 the individual would be…。
5. (C) if taken = if the individual were taken

要點 5

聯考題型

1. (C) in order (for sb/sth) to …
2. (A) so that + S + V … 表「目的」。
3. (B) such + adj + 不可數/複數名詞。
4. (A) 同第2題。
5. (A) so as to = in order to（為了…目的）。
6. (C) as 為準關代，作 watching 的受詞。
7. (B) such … that … 表「如此…以致於…」。
8. (C) 同第3題。
9. (C) 此處的 such 是代名詞。
10. (B) so 作副詞修飾形容詞 careless。

克漏字

1. (B) be based on …（以…為基礎）。

2. (D) all walks of life（各行各業的人）。
3. (C) a striking difference（極大的不同）。
4. (A) so that … 表「目的」。
5. (B) the latter（後者）搭配 the former（前者）。

翻譯造句

1. It was such a boring speech that I fell asleep.
2. We take a rest so that we can go farther.
3. She opened the window so as to let some fresh air in.
4. TV is so influential that it can make anyone famous overnight.
5. I got up early in order to see the sunrise.

要點 6

聯考題型

1. (B) for fear of + V-ing（唯恐…）。
2. (D) lest + S + (should) + 原形 V.
3. (C) 同上。
4. (A) in case (that) …（以防/備…）。
5. (A) for fear that …（唯恐…）。

克漏字

1. (B) complexity（複雜性）。
2. (A) lest + S + (should) + 原形 V.
3. (C) in + 衣服（穿著…的衣服）。

4. (B) the same … that …（相同的）

5. (D) liking（喜歡）。

要點 7

聯考題型

1. (A) Just because …, it doesn't mean … 固定句法。

2. (C) as 表「因為」。

3. (D) for + n/V-ing表「因為」。

4. (A) because 表「因為」，是連接詞。

5. (B) since 表「因為/既然」。now that 需搭配現在式 V。

6. (A) as 表「因為」。

7. (A) out of … 表「由於…」。

8. (C) because 表「因為」，是連接詞。

9. (B) seeing that … 表「因為」。

10. (A) 同第4，8題。

克漏字

1. (B) in part because = partly because（部分原因是…）

2. (A) so that … 此處表「結果」。

3. (C) one = generation，避免重複。

4. (A) offspring（後代），單複數同形。

5. (D) limited（有限的）。

聯考題型

1. (C) Given that … （要是考慮到…）。
2. (D) unless 表「除非…」。
3. (D) as long as … （只要…）
4. (D) blood circulation 指「血液循環」。
5. (A) suppose/supposing (that) = if
6. (C) in the long run/term 表「將來」。
7. (B) assuming (that) = if
8. (C) if 表「假定/如果」。
9. (D) in case … 表「以免/防」。
10. (A) 同第1題。

克漏字

1. (A) live up to sb's expectations（達到某人的期望）。
2. (C) individual（個體/人）。
3. (B) as such = as an individual
4. (D) if + S + should … 表「萬一…」。
5. (A) what sb is 表「某人的身分/能力等」。

1. (C) dependable（可靠的）；dependent（依靠人的）。
2. (A) rarely 表「很少」。
3. (A) sound strange 表「聽起來很奇怪」。
4. (B) visualize（在心中形成圖像）。
5. (B) in spite of …（儘管…）。
6. (B) be confirmed（被證實）。
7. (D) not always（不總是）；not necessarily（未必）。
8. (D) even though = even if（即使）。
9. (D) economize（節約）是動詞。
10. (B) but 是表「相反/對照」的連接詞。

克漏字

1. (A) though 置於句末作副詞表「不過」。
2. (D) 此處 as 表「雖然」。
3. (B) exert/exercise influence（發揮影響力）。
4. (A) their 呼應其後的主詞 advertisers。
5. (C) 此處 classified 為 have classified 之略。

翻譯造句

1. Much as the twins look alike, I can distinguish between them.
2. Despite his old age, my grandfather likes making jokes.
3. I'll make my own choices even though my parents do not agree.
4. Although the boss has given her a raise, she keeps complaining.

5. He is tall and strong, but in fact he is very shy.

聯考題型

1. (C) whenever = no matter when（不論何時）。
2. (B) whether or not … = whether … or not（是否…）。
3. (C) consequence 應搭配 what。how 是副詞。
4. (D) regardless of …（不論…）。
5. (A) whoever = no matter who（不論誰）。
6. (B) believe it or not = whether you believe it or not
7. (C) rain or shine（不論雨晴），為固定說法。
8. (C) 此處 whoever = anyone who
9. (A) kick a habit（戒除一種習慣）。
10. (C) whichever = no matter which，表「一堆中的任一」。

克漏字

1. (A) as far as A is concerned（就 A 而言）。
2. (B) whatever = no matter what（不論什麼）。
3. (D) irrespective/regardless of …（不論…）。
4. (B) whether … A, B, or C（不論是 A, B 或 C）。
5. (B) when it comes to + n/V-ing（說到…）。

Unit 6

要點 1

聯考題型

1. (A) 子句是一個恆真的命題，其主詞為 the planets，搭配複數動詞 go。
2. (C) maintenance work（維修工作）。
3. (C) do not bite 於此處表蛇類「不主動攻擊人」。
4. (B) recycle sth（回收某物再利用）。
5. (B) be being + pp 表「正在被⋯」。
6. (B) inquisitive（好奇的）。
7. (B) 颱風來襲，動詞用 hit。
8. (A) spiritually 表「在精神上」。
9. (B) be being + adj 表「一時的行為」。
10. (A) make-believe 是形容詞，意為「虛構的」，故選 (A)。

克漏字

1. (C) go our way（照我們的方式發生）。
2. (B) imaginary（假想的）；imaginative（想像力豐富的）；imaginable（可想像而知的）。
3. (C) win the hand of sb（娶回某人當妻子）。
4. (A) A and B alike 表「AB 都一樣」。
5. (A) take revenge on sb（向某人報復）。

1. (D) get married 表「動作」，be married 表「狀態」。
2. (A) blossom (Vi) 表「開花；大放異彩」。
3. (C) Where <u>did</u> you come from? 問「你從哪裡來這兒？」Where <u>do</u> you come from? 或 Where are you from? 問「你是哪裡/國人？」
4. (A) headline sth（在…當中名列最前茅/表現最優）。
5. (B) shortly = soon（不久）；recently（過去的最近）。
6. (B) bring about = cause（造成）。
7. (D) 主詞 hurricanes 是複數，時間副詞表「最近幾個月以來」，故選 (D)。
8. (A) bring sb sth = bring sth to sb（為某人帶來某物）。
9. (D) 現在完成進行式強調「仍繼續下去」。
10. (B) must 是現在/未來「必須」，had to 是過去「必須」。

文意選填

1. (I) 空格前有 be，須接形容詞。(I) 項是唯一的形容詞。
2. (E) in + V-ing，就文意應用 managing（管理）。
3. (H) that 為關代，引導形容詞子句。
4. (G) reaction to sth 表「對某物的反應」。
5. (B) from sth 表「來/源自」某物。
6. (J) leading 作形容詞，表「主要的」。
7. (A) about + 數量詞，表「大約…」。
8. (C) even 表「甚至」。
9. (F) like = such as（像…），舉例用。
10. (D) as … as 表「相同程度」的比較。

1. (D) 因孩子沒見過野生動物在先。
2. (C) 過去完成式搭配 by + 過去的時間。
3. (A) when 引導另一個過去式子句與主要子句對比。
4. (A) by age 21 表「在21歲」之前。
5. (B) 連接詞 but 表對照。
6. (B) disconnected 表（電源）「被切斷」。
7. (C) ago 搭配過去簡單式；before 可搭配過去完成式。
8. (D) had never used … 比 said 早。
9. (C) had not eaten anything 在先。
10. (A) sue sb 表（到法院）「告某人」。

克漏字

1. (C) 家中發生的事情較 returned home 早。
2. (A) without a trace 喻東西消失得「無影無蹤」。
3. (B) vanish = disappear（消失）。
4. (C) walk away with = steal（偷走）。
5. (D) ransack 表「到處翻找」。

1. (C) 未來完成式搭配 by + 未來時間。
2. (D) 時間是 next Tuesday，所以要用未來完成式。
3. (B) 同第1題。
4. (C) 同第1題。
5. (A) 同第1題。

1. (B) 搭配 said 用 would。
2. (B) 同時。
3. (D) 正在用晚餐時故用過去進行式。
4. (D) be arrested（被逮捕）。
5. (D) 下雨較早並持續進行中。
6. (B) fail to + V 表「未能/沒有…」。
7. (B) fall 的過去式是 fell。
8. (B) 搭配 came 用 could …
9. (B) what I meant（我當時的意思）。
10. (D) had belonged to …（曾經屬於…）。

1. (B) beings 表（來自外太空的）「生物」。
2. (H) originated（起源）。
3. (E) keep an eye on …（監視…）。
4. (A) as well as（以及…）。
5. (G) still others 表「另有其他人」。
6. (I) since 作副詞，搭配現在完成式。
7. (F) like = such as（像…），舉例用。
8. (C) drawings（圖畫）和 writings 對舉。
9. (J) intend sb harm（有意傷害某人）。
10. (D) in any way（以任何方式）。

翻譯造句

1. My husband and I have been married for almost a year.
2. We were very happy in the first 8 months.
3. But it seems that he has been more interested in his work recently.
4. He works overtime almost every night.
5. What should I do to make him spend more time with me?

Unit 7

要點 1

聯考題型

1. (A) 動名詞作主詞表「一般」的行為。不定詞作主詞時表「計畫/意圖」的行為。
2. (C) being + adj = n 可作主詞或受詞。
3. (B) 動名詞（片語）作主詞一律接單數 V。
4. (D) 用 taking … 呼應之前的 reading …
5. (A) have a drinking problem（有酗酒的習慣）。
6. (C) 動名詞之前可用形容詞修飾。
7. (C) being sensible 表「明智的作為」。
8. (B) spend 搭配 V-ing 形式，snooze（打瞌睡）；sneeze（打噴嚏）。
9. (C) drunk driving（酒醉駕車）為固定說法。
10. (D) cloning（基因複製）。

文意選填

1. (F) forever 修飾動詞 last。
2. (I) be free from …（擺脫…）。
3. (H) take over 表「接管/手」。
4. (C) similarly（同樣地）。
5. (G) instead of + V-ing …（非但沒有…反而…）。
6. (B) consequently 表「結果，…」。
7. (A) break down（故障/破壞）。
8. (E) few + 複數名詞，表「很少…」。
9. (J) as long as（只要…）。
10. (D) indeed（的確）。

1. (B) being left alone 表「一個人獨處，不要有人陪」。
2. (A) 根據前後文意，應選 dying（死亡）
3. (D) speeding 指「開車超速」。
4. (B) bird watching（賞鳥），為固定說法。
5. (D) being nicknamed …（被取綽號為…）。

翻譯造句

1. I admit having been wrongly accused several times.
2. He is proud of having been a soldier.
3. I am ashamed of being a/your teacher.
4. She denied having been married.
5. I have a feeling of being cheated.

要點 3

聯考題型

1. (C) consider + V-ing（考慮從事…）。
2. (C) mean + V-ing（意謂…）。
3. (B) suggest + V-ing（建議做…）。
4. (D) distort（歪曲/扭曲…）。
5. (A) anticipate + V-ing（期望…）。

6. (A) avoid + V-ing（避免…）。

7. (B) resist + V-ing（抗拒…）。

8. (A) imagine + V-ing（想像一下…）。

9. (B) passive smoking = secondhand smoking（二手菸）。

10. (C) make up stories（虛構故事）。

克漏字

1. (A) do the/some shopping（購物）。

2. (B) in rags（衣衫襤褸）：rags 是「破舊的衣服」。

3. (D) judging from …（由…來判斷）。

4. (C) inviting 作形容詞，表「很吸引人的」。

5. (D) cannot help + V-ing（身不由己就…起來）。

要點 4

聯考題型

1. (A) not above asking questions（很樂於問問題）。

2. (B) in + V-ing 表「在…之時」。

3. (D) between V-ing and V-ing（因…又因…）。

4. (C) such as = like（像…），舉例用。

5. (A) against + V-ing 表「禁止/反對…」。

6. (C) instead of …（替代/而非…）。

7. (C) before crossing = before you cross

8. (B) like（像）為介系詞，應接 V-ing。

9. (A) be past + V-ing 表「不再…」。

10. (B) as 為介系詞，應接 V-ing。

文意選填

1. (C) leave sth behind（把某物留下，不帶走）。
2. (G) quite + adj/adv 表「十分…」。
3. (A) be sorry about …（對…很抱歉）。
4. (J) in the way（妨礙他人）。
5. (B) leave sth outside（把某物留在外面）。
6. (F) under normal circumstances（在正常的情況下）。
7. (I) make/cause a disturbance（製造糾紛）。
8. (D) securely（安穩地）修飾過去分詞 fixed（固定著）。
9. (H) come off（脫落）。
10. (E) not … any more than … 表「不…也不…」。

翻譯造句

1. Besides being a reporter, he is also a famous novelist.
2. The result is far from (being) satisfactory.
3. I feel like having/eating some ice cream.
4. What/How about having/eating lunch together?
5. She never goes to see a movie without buying some popcorn.

要點 5

聯考題型

1. (B) be accustomed/used to + V-ing（習慣於…）。
2. (C) devote one's life/time to + V-ing（致力於…）。
3. (D) be addicted to + V-ing（沉湎於…）。
4. (C) at the cost of …（耗費了…）。

5. (B) dye（染色）的動名詞形式為 dyeing。
6. (B) take to + V-ing（開始）喜歡從事…。
7. (A) amount to + V-ing（等於是…）。
8. (C) devote one's time to + V-ing（致力於…）。
9. (B) come close to + V-ing（差一點就…）。
10. (A) entertain sb（娛樂/招待某人）。

翻譯造句

1. When it comes to cooking, she is all thumbs.
2. I object to being treated like this.
3. He is not equal to running such a business.
4. I prefer brisk walking to jogging.
5. David moved to the countryside with a view to leading a simpler life.

要點 6

聯考題型

1. (B) cease to beat = stop beating（停止跳動）。
2. (D) begin + V-ing/to + V。
3. (A) novel 作形容詞表「新奇的」。
4. (B) 已經將衣服送洗。
5. (C) regret + V-ing 表「後悔曾/已經…」。
6. (A) regret + 不定詞，表「抱歉將要…」。
7. (D) 記得曾經被人介紹給他認識。
8. (C) hum a tune（哼支曲子）。
9. (B) 接著做另一件事用 go on to do sth。
10. (B) mean + V-ing 表「意謂」…
11. (B) watering（澆水）。

12. (D) need + V-ing = need to be + pp（需要被…）
13. (D) deserve to be well paid = deserve a good pay
14. (B) remember to do sth（要記得做某事）。
15. (A) cannot bear + V-ing（無法忍受…）。

翻譯造句

1. A pedestrian stopped to pick up a coin.
2. Let's go on doing what should have been finished yesterday.
3. The man run down by a motorcycle tried to stand up, but in vain.
4. I remember being chased by a mean dog.
5. She deserves to be handsomely rewarded.

要點 7

聯考題型

1. (A) keep body and soul together（維持生計），固定說法。
2. (C) have (good) fun + V-ing
3. (A) make oneself understood（使別人瞭解自己的意思）。
4. (B) do the/some + V-ing（做…的事）。
5. (C) go + V-ing（從事…活動）。

翻譯造句

1. They had a good time making jokes last night.
2. We had no difficulty fnding your home.
3. Peter and his girlfriend will go whitewater rafting this weekend.

4. It's your turn to do the ironing.
5. Let's go surfing this afternoon, shall we?

Unit 8

要點 1

聯考題型

1. (A) 不定詞（片語）作主詞接單數 V，故選 is。用has 無意義。
2. (C) remind sb of sth（提醒某人某事）。
3. (B) make it a rule + 不定詞（養成⋯之習慣）。
4. (C) seek to do sth（設法去⋯）。
5. (B) It is + adj. + for + O + 不定詞，固定句法。
6. (D) observe（觀察）。
7. (D) believe + O. + 不定詞 = believe (that) + S + V
8. (C) seem + 不定詞，be driven by ⋯（為⋯所驅使）。
9. (A) choose to do sth（寧願⋯）。
10. (A) 主詞 purpose 搭配不定詞作補語。

克漏字

1. (C) 用 shout（吼叫）呼應之前的 yell（喊叫）。
2. (A) raise one's voices（提高嗓門）。
3. (C) someone superior（上司/主管）。
4. (D) 用 them 呼應前文的 friends。
5. (C) likewise（同樣地）。
6. (C) kisses（親吻）呼應前文的 hugs（擁抱）。
7. (B) get uneasy（覺得不自在）。
8. (A) by（憑藉）。by which 指 by these obvious signals。
9. (D) Besides ⋯, there are ⋯（除⋯之外，還有⋯）。
10. (B) whether ⋯ or ⋯ 形成相反的「對照」，故須用 distant 來跟前文的 close 形成對比。

1. (C) to read by = by which I could read（藉燭光來閱讀）。
2. (B) replace（取代）= take place of
3. (D) to cook in = in which we can cook
4. (A) 名詞 + 不定詞片語（作形容詞用）。
5. (A) turn to sb for help（求助於某人）。
6. (A) 同第4題。
7. (A) write … down（把…寫下來）。
8. (B) have much/a lot to do with …（與…大有關係）。
9. (B) to kill time with = with which she could kill time
10. (B) to live in = in which they could live

翻譯造句

1. He is not a man to break his word.
2. To skip breakfast is not a good way to lose weight.
3. Thank you for giving me the chance to make the speech.
4. They are to get married next month.
5. There is nothing to worry about.

1. (B) so as to = in order to（為了…目的）。
2. (A) publicity（曝光/知名度）。
3. (A) such 為代名詞，表「到如此程度/地步」，作主詞補語。
4. (B) commonplace（普遍的）是形容詞，須用副詞 so 修飾。
5. (D) only to + 原形 V 表「意外的結果」。
6. (C) To contribute … = If you'd like to contribute…
7. (A) Keep sb waiting（讓某人等）；be sorry + 不定詞。
8. (C) be in place（就緒）。
9. (C) with a view to + V-ing（為了…）。
10. (A) promote products（促銷產品）。

翻譯造句

1. He is anxious to know the examination result.
2. Michael is easy to get along with.
3. We are perfectly willing to cooperate with the police.
4. I hurried to the station, only to discover the train had gone.
5. Her misery was such that everybody was in tears.

1. (C) 不定詞完成式的動作早於主要 V。
2. (A) pretend to be playing …（假裝正在彈…）。
3. (D) 同第1題。
4. (D) (which is) about to be launched …（即將被發射出去…）。
5. (A) need + 不定詞（需要…）。
6. (C) be here to + 原形 V（來/在這裡…）。
7. (D) 同第1題。
8. (A) last（持續）無被動式。
9. (D) 同第1題。
10. (C) 同第1題。

1. (A) address + 一群人（向一群人演講）。
2. (B) with … in mind（鑑於…）。
3. (B) be delighted to + V …（很高興…）。
4. (C) be covered（被報導/刊載）。
5. (D) glance at sth（很快地掠過…一眼）。
6. (A) 分詞構句。
7. (D) expect to be surrounded …（期望被包圍著）。
8. (A) alone（孤單地）。
9. (C) an audience（一群聽眾）。
10. (B) everyday = daily（日常的）。

1. (B) never too old to learn（學習永不嫌老）。
2. (C) too … to（太…以致於不…）。
3. (B) too … for + n.（太…以致於不…）。
4. (A) be busy + V-ing …（忙於…）。
5. (B) 根據語意應選 perceptible（可以覺察的）。大意為：人類歷史太短暫了，所以人性有任何改變也覺察不出來。

翻譯造句

1. It is never too late to give up smoking.
2. I am too poor to afford such luxuries.
3. She is too young to know about love.
4. My younger brother is only too happy to see you again.
5. He is too careful not to have noticed that mistake.

要點 6

聯考題型

1. (B) crawl（爬行）。
2. (A) make sb do sth，make 為使役 V。
3. (A) run over（被輾過），這個 run 是 pp.。
4. (A) why not + 原形 V…? = Why don't we + 原形 V …?

5. (B) make sb's dream come true（使某人的夢想成真）。
6. (C) let + O + 原形 V。
7. (A) All you have to do is + 原形 V。
8. (B) 根據文意應選 overtired（過勞的）。
9. (A) Let that be a lesson to you … 為固定說法。
10. (B) desire nothing but + 不定詞（只想要…）。

克漏字

1. (D) being shy = shyness，此處作 be 動詞的補語。
2. (B) named 為 who is named 之略。
3. (C) tell sb to do sth。take it easy（放輕鬆點）。
4. (C) all sb has to do is + 原形 V。
5. (D) remain = continue to be。

要點 7

聯考題型

1. (D) let alone = not to speak of（更不必提…了）。
2. (C) to do sb justice（為某人說句公道話）。
3. (A) to cut/make a long story short（長話短說）。
4. (C) to say the least（說最輕微的）。
5. (A) strange to say（說來奇怪），固定說法。

1. (C) to define it（要是給它下個定義）。
2. (A) what = the thing(s) which。
3. (C) make a living（謀生）。
4. (B) the kind = the kind of work。work（工作）不可數，不能用 (the) one。
5. (A) in line with = similar to（與…相似）。

Unit 9

要點 1

聯考題型

1. (B) a lost/missed opportunity（失去的機會）。
2. (C) baked（被烘烤過的）。
3. (B) interested 表「本身感到有興趣的」。
4. (A) opposing (= opposite)，表「完全相反的」。
5. (C) a required course（一門必修課）。
6. (A) stand by（在一旁待命）。
7. (B) canned food（罐頭食品）。
8. (A) forthcoming（即將出現/版的）。
9. (A) running water = tap water（自來水）。
10. (B) practiced（訓練有素的）；practical（實用的）。

克漏字

1. (B) increasing 表「逐漸增加的」。
2. (D) 用現在完成式搭配 in recent years。
3. (D) the authorities concerned（相關主管機關）。
4. (A) pursue（追求）。
5. (A) be free from（免除/擺脫）；be freed from（被從⋯釋放）。

1. (D) changed 表「已有/被改變」。
2. (B) wanting = who want 之略。
3. (C) catch sb doing sth（逮到某人正在做…）。
4. (D) 此處 scattered = which are scattered。
5. (B) leave sb wondering …（使某人想知道…）。
6. (C) expressing = which expresses。
7. (A) hear it said that …（聽說…）。
8. (C) 此處 applying = who were applying。
9. (A) accusing（主動）指控…。
10. (B) exploded 本義為「爆炸」，引申為「氣炸了」。
11. (A) 本句為倒裝句，主詞為 a school teacher，須用動詞sat。
12. (C) those interested 為 those who are interested 之略。
13. (B) dozing/dropping off（主動）表「無意中睡著」。
14. (A) make a U-turn（汽車）作 U 字形迴轉。
15. (A) watered（被灌溉）為 which is watered 之略。

克漏字

1. (B) 此處 shot 表「被拍攝」。
2. (A) hit on an idea（突然有個想法/心血來潮）。
3. (C) a leading man/lady = a male/female lead（男/女主角）。
4. (C) come along with sb（跟某人一道過來）。
5. (C) expected（被期待的）。

1. (B) n. + included（…也被包含其中）。
2. (A) 主詞是 pictures，用複數 V include。
3. (D) n. + excluded（不包含…）。
4. (A) regarding sth（關於某事/物）。
5. (B) pending + n. 表「等候…處理」。
6. (A) following … = after … 表「在…之後」。
7. (D) failing that 表「如果那樣不行的話」。
8. (A) including + n.（包含…）。
9. (B) barring + n. 表「除非…發生」，為介系詞。
10. (C) touching = concerning = regarding（關於）。

1. (A) a growing phenomenon（一個日益普遍的現象）。
2. (A) including + n.（包含…）。
3. (C) while moving 為 while they are moving 之略。
4. (D) choose from + 一堆東西/人物，表「從中選擇…」。
5. (B) anywhere 呼應前文的 home 和 to a picnic area 等副詞（片語）。

1. (A) cooking 引導分詞構句修飾 my mom。注意：本句如去掉逗點，cooking 引導分詞片語修飾 the thief，句意全然不同。
2. (B) while searching for … = while they are searching for …。
3. (B) weather permitting = if weather permits（如果天氣許可）。
4. (C) squeezing（將…擠入），表「主動」。
5. (C) it being fine 為 because it was fine 之略。
6. (A) recognizing（認出…），表「主動」。
7. (C) not + V-ing 或 not being + pp 為固定語法。
8. (D) starting around …（約自…開始），表「主動」。
9. (C) 此處 being fine 為 because it is fine 之略。
10. (D) while singing 為 while she was singing 之略。
11. (C) there being no taxi … 為 because there was no taxi … 之略。
12. (C) based on sth（按照…），固定語法。
13. (C) when asked .. 為 when she was asked … 之略。
14. (B) 此處 faced with = because they are faced with …。
15. (A) 此處 told = after the traveler was told。

克漏字

　　某公司冒險投入新的市場時，需要面對各種不同的問題。這些問題可以概括區分成幾類，包括(1)文化因素，(2)經濟問題，(3)地理因素，(4)政治/法律問題，(5) 宗教因素，以及(6) 科技問題。請為下列每一段文章所討論的問題找出適當的分類。

　　某公司與該國的商業氣候相較時，由於它是個外國公司，這時該公司就會面臨這類問題。比方說，可口可樂在印度被要求做個選擇：不是透露它的秘方就是離開印度，因此就面臨了這樣一個問題。可口可樂選擇一走了之。不過幾年後印度歡

迎可口可樂再度回來時，該公司卻遭到政治活躍份子的騷擾及不斷的干預。

1. (D) 上列一段文章最恰當的歸類就是 ＿＿＿＿＿。
   (A) 宗教因素　　　(B) 經濟問題　　　(C) 地理因素　　　(D) 政治/法律問題

　　　　這類問題會對產品的屬性造成衝擊。這種衝擊會迫使公司調整產品以符合當地市場的需求。要解決這些問題，就應評估市場經濟發展的程度，例如可藉由收益數值、當地消費者的購買力及該外國市場的基礎建設狀況來評估。這些指數可為公司的行銷策略提供重要的訊息。

2. (B) 上列一段文章最恰當歸類是 ＿＿＿＿＿。
   (A) 文化因素　　　(B) 經濟問題　　　(C) 地理因素　　　(D) 技術問題

　　　　研究人員在研究新市場時，這些問題可能是他會遭遇到的最大問題。此乃因為基於種種不同的理由，那些被歸類成屬性相同的市場，在談到這一方面時，往往就成了屬性迥異的市場。即使在同一個國家，也有相異之處。因此，加拿大的旅遊廣告就被劃分成英語觀眾及法語觀眾兩塊區域。為英語觀眾所設計的旅遊廣告畫面只顯示妻子一個人，而為法語觀眾所設計的畫面則是夫妻檔。之所以這樣做乃因法國人的家庭關係比較密切。

3. (A) 上列一段文章最恰當的歸類是 ＿＿＿＿＿。
   (A) 文化因素　　　(B) 經濟問題　　　(C) 地理因素　　　(D) 政治/法律問題

要點 5

聯考題型

1. (C) a blue-collar work（工人），固定說法。blue-blooded 表「貴族的」。
2. (A) high-tech（高科技的）。
3. (B) one-armed（獨臂的），固定說法。
4. (A) one-month/two-week/three-day 皆固定說法。
5. (D) be caught red-handed（被當場逮到）。
6. (B) insecticide-treated（經過殺蟲劑處理過的）。
7. (B) a red-carpet welcome（隆重的歡迎）。
8. (C) eagle-eyed（鷹眼般的；目光銳利的）。

9. (D) a candle-lit dinner（燭光晚餐），為固定說法。

10. (C) bright-colored（顏色鮮明的）。

11. (A) off-putting 表「令人分心的」。

12. (A) dress-down（非正式穿著的），與 dress-up（盛裝的）相對。
    另外，dressing-down 表「申斥/責罵」。

13. (C) a two-headed snake 即「雙頭蛇」。

14. (A) a red-letter day（特別重要的日子）。

15. (A) well-meaning（善意的），修飾人。well-meant（善意的），修飾言行。

要點 6

聯考題型

1. (A) speaking of … = when it comes to …（說到…）。

2. (B) biological clock（生理時鐘）。

3. (A) speak of the devil！（說曹操，曹操到）。

4. (C) judging from …（由…來判斷），固定說法。

5. (B) all things considered（全盤考慮之後）。

克漏字

1. (B) broadly/generally/roughly speaking（一般而言）。

2. (C) leading factors（主要的因素）。

3. (A) a breadwinner（賺錢養家活口的人）。

4. (B) on the increase = increasing（增加中）。

5. (D) comparatively speaking（比較而言）。

Unit 10

翻譯造句

1. Will you run a bath for me?
2. My son shall not be treated like that.
3. I will/shall come of age next month.
4. Shall I do the dishes for you?
5. Let's eat something different, shall we?

要點 2

翻譯造句

1. They would sometimes invite us over for the weekend.
2. She used to be an actress; therefore, she is used to such an occasion.
3. Now a lot of cellphones can be used to take pictures.
4. Would it be OK if I left now?
5. I would like to have a glass of mineral water.

翻譯造句

1. Those who park illegally should be fined.
2. You ought not to do anything by halves.
3. You should have called the police.
4. It's a pity that she should have given up hope.
5. I would/should like to see more of you.

要點 4

翻譯造句

1. My father is getting older. He can't read without wearing glasses.
2. Kids at his age can be very rebellious.
3. My grandfather could swim across the river when (he was) young.
4. Can you help me do the laundry?
5. Only Tom was at home then. He can't have eaten all the food.
6. Who stole my car? It could have been my younger brother, but I'm not sure.
7. You could have been fired !
8. Could I have a drink of water, please?
9. Their lifestyles couldn't be more different.
10. I know he is as rich as can be.

要點 5

翻譯造句

1. Since it is getting late, we may as well go home.
2. Sorry, he's not in. May I take a message?
3. The child may have gotten lost.
4. This is a phenomenon (that) we might well worry about.
5. A bad cold may easily lead to some complications.

要點 6

翻譯造句

1. Rich people need not worry about their meals.
2. I need not have written the letter because I sent her a text message right after that.
3. You need only sign your name here to get a free gift.
4. Do I need to buy tickets for the kids?
5. David will work overtime, if need be.

要點 7

翻譯造句

1. All passengers aboard must have their seat/safety belts fastened.

2. Her grandfather must be nearly 90 now.
3. I had to leave earlier yesterday afternoon in order to pick up my kids.
4. I can't find my purse. It must have been stolen.
5. This film/movie is a must-see.

要點 8

翻譯造句

1. I dare not reveal/disclose the secret.
2. Only a few students dare to answer the teacher's questions.
3. Last night they dared me to steal a bottle of whiskey from the supermarket.
4. Don't you dare talk to me like that !
5. How dare you say I'm a thief !

Unit 11

要點 1

聯考題型

1. (B) 用簡單式（被動）搭配 every day/week/year 等。
2. (D) be arrested（被逮捕）。
3. (C) is/are being + pp 表「現在正被…」。
4. (B) 交通系統 + be paralyzed（交通系統癱瘓）。
5. (D) is being grilled（正在被燒烤）。
6. (A) be held = take place（舉行）。
7. (D) enjoy being + pp 表「喜歡被人…」。
8. (A) be offered the opportunity（被提供機會）。
9. (B) 此處 once believed = which was once believed。
10. (B) be injuried（由於意外所傷）；be wounded（被武器所傷）。

要點 2

聯考題型

1. (A) do away with …（廢除…）。
2. (C) inhabit (= live in)，是 Vt，可用被動式。
3. (B) put up with … 表「忍受…」，其被動式是 be put up with。
4. (A) break down（故障/停擺），沒有被動式。
5. (D) be taken care of（被照顧）。
6. (A) read（主動）like…（讀起來像…）；be read as …（被解讀為…）如：Her silence can be read as refusal.（她的沉默可以被解讀為拒絕）。
7. (D) believe in God（相信上帝）。

8. (A) be transformed into …（被轉變成…）。
9. (B) be taken advantage of（被利用/佔便宜）。
10. (D) be isolated（被隔離）。本句搭配 since then 須用現在完成式。

要點 3

聯考題型

1. (A) deserted 表（房屋）「被遺棄」，沒人住。
2. (C) hurry out of somewhere（自某地匆忙離開）。
3. (D) be heard/seen/felt + 不定詞/V-ing …。
4. (A) have sb do sth（使某人做…），have 為「使役 V」。
5. (D) be made + 不定詞（被迫…）。
6. (A) be pictured + V-ing（被拍攝到正在…）。
7. (D) let sth be + pp 表「讓某物被…」。
8. (B) 同第3題。
9. (C) 同第3題。
10. (A) 同第3題。

要點 4

句子改寫 / 填充

1. Has the movie seen by you?
2. At what
3. To whom
4. With which
5. In what

1. (A) be frightened/scared/afraid of …（害怕）。
2. (B) be excited at + 機會/希望。
3. (A) be engaged to sb 表「與某人訂婚」。
4. (A) be covered in/with …（被一層…覆蓋著）。
5. (B) be occupied by sb …（由…佔/使用）。
6. (A) be occupied with …（忙著…）。
7. (D) be made into + 成品。
8. (C) be adapted for television（改編成電視劇）。
9. (A) be known as … 表「以…的身分/場所有名」。
10. (D) 本句為諺語，意為「觀其友知其人」。

1. (A) resemble = look like（像…），沒有被動式。
2. (C) take place = be held（舉行）。
3. (A) consist of = be made up/composed of（由…組成）。
4. (B) 主詞是 a bouquet，用單數 V。
5. (A) taste/look/sound 表「嚐/看/聽起來…」時沒有被動式。

Unit 12

要點 1

聯考題型

1. (B) 恆真命題，用現在式 V。
2. (D) 本句亦屬 if 引導的恆真命題。
3. (B) 條件句的未來用現在式代之。
4. (A) 同上。
5. (C) 同第1題。
6. (C) 本句屬未來可能發生的情況。
7. (A) 吃/服藥一律用 take。
8. (B) 不變的事實。
9. (C) 同上題。
10. (A) 同第6題。

要點 2

聯考題型

1. (B) do likewise 表「（也）有同樣的做法」。likewise 為副詞。
2. (C) 本句屬與過去事實相反的假設。
3. (D) 本句屬與現在事實相反的假設。
4. (A) 同上題。
5. (D) 同第2題。
6. (C) 假設語氣。
7. (D) 同第3題。happen to + V 表「恰好…」。
8. (D) 同第2題。

9. (C) 同第3題。
10. (A) 過去的假設影響至目前。

要點 3

聯考題型

1. (D) 不（太）可能的未來假設用 If + S + were to …。
2. (C) 問題的「產/發生」，英文用 arise 或 come up。
3. (A) would rather 表「寧願」。
4. (A) there + be 動詞，表「有…」。
5. (D) 絕不可能的未來假設。
6. (A) 不確定的未來假設用 If + S + should …。
7. (D) 與過去事實相反的假設。
8. (B) 火山「爆發」的英文動詞是 erupt。
9. (D) 同第1題。
10. (D) If + S + should …, + 祈使句。

要點 4

聯考題型

1. (A) If + S + 現在式 V，+ 祈使句。
2. (C) 直說法，動詞如實反映時間。
3. (A) 同上。
4. (D) 同上。
5. (B) 同上。

1. (A) 表「若非…」用 but for/without + n.。
2. (B) 同上。
3. (C) If it had not been for … 表「若非過去…」。
4. (C) S + should/would + have + pp …, but/only + S + 過去式 V。
5. (D) 同上。

翻譯造句

1. But for my bad cold, I wouldn't have called in sick.
2. Without the typhoon, all the summer camp activities would have taken place as scheduled.
3. But for a flight delay, we would be at home now.
4. Without a few grammatical mistakes, the composition would be a good one.
5. Many victims would have starved to death, only/but the government took emergency measures.

要點 6

聯考題型

1. (D) I wish I did. = I wish I liked it。
2. (D) 與過去事實相反。
3. (B) wishful thinking 表不切實際的「如意算盤」。
4. (C) 祝福的句型：S + wish + O + n./well.。

5. (B) 同上。
6. (A) I wish I could … = I cannot …。
7. (D) I wish (that) sb could/would …。
8. (D) 同第2題。
9. (A) 同第4題。
10. (B) If only you knew … = I wish you knew …。

要點 7

聯考題型

1. (B) 與現在事實相反，用過去式 V 表現在。
2. (C) 接近事實。
3. (B) As if it mattered！= It doesn't matter at all.。
4. (C) by magic（藉魔術）。
5. (A) 接近事實。
6. (B) 與事實相反。
7. (A) as though = as if（好像…似的）。
8. (B) 省略句型，不定詞表「目的」。
9. (B) 與事實相反。
10. (B) 同上。

要點 8

聯考題型

1. (C) It's (about) time + (that) + S + 過去式 V …。
2. (D) 同上。

3. (B) It's (high) time + (that) + S + 過去式 V …。
4. (D) to be maintained 表汽車「被維修」。
5. (B) 同第1題。

要點 9

聯考題型

1. (A) would rather/sooner/as soon + 原形 V。
2. (D) 表「寧願他人/物…」，用過去式 V 或 had + pp.。
3. (D) 同上。
4. (C) 同第1題。
5. (B) 同第2題。

翻譯造句

1. He would rather go to another restaurant than stand in line here.
2. I would rather (that) you stayed at home tomorrow.
3. I have much to say (that) I would rather not.
4. She would sooner keep silent.
5. These soldiers would as soon sacrifice their lives as surrender.

1. (A) 表「建議/要求/命令/堅持」所接的子句用 (should) + 原形 V。
2. (C) be given 為 should be given 之略。
3. (D) 同第2題。
4. (A) 此處的 suggested 表「暗示」，接直說法 V。
5. (C) 同第2題。
6. (A) 同第1題。
7. (C) 同第1題。
8. (D) be on sick leave（請病假），此處用直說法。
9. (A) 同第1題。
10. (B) 同第1題。

Unit 13

要點 1

聯考題型

1. (B) 主詞是 the technological development，單數。
2. (A) driving cars 指「開車的行為」，單數；driving lessons 是「駕駛訓練的課程」，複數。
3. (A) 主詞是 the products，複數。
4. (A) many a(n) + n + 單數 V，此處為「被動」。
5. (A) bacon and eggs（培根蛋）視為一道早餐，單數。
6. (D) 主詞為複數，用完成式搭配 up to the present time。
7. (B) 動名詞片語作主詞，接單數 V。
8. (D) 名詞片語作主詞接單數 V。pose（構成）；pause（停頓）。
9. (A) 不定詞作主詞接單數 V。另外，always 須置於 has 和 been 之間方可。
10. (B) 名詞子句作主詞接單數 V。sth is anybody's guess 表「沒有人知道這回事」。

要點 2

聯考題型

1. (A) a number of …接複數 V。
2. (B) the number of …接單數 V。
3. (A) be composed of …（由…組成）。此處 family 指「家庭」。
4. (A) 學科名稱作主詞 + 單數 V。
5. (C) 金額作主詞 + 單數 V。
6. (A) politics（政治學）作主詞接單數 V。
7. (A) statistics（統計學）作主詞接單數 V。

8. (B) statistics（統計數字）作主詞接複數 V。

9. (B) the police 搭配複數 V，此處用被動。

10. (A) 主詞為 a list 接單數 V，此處用被動。

11. (A) measles（麻疹）搭配單數 V。

12. (B) acoustics 指「音響效果」時搭配複數 V。

13. (A) this species 指「這一種」，搭配單數 V。如果是 these species（這幾種）則搭配複數 V。

14. (B) 此處的 ethics 指「道德原則」，接複數 V。

15. (B) 此處的 politics 指「政治理念」，接複數 V。

要點 3

聯考題型

1. (B) 主詞為 two $100 bills and a few coins，複數。

2. (A) there/here you go 用於將某物交給某人時。

3. (D) time 為不可數名詞。

4. (A) 百分比 + 單數 n. + 單數 V。

5. (B) some of the/my + 複數 n. + 複數 V。

6. (C) damage（破壞），不可數，搭配單數 V。

7. (B) damages（賠償金）作主詞時用複數 V。

8. (B) crew 指船/飛機上的所有組員，是複數名詞。

9. (A) (a large/small) part of + 單數 n. + 單數 V。

10. (A) 主詞複數 (a famous host … and his wife)，用 are。

1. (B) that 的先行詞是單數名詞 oratory（逞口舌之能），接單數 V。
2. (B) A as well as B，動詞單複數與 A 一致。
3. (B) 靠近 the cat 搭配單數 V。
4. (A) 靠近 a machine gun，用單數 V。
5. (D) not only A but (also) B + V（與 B 一致）。
6. (A) 與靠近的 tap water 一致。
7. (B) 主詞是 the woman，搭配單數 V。
8. (D) be missing 指（東西）「不在原來的地方」；be lost 指東西「搞丟了」。A together with B + V.（與 A 一致）
9. (A) be reported to have been + pp（據傳已被…）。
10. (B) A along with B + V（與 A 一致）。

Unit 14

聯考題型

1. (B) 指機會被給。
2. (D) loss 是名詞，lose 是動詞。
3. (D) 此處 mine = my fault，其它選項不合慣用。
4. (C) sth cannot be found everywhere 表「某物只能在某些地方找到」。
5. (D) neither（兩者任一）。

克漏字

1. (B) not … entirely（不完全）。
2. (C) contact（接觸）；contract（契約）。
3. (A) not necessarily 表「未必」。
4. (B) adopt（採用/取）。
5. (C) past and present（過去和現在），固定說法。

要點 2

聯考題型

1. (A) be otherwise engaged 表「已另有安排」。
2. (D) not … because …（不因…才…）。
3. (A) be equal to sth 表「有能力勝任…」。

4. (D) Just because … doesn't mean … 為固定用法。

5. (D) not because …, nor because …, but because … 表「不是因為…，也非因為…，而是因為…」，固定說法。

引導寫作

1. not, but, less, effort, itself
2. to, lie, in, but, from

要點 3

聯考題型

1. (C) cannot be too + adj = cannot be + adj + enough。

2. (C) 同上。

3. (D) cannot … too quickly 表「愈快愈好」，指「速度」。

4. (A) 本句為 cannot … too … 的變體。

5. (A) cannot … too soon 表「愈快愈好」，指在最短的時間內，無關「速度」。

6. (B) cannot be overemphasized（再怎麼強調也不為過）。

7. (C) cannot get enough of sth 表「極為喜歡某物」。

8. (D) cannot thank you enough = cannot thank you too much。

9. (C) can't be overestimated/overemphasized，同第6題。

10. (B) 同第7題。

1. (C) S + never + V + but + S + V … （不…則已，一…就…）。
2. (B) 本句屬 not so/such … but … 的變體。
3. (D) 本句屬 not so/such … but … 的變體。
4. (C) 同第1題。
5. (D) 同第1題。

克漏字

1. (B) not so/such … but … 的變體。
2. (C) not/never … until …（直到…才…）。
3. (A) regarding = concerning = about（關/對於…）。
4. (C) regained（復得）。
5. (D) treasure sth 表「珍惜某物」。

1. (C) none but + 人，表「只有某人」。
2. (A) 本句意為：除了少數的幾個親信外，所有的人都痛恨這位政治強人。
3. (C) none other than …（不是別人，正是…）。
4. (A) anything but 表「絕非…」。
5. (D) enjoy nothing but + V-ing 表「只喜歡從事…」。

6. (B) nothing but + 事物/身分。A pavement artist（英式）是一名「街頭藝術家」；美式的說法是 a sidewalk artist.。

7. (A) 同第4題。

8. (B) all but = almost（幾乎）。

9. (D) 同第1題。

10. (C) 同第4題。

要點 6

聯考題型

1. (C) for free = for nothing = free (of charge) 表「免費地」。

2. (B) sb does not help you for nothing（某人不是平白無故幫忙你）。

3. (C) nothing like …（一點都不像…）。

4. (A) there is nothing like + n/V-ing 表「（做）…最好」。

5. (C) there is nothing in/to sth 表「某事非真」。

6. (C) there is nothing to it 表「這事太簡單了」。

7. (D) nothing less than … = nothing short of …（簡直…）。

8. (B) 此處 He has nothing on you … 表「他不比你強」。

9. (C) 此處表「警方沒有 Brad 的犯罪記錄」。

10. (D) It's nothing 表「這不算什麼」。

要點 7

聯考題型

1. (D) A rather than B（是 A 而非 B）。

2. (A) cannot so much as + 原形 V（甚至都不會…）。

3. (C) how he looks = what he looks like（他的長相）。

4. (D) get a wink of sleep 表「闔一眼」。
5. (C) not so much that … but that …（與其說是…不如說是…）。

克漏字

1. (B) viruses（病毒）。
2. (A) a sufficient number 表「一個足夠的量」。
3. (C) not so much that … but that …。
4. (A) get the upper hand（佔上風/優勢）。
5. (B) fall prey/victim to sth（成為…的受害者）。

要點 8

聯考題型

1. (B) No + V-ing/n 表「禁止/反對…」。
2. (A) there is no + V-ing …（不可能…）。
3. (C) 同第2題。
4. (B) the last + n. + (that) + S + V … 表「絕/最不…」。
5. (A) the last + n. + 不定詞…表「絕/最不…」。
6. (C) 同第1題。
7. (C) there is no knowing/telling …（不可能知道…）。
8. (A) how much longer 表「還有多久」。
9. (D) 同第4題。
10. (B) 同第5題。

1. (B) on + adj + terms 表「處於…之關係」。
2. (A) drop by/in（臨時來訪）。
3. (C) while = although。
4. (D) waste money on sth（浪費錢在某物上）。
5. (A) the last + (n) + 不定詞（絕/最不可能…）。

Unit 15

要點 1

聯考題型

1. (C) not so … as …（不如…一樣…）。
2. (A) be best known for（以…最為有名），固定說法。
3. (D) 最高級的比較須包含自己於其中。all her sisters 不包含 Jane。
4. (B) 比台北 101 高 180 呎，用比較級。
5. (C) 絕對最高級不加 "the"。
6. (B) both more … and more …。
7. (B) 兩方面的比較用比較級。
8. (A) as + 原級 adj + as …。
9. (D) the least + adj. + (n) →最不…的…。
10. (D) the most + adj. + (n) →最…的…。

翻譯造句

1. Tony is taller than everyone/anyone else in his class.
2. He is not so honest as he looks.
3. He is not as diligent a student as his younger brother.
4. His younger brother is the more dependable of the two.
5. I like Tony less than his young brother.

聯考題型

1. (C) the same age as … = as old as …。
2. (A) as … as possible（儘可能…）。
3. (B) as … as can be 表「極為…」。
4. (B) as … as ever（…一如往常）。
5. (B) a lame duck（跛腳鴨），喻已失去權勢的人。
6. (D) as good as = almost（簡直…）。
7. (A) as it is = in fact（事實上）。
8. (B) as it is（句末）= already（已經）。
9. (B) so to speak = as it were（可以說是）。
10. (C) as … as ever lived（有史以來最…的…）。

要點 3

聯考題型

1. (B) 本句為諺語，意為「自作自受」。
2. (A) eagle（老鷹）。
3. (B) 意為：護士之於病人如同母親之於孩子。
4. (B) lung（肺）；liver（肝）；kidney（腎）；spleen（脾）。
5. (C) As …, so …（正如…，所以…）。

1. (D) Just as …, so … 固定句型。
2. (B) be capable of + V-ing/n→能夠（做）…。
3. (B) considerable（相當多的）。
4. (A) by itself = alone（單獨）。
5. (A) rather than …（而非…）。

要點 4

翻譯造句

1. The government is nothing/little more than a puppet regime.
2. I'm no more a millionaire than you are a philanthropist.
3. No less/fewer than ten mountain climbers are missing.
4. It seems you are no less jealous of me than she.
5. It's no better than a case of blackmail.

克漏字

1. (C) nothing more than = nothing but = only（不過）。
2. (A) achieve the goal 表「達成目標」。
3. (C) assure sb of sth（保證某人擁有/獲得某物）。
4. (B) cannot last long（無法維持長久）。
5. (B) no less … than …（與…一樣…）。

1. (A) take a hot bath（洗個熱水澡）。
2. (B) 本句是I have never met a more funny person than him 的倒裝。
3. (D) 此處的 than 為介系詞，故接受格形式的 whom。
4. (B) nothing is less valued 是 nothing is less valued than time 之略。
5. (B) couldn't care less 表「最不在乎」。
6. (A) none the wiser 表「還是不明白」。
7. (B) not/nobody … any the wiser = none the wiser。
8. (D) know better than + 不定詞。
9. (C) couldn't … + 比較級 表「最為…」。
10. (A) bore holes 表「鑽孔/挖洞」。

要點 6

1. (C) 本題意為：吃得越少，就越健康。
2. (B) at the mercy of … 表「受制於…」。
3. (D) less and less「越來越不…」。
4. (D) less A than B = more B than A。
5. (D) 大意：專家就是對於越來越小的範圍懂得越來越多的人。
6. (A) 根據前文應選 more。
7. (C) more or less = almost（幾乎）。
8. (B) more A than B 表「與其說是 B 不如說是 A」。
9. (A) the more …, the more …（愈…就愈…）。
10. (A) for health reasons（為了健康之故），固定說法。

翻譯造句

1. Drug abuse is getting more and more serious.
2. I've become less and less interested in politics.
3. After we drove into the forest, it was getting darker and darker.
4. The older you are, the poorer your memory will become.
5. Our boss is more frugal than stingy.

要點 7

聯考題型

1. (D) senior 用名詞形式或用 older than me。
2. (C) be superior to … 表「優於…」。
3. (B) be junior to … 表（職位）「低於…」。
4. (A) prior to = before（在…之前）。
5. (D) be inferior to …（劣於…）。
6. (A) 表「差距」的介系詞用 by。
7. (C) senior citizens（年長者）。
8. (C) 同第2題。
9. (D) 此處 mine = my position。
10. (C) prior to（介系詞）須接V-ing或n。

1. (C) 可數名詞用倍數詞 + the number of …。
2. (C) 倍數詞 + the size of … 表「…為…的幾倍大」。
3. (A) faster than …（比…快）。
4. (C) 設 Black 女兒年齡為 X，則 Black 的年齡為 X + 24。根據文意列出方程式為 X + 24 + 2 = 4 (X + 2)，所以 X + 26 = 4X + 8，因此得 18 = 3X，即 X = 6。所以母親年齡 為 6 + 24 = 30，為女兒的 5 倍。
5. (C) 前者為後者的三倍，則後者為前者的三分之一。

克漏字

1. (C) improve 表「改善」。
2. (A) accumulate（累積）。
3. (B) contribute to … 表「對…有貢獻/幫助」。
4. (B) 倍數詞 + as … as …。
5. (A) do/work wonders 表「製造奇蹟」。

Unit 16

要點 1

聯考題型

1. (D) little（否定副詞）置於子句句首須倒裝。
2. (B) much less 為 little 的比較級。
3. (D) 警方要求民眾不要接近該越獄的犯人。
4. (A) 人 + be grounded 表「…被禁足」。
5. (B) by no means = in no way = under no circumstances（絕不/非）。
6. (D) nowhere else置句首才須倒裝。
7. (B) Hardly had + S + pp … when + S + 過去式（一…就…）。
8. (A) go by 表時間的「經過」。
9. (D) Not until … + 倒裝。
10. (A) at no time = never，置於句首須倒裝。

要點 2

聯考題型

1. (C) only then = only at that time。
2. (D) only = 副詞置於句首須倒裝，recently 搭配現在完成式。
3. (A) does + 單數 S + 原形 V。
4. (D) could 表過去的能力。
5. (D) be aware that … = know that …。
6. (B) 忘記在前，發現在後。
7. (A) only last week 置於句首須搭配過去式的倒裝。
8. (B) be awake/wake up to sth 表（開始）「瞭解」某物/事。

9. (A) crack down on …（掃蕩/打擊…）。
10.(D) 搭配完成式倒裝。

聯考題型

1. (A) 主詞為 the best time …，搭配單數動詞 is。
2. (B) lie in …（在於…），此處搭配單數的 lies。
3. (D) 主詞 the pure = pure people，搭配複數的 are。
4. (C) be laid 表「被放置」，主詞複數故選 (C)。
5. (B) be not above + V-ing（不會不屑於…）。
6. (A) 主詞 the man 單數，用 is 搭配 interested …。
7. (A) Here you go. = Here you are.（拿去吧。）
8. (C) 主詞 several pictures，用 were 搭配 enclosed …。
9. (B) Such is/was … that …（如此…以致於…）。
10.(A) gone are those … 為 those … are gone 的倒裝。

要點 4

聯考題型

1. (C) Had it not been for … = If it had not been for …（當時要不是因為…）。
2. (A) Should he change … = If he should change …。
3. (C) Had the management acted … = If the management had acted …。
4. (A) 同第1題。
5. (B) have to … 用 do 代替。
6. (B) so do I. = I do, too。

7. (C) money 為不可數名詞，故搭配 nor will it。

8. (D) 搭配前文的 haven't 用 has。

9. (D) 搭配否定句用否定連接詞 nor。

10. (A) 同第3題。

要點 5

聯考題型

1. (D) predict 表「預測」。

2. (C) 本句為 I have never heard a more funny joke. 之倒裝。

3. (A) what (= the thing which) 引導名詞子句作 finished 的受詞。

4. (C) whatever 引導的名詞子句作 give 的直接受詞（you 為間接受詞）。

5. (C) 此處 does = speaks English。

6. (C) as are their teenaged kids = as their teenaged kids are interested in playing computer games.

7. (A) what is actually impossible 作 considers 的受詞。

8. (A) does = loves the kids。

9. (B) What should have been a carefree childhood 作 I spent 的受詞。

10. (D) do = eat meat，表「一些其它種類的猿猴吃肉」。

要點 6

聯考題型

1. (C) 主句帶 seldom, hardly, few, nothing 等視為否定句，附加問句須用肯定形式。

2. (D) I think/suppose/believe/am afraid (that) + S + V …的附加問句，由 that 子句的主詞、動詞形成。

3. (B) 主句肯定，附加問句否定。

4. (B) 同上。
5. (C) 同第1題。
6. (D) 同第3題。
7. (D) 同第3題。
8. (D) 同第3題。
9. (D) used to …的否定形式為 didn't use to …。
10. (D) 同第2題。

Unit 17

要點 1

聯考題型

1. (D) experience 表「遭遇/經歷」時是可數名詞。
2. (D) experience 作「經驗」解時為不可數名詞。
3. (C) change trains/planes（恆用複數）。
4. (A) be satisfied with（對⋯滿意）。people接複數 V。
5. (D) an audience 是「一群觀眾」，audiences 是「很多群觀眾」。
6. (B) be ferried ashore（被運送上岸）。crew 是複數用法。
7. (A) the aristocracy 是「貴族」的總稱。an aristocrat 是一名「貴族」。
8. (B) on + adj/V-ing + terms 表「處於⋯之關係」。
9. (B) cattle（牛，集合名詞）作主詞時接複數 V。
10. (A) vermin（害蟲）作主詞時接複數 V。
11. (C)「滑鼠」的複數形為 mice 或 mouses。「老鼠」的複數形為 mice。
12. (A) this species（這個品種）單數。
13. (B) offspring（子女），單複數同形。
14. (A) a real treat 是一件「特別愉快的事物」。
15. (A) a man of his word（恆用單數），指一個「講信用的人」。

要點 2

聯考題型

1. (C) a whole chicken 表「一整隻雞」。
2. (B) a glass（一個玻璃杯）。一整片玻璃需說 a sheet/pane of glass。
3. (B) a slice of toast（一片土司麵包）。

4. (A) egg on sb's face（尷尬；難堪），猶台語「滿臉豆花」，不可數。

5. (C) have several/different/other irons in the fire 表「正忙著做好幾件事情」。

6. (B) a pot of oolong tea（一壺烏龍茶）。A cup of tea 是「一杯茶」，怎麼請大家呢？

7. (C) advice（勸告），不可數，但可以說 a bit/word of advice。

8. (A) take sth with a pinch of salt 表「對某物的真實性持懷疑的態度」。

9. (B) under the weather（身體不適），慣用語。

10. (C) Do you have a light?（你有火嗎？），固定說法。

11. (A) bring sth to light（揭發某事）。

12. (B) a helping/serving (of …) 是「一客（食物）」。

13. (A) 汽車/機器的「廠牌」用 make。

14. (D) It's a breeze.（這太容易了。）= It's a piece of cake. = It's (as) easy as pie. = It's a cinch. = No sweat.

15. (A) as luck would have it（幸好）。

要點 3

翻譯填充

1. airs	15. depth
2. arms	16. duties
3. ash	17. effect
4. ashes	18. effects
5. attentions	19. fact
6. authorities	20. facts
7. brains	21. future
8. cloth	22. futures
9. colors	23. good
10. content	24. goods
11. contents	25. green
12. customs	26. greens
13. damage	27. grounds
14. damages	28. head

29. heads	40. ruin
30. heights	41. savings
31. honors	42. saving
32. looks	43. spirit
33. manners	44. spirits
34. mean	45. sweat
35. pains	46. sweets
36. rags	47. talk
37. ranks	48. talks
38. rating	49. times
39. ratings	50. utilities

要點 4

聯考題型

1. (C) of an age = (of) the same age（同年齡）。
2. (A) by the hour/day/week（按小時/天/週計算）。
3. (C) 強調數字對比時用 one 不用 a(n)。
4. (B) 不強調數字對比時用 a(n)。
5. (C) What a surprise！表「真是意外！」，固定說法。
6. (C) 流感用 flu 或 the flu。
7. (C) 特定的人物之前加定冠詞。
8. (B) the tip of the iceberg（冰山之一角），固定說法。
9. (A) 日期，星期，月份，假日之前不加冠詞。
10. (C) 表「真相」用 the truth。
11. (D) most of the + n.（大多數的…）；most of + 代名詞。
12. (C) 此指特定的「數」。Number twenty-seven 是 27 號。
13. (A) a(n) + n. + or two 或 one or two +（複數）n. 是「一兩個…」的固定說法。
14. (B) 作「抽象名詞」時 education 不可數。指一段受教育過程時，可數
15. (A) 成對的人事物不加冠詞。
16. (B) make a fool of sb/oneself 表「愚弄某人/自己」。

17. (A) spread from mouth to mouth（口口相傳），慣用法。

18. (A) arm in arm（臂挽著臂），慣用法。

19. (B) 同第15題。

20. (A) 三餐一般不加冠詞於其前，除非指「特殊/定的」早/午/晚餐，如：a light lunch（一份輕淡的午餐）或 a big dinner（一份大餐）。

Unit 18

要點 1

聯考題型

1. (A) charge it 表「以信用卡支付」。
2. (C) 在別的地方/國家用 they。
3. (B) Lucky you/me/her！表「你/我/她真幸運！」，用受格。
4. (D) It's = It is，此處 it 呼應前句的 that。
5. (A) They/People say … 表「據說…」。
6. (C) your own = yours，此指 your comb。
7. (C) 此處 mine = my dad。
8. (B) blame oneself 表「自責」。
9. (D) (strictly) between ourselves/you and me 表「（絕對）不要告訴第三者」。
10. (C) be/look oneself 指「身心正常」。

要點 2

聯考題型

1. (B) 電話中自我介紹用 This is …。
2. (A) 電視/收音機播報人員結束播報內容時說。
3. (B) 指對方的衣物用 that（＋單數 n）或 those（＋複數 n）。
4. (B) 此處 that = the voice。
5. (D) 此處 those = the wines。
6. (A) and all that = and so on 表「等等」。
7. (B) … at that 是附加一句話後的強調。
8. (A) 此處 That's it！表「我受夠了！」。

9. (C) That's a good boy/girl.（這才乖）。
10. (C) I hope not. 表「希望不會…」。

聯考題型

1. (B) 否定句，疑問句，條件句的「一些」，用 any。
2. (A) 同上。
3. (C) 兩者任一用 either。
4. (A) in all = all told（總共）。
5. (A) have none of sth 表「不接受/理會…」。
6. (D) 路只有兩旁，用 on either side 或 on both sides。
7. (C) others = other people（別人）。
8. (C) as such 表「如此」。
9. (D) they both = both of them。
10. (B) 表「如此…以致於…」，此處 such 是代名詞。

要點 4

聯考題型

1. (B) A presuppose B 表「A 須以 B 為前提」。
2. (C) What matters（重要的事）是名詞子句作主詞。
3. (D) Report has it (that) … = It is reported (that) … 表「據報導，…」。
4. (B) It occurred to sb that …（某人突然想到…）。
5. (D) it follows that … 表「可以推論出某種情況」。
6. (A) 該 adj 指人時用 of。

7. (C) 強調用法。

8. (A) take it for granted (that) + S + V …（視…為當然）。

9. (B) make + O + possible = make possible + O，此處 the improvement of …作 made 的受詞，possible 為受詞補語。

10. (D) It cost +（人）+ 金錢 + 不定詞。此處 a small fortune 表「一大筆錢」。

Unit 19

要點 1

聯考題型

1. (C) A looks <u>like</u> B. = A and B look alike。

2. (A) sleeping（正在睡覺的），asleep（睡著的）只能接在 be/seem 之後。

3. (B) imaginative 表「想像力豐富的」。

4. (D) unwilling（不願意的）。impossible 一般須用 it 引導，如：It is impossible for these people to trust you.

5. (A) money alone = mere money（光是金錢）。

6. (B) a frightened man 是一個「受到驚嚇的人」，afraid 只能作「敘述用」，即接於 be/seem 之後。

7. (A) heavy traffic（車流量很大），是固定說法。

8. (D) living creatures（生物），alive 只有「敘述用法」。

9. (B) 此處 live 是形容詞，表「現場（轉播）的」。

10. (C) be still alive and kicking（仍活得好好的），敘述用法。

11. (A) a life sentence 是「無期徒刑/終身監禁」。

12. (B) sensible（明智的）；sensitive（敏感的）；sensory（感官方面的）；sensuous（感官之娛的）。

13. (C) literate（識字的）；literal（字面上的）；literary（文學的）；literature（文學）。

14. (B) be respectful of …（尊敬…）。

15. (D) be/seem favorable for（有利於…的）。

16. (C) sickening（令人作嘔的）；sickly（體弱多病的）。

17. (D) endangered species（瀕臨絕種的物種）。

18. (B) industrialized（已工業化的）。

19. (D) respective（個別的）；respectable（可敬的）。

20. (A) health problems（健康問題），固定說法。

21. (D) historical（根據歷史的）；historic（史上有名的）。

22. (A) considerable（相當多的；可觀的）。

23. (B) honorary degrees（榮譽學位）；honorable（值得尊敬的）；honored（感到榮幸的）。

24. (B) continual（一直的；時續時停的）；continuous（連續不停的）。

25. (D) marriageable（適婚的）。unmarried 前置 an。

要點 2

聯考題型

1. (B) need/want sth badly（急需某物），固定說法。

2. (D) 副詞 + enough 置於句首/末可修飾整句。

3. (A) travel light（轉便地旅行）。

4. (A) 作副詞時 close 表地方的「接近」，closely 表關係的「接近」。closer 是副詞的比較級。

5. (A) send sth express（副詞）= send sth by express（名詞），表「以快遞方式寄出某物」。expressly（特別地）。

6. (D) go outdoors/indoors（到戶外/進室內）。outdoor/indoor 為形容詞

7. (C) not a little（非常…）；not a bit（一點也不…）。

8. (A) cut sb short（突然打斷某人的談話）。shortly 是「不久」之意。

9. (B) deep down 猶言在（某人）的「骨子裡」。

10. (B) directly = immediately（立即）；direct 作副詞時表「直接/達」。

11. (A) stop dead (in one's tracks) 表「愣住」。

12. (D) deathly pale（臉色死白）；deadly（致命的）。

13. (C) mostly 表「十之八九」。

14. (A) clean forget（完全忘記…），是固定說法。

15. (B) burn cleanly 指（汽油）燃燒得很乾淨，不會造成污染。

16. (A) still going strong（仍很強勢），是固定說法。

17. (A) open wide（張得很開）；widely 表「廣泛地」。

18. (A) travel free（免費搭車/旅遊）。

19. (A) 指地方/價格的「高」用 high；指程度上的「高」用 highly，即「非常」之意。

20. (B) a highly efficient secretary（非常有效率的秘書）。

Unit 20

要點 1

聯考題型

1. (A) at + 地址。
2. (A) at the dentist's（在牙醫診所）。
3. (C) in space（在太空中）。
4. (B) in the center of …（在…中央）。
5. (B) on the cheek（在臉頰上）。
6. (D) over …（在…正上方）。
7. (C) above average（在平均值之上）；on average（平均/一般而言）。
8. (D) under the table（在桌子底下）。
9. (A) beside …（在…之旁）。
10. (B) before + 地方（在…之前）。
11. (B) shut/close the door behind you（出去時將門關上）。
12. (C) among other things（其中之一）。
13. (B) between you and me.（不要告訴別人）。
14. (A) around the clock 表「全天候」。
15. (B) who was behind the murder（誰是這謀殺案背後的主使）。
16. (A) across（介詞）表「跨越…」。
17. (B) get along with + 事物，指某事物的「進展」。
18. (C) be into sth 表「對某學科/活動有興趣」。
19. (D) (much) to one's + 情緒名詞（使某人感到…）。
20. (D) 此處的 against 表「倚靠」。

聯考題型

1. (D) 此處 toward 表「將近…」。
2. (A) be good at（擅長…）。
3. (A) at night（在夜晚），固定用法。
4. (C) in a minute or two（再過一兩分鐘）。
5. (D) by the hour/day/week（按小時/天/週計算）。
6. (C) save … for a rainy day 猶言「未雨綢繆」。
7. (B) at the age of + 數字（在…歲時）。
8. (B) on + 日期。
9. (D) by the time …（到了…之時/前）。
10. (B) after dark 指「天黑後」。
11. (A) at dawn/dusk（在黎明/黃昏時）。
12. (A) by night = at night（在夜晚）。
13. (B) in the night = during the night（在夜晚某特定時間）。
14. (A) a quarter of/to 6 即「六點差一刻」。of 為美式用法。
15. (D) 現在完成式搭配 since。
16. (D) Monday through Friday（從星期一至星期五）。
17. (B) throughout one's life（終某人一生）。
18. (C) It was not until … that …（直到…才…）。
19. (B) It is (about) time …（該是做…的時候了）。
20. (A) around 此處表「大約在…」。

1. (C) be made into + 成品。
2. (D) be dying for sth（很想要某物）。
3. (D) out of curiosity（由於好奇）。
4. (A) die by one's own hand（自殺）。
5. (B) come down with …（罹患…）。
6. (A) 在北邊用 on the north of …。
7. (C) 在南部用 in the south of …。
8. (B) 在…西方用 to the west of …。
9. (A) run after sb（追求異性）。
10. (C) be aimed at …（目的為…）。
11. (A) at half price（以半價）。
12. (A) with one's/the + n + pp 表「附帶狀況」。
13. (B) in charge 表「負責/管理」某地方。
14. (B) under/in … circumstances（在…的情況下）。
15. (B) be sentenced to life/death/3 years（被判無期徒刑/死刑/三年）。
16. (D) by the way 表「順便一提」。
17. (A) to the point（切題）。
18. (B) for free = free (of charge) 表「免費地」。
19. (D) bring on sth 表「造成…」，通常是負面的結果。
20. (B) take on = employ（僱用…）。
21. (C) put sth away（將某物收好/歸位）。
22. (D) give out（散發傳單/小冊等）。
23. (A) be hard on sb 表「對某人很嚴苛」。
24. (D) for certain（有把握地）。
25. (D) get into a car/taxi;get on a bus/train。
26. (A) hang up on sb（掛某人的電話）。
27. (B) a … man/person at heart（本質上是一個…的人）。
28. (C) count on sb …（指望某人…）。
29. (C) get over + 疾病（自某種疾病恢復/痊癒），接近 recover from …的用法。
30. (A) grind to a halt 指汽車等因特殊路況或天候不佳而慢慢停下來。

常春藤升大學系列　A62

高中英文句型總整理

編　　著：李端
編　　審：常春藤中外編輯群
封面設計：黃振倫
電腦排版：環涓排版設計坊
顧　　問：賴陳愉嫻
法律顧問：王存淦律律・蕭雄淋律師
發行日期：2008 年 9 月　再版／二刷

出 版 者：常春藤有聲出版有限公司
台北市忠孝西路一段 33 號 5 樓
行政院新聞局出版事業登記證
局版臺業字第肆捌貳陸號

服務電話：(02) 2331-7600　　服務傳真：(02) 2381-0918
信　　箱：臺北郵政 8-18 號信箱
郵撥帳號：19714777　　常春藤有聲出版有限公司
定價：365 元

＊如有缺頁、裝訂錯誤或破損　請寄回本社更換

國家圖書館出版品預行編目資料

高中英文句型總整理 / 李端編著 . -- 初版 . --
　　臺北市：常春藤有聲，2006[民 95]
　　　面；　　公分 . -- (常春藤升大學系列；A62)
　　ISBN　986-7008-00-6 (平裝)
　　1. 英國語言 - 句法　2. 中等教育 - 教學法
524.38　　　　　　　　　　　　　95007429

常春藤有聲出版有限公司
讀者回函卡

✍感謝您的填寫，您的建議將是公司重要的參考及修正指標！

我購買本書的書名是		編碼	
我購買本書的原因是	□老師、同學推薦 □家人推薦 □學校購買 □書店閱讀後感到喜歡 □其他		
我購得本書的管道是	□書攤 □業務人員推薦 □大型連鎖書店 □書店名稱＿＿＿＿＿＿ □其他		
我最滿意本書的三點依序是	□內容 □編排方式 □雙色印刷 □試題演練 □解析清楚 □封面 □售價 □促銷活動豐富 □信任品牌 □廣告 □其他		
我最不滿意本書的三點依序是	□內容 □編排方式 □雙色印刷 □試題演練 □解析不足 □封面 □售價 □促銷活動貧乏 □廣告 □其他		
我有一些其他想法與建議是			
我發現本書誤植的部份是	□書籍第＿頁，第＿行，有錯誤的部份是		
	□書籍第＿頁，第＿行，有錯誤的部份是		
◡◠◡			

✍我的基本資料

讀者姓名		生　日		性別	□男 □女
就讀學校		科系年級	科 年級	畢業	□已畢 □在學
聯絡電話		E-mail			
聯絡地址					

請您填寫完後寄至：
台北市忠孝西路一段33號5樓　　**常春藤有聲出版有限公司**　　**出版部收**
填寫日期：西元＿＿＿＿年＿＿＿＿月＿＿＿日